STEREO REALIST
MANUAL

The ultra modern Stereo Realist
camera. Below, an early wooden
stereo camera, circa 1870, from
Monckhoven, "Traité Generale de
Photographie."

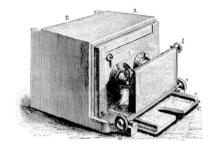

STEREO REALIST
MANUAL

WILLARD D. MORGAN

HENRY M. LESTER

and 14 Contributors

MORGAN & LESTER   *Publishers*   NEW YORK

THE FOUNTAIN PRESS, LONDON

First Edition October 1954

Copyright 1954
by
WILLARD D. MORGAN
and
HENRY M. LESTER

Library of Congress Catalog Number 54-11905

All black-and-white and color stereos in this book have been reproduced from original Stereo Realist color transparencies.

Typographic Design by John S. Carroll
Type set by Albert O. Jennings, Inc.
Color by The Beck Engraving Company
Printing and Binding by American Book—Stratford Press
Jacket Design by Seymour Robins
Viewers by American Optical Co.
Printed in U.S.A.

Introduction

HAROLD LLOYD

I have been a stereo fan from the very day when two friends—stereo friends, of course — looped the strap of a Stereo Realist camera over my neck and said, "Just do what we do." I took nearly ninety pictures that day, and that was only the beginning. I have taken untold thousands since.

Years have passed, and I still get as much pleasure out of shooting each new roll of stereo pictures as I did on that first exciting day. There is the thrill, not only of shooting the pictures, choosing the most interesting subject and the most effective angle from which to take it, but the excitement of opening the package when the film comes back from processing. There is the first big moment when the pictures are examined as the roll of film is unwound, and the really big thrill comes when I get my first good look at the mounted pictures in full relief through the stereo viewer. The joy is not always undiluted — stereo viewers are exacting and magnify faults as well as virtues. But even if the entire roll is not as wonderful as I had hoped, there are always a few better-than-average pictures, and now and then a near-masterpiece to make up for the disappointments.

The stereo camera adds joy to other activities too. I always have it with me on my trips, and I find, as a result, that I go to places that otherwise I might have never seen. Before stereo, I preferred to sleep later in the morning; now I find myself rising at the crack of dawn to take advantage of an unusual light effect or, perhaps, for some special early morning activities. I have climbed mountains, trudged through snow, splashed through rain, sought out places and done things that I would never have dreamed of doing before the stereo bug bit me.

Living as we do in a world of color, we know it as a spacious world. Pictures in color make things look more like we know them. Stereo pictures in color make them real, live and fairly breathing in space. And colors need not be vivid and glaring; they are good when harmonious and not distracting: even a gray day makes things look well for a stereo camera, when one would not think of taking a color picture with an ordinary camera.

There is something about stereo color photography which makes it alive for me as compared with ordinary photography. Take the artist at his easel in a Paris street (Fig. 12, Page 102): seen through the stereo viewer, it is an actual scene in suspension, just as I viewed it when I was there. For me, the world must be seen in color stereo! (See Fig. 3, p. 98 and Fig. 5, p. 99.) In Europe, particularly, I find myself more alert to beauty, to pageantry and to tradition now that I can record it in color stereos. People ask me what these shots mean, so now I try to learn some of the history and background of the places, people and things I photograph while traveling. The result is that my pictures are not only fascinating to my friends, but they mean more to me too. Every stereo slide becomes a little bit of history or legend, and brings my travels back into my library with me. Of an evening, I can sit, looking into the stereo viewer, as if I were looking out of a window upon the things I have seen, places I have been to; the pleasures, thrills and experiences of the past are vividly recreated for me.

Through the magic of the stereo viewer, my friends enjoy my journeys, though they have not traveled with me. If they are planning a trip, an evening with my stereo views will prepare them for the places they will visit and suggest other places they have not included in their plans.

A friend recently helped me to sort out and choose the best slides from about 90 rolls of film I had shot in Europe. (A friend, indeed—ninety rolls of film; twenty eight pictures to a roll!) When some time later she too went to Europe, she found her appreciation heightened beyond measure, as she visited spots I had photographed. It was just as though she were recognizing old friends, friends she knew and loved. Often too, she found details not shown in my pictures (I could not shoot *everything*, even on 90 rolls of film!) and made notes to point them out to me. Naturally, I'm going back again—I have a list of just what I want to photograph in stereo the next time I am there!

It's hard for me to stop here . . . I could go on like this for hours. But I am most grateful and thankful to those friends who hung the stereo camera around my neck and said: "Just do what we do." That's just what I have done, and a new world of stereo wonders and beauty has unfolded before my delighted eyes. I hope that the contents of this book will open your eyes too—open them to this fascinating way of recording the world around you—and that your forthcoming excursion into the colorful three-dimensional world of stereo photography will give you as much pleasure as it has given me.

HAROLD LLOYD

AUGUST 1954
BEVERLY HILLS, CALIFORNIA

Contents

Viewing The Stereos In This Book

The Stereo Viewer included with this book was devised for a very good reason. A book about stereo photography would not be very convincing if it just *told* you about three-dimensional pictures, and didn't *show* you what they are all about. You want to *see stereo pictures* in a stereo book, and you can do it with this viewer. It's new, of course, and like anything new, you'll have to learn to use it at first. Some people will get the knack right away; others may need a few hints.

It may seem peculiar but there is a *way* to read and to enjoy this book! When you're reading type, your eyes are focused at about 10 inches. However, when you look through the viewer, your eyes relax to infinity focus, the same as looking out of the window at something far away. If you read a while, then look at a few pictures—the effect will be relaxing. On the other hand, frequent looking back and forth between pictures and text may prove tiring. So — read a while, then look at some pictures.

The first time you use the Stereo Viewer you may not see all the depth in some of the pictures, especially if you are used to the Stereo Realist slide viewer. The reason is psychological: with the Realist slide viewer you look *into* a box. Here the pictures are flat on the page, and there is a mental contradiction. As you get used to the viewer, this contradiction will disappear, and the pictures will gain much in depth perception for you.

One word of advice. This viewer has been designed for one purpose only: *to view the stereo pairs in this book*. Don't try to look around the room with it! Don't take it to the movies. You won't see a thing. And don't try to read the text or look at the single pictures in this book with it. You can, however, read the picture caption with a stereo pair because the captions appear on one side only, placed there purposely for your information and convenience.

How to Use the Stereo Viewer

1. Put the book directly in front of you, so that the pages are in good light, and at a comfortable reading distance. The pages should lie flat — *this is important.* If you wear glasses for reading, wear them now.

2. Make sure the page is square to you, not tilted so that one picture is farther away than the other. And most important, *both pictures should be level* — one must not be higher than the other.

3. Now look at the stereo pair below for your first trial. Place the stereo viewer over the bridge of your nose directly in front of your eyes while looking at the stereo pair. Most people will find that the two pictures merge immediately into one — a three-dimensional scene. If you don't see stereo immediately, the next step is the key to the whole matter.

4. While keeping the picture at the comfortable reading distance, *slowly* move the stereo viewer away from your eyes, toward the picture, with your eyes relaxed as if gazing into the distance. Before you have moved the viewer an inch or so, the pictures will "float" together and combine into one.

OR — you may hold the viewer steady and slowly move the book to and from your eyes.

AND — you can tilt the viewer slightly one way or the other if one picture seems higher than the other.

5. You only need to go through the above procedure once. After you've once had a pair of pictures fuse into a stereo, all the others will do the

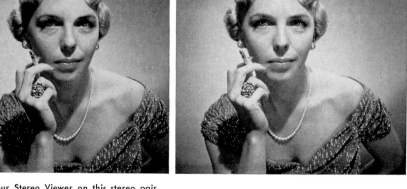

1. Try out your Stereo Viewer on this stereo pair, following the suggestions above. Adjust the picture and viewer distance for your own eyesight, as described in the text. Stereo by John Meredith.

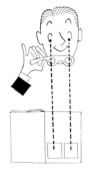

RIGHT!

2. Always have the book, the viewer and your eyes lined up straight. Adjust the distance for your own eyesight.

same thing without effort. Finding the proper distance for the viewer and for the pictures will become instinctive.

6. Most people can fuse the pictures through the viewer right away. However, if you have any trouble, relax, and start from the beginning. You will get it on the second or third try.

7. Depending upon your particular viewing distance, you may see an extra strip of picture on each side of the fused stereo. If you do, just disregard it . . . or move the viewer just a little further away from your eyes to make the strips disappear.

8. The Stereo Viewer should be cleaned only with a soft dry cloth or with soap and water if it gets dirty. Do not use carbon tetrachloride or benzine, or silicone-treated lens papers: they will ruin the polish on the lenses.

9. If you lose or damage your Stereo Viewer, or want additional viewers you can obtain them for 50¢ each postpaid from Morgan & Lester, the publishers of this book, or from the store where you bought this book.

3. This will never do! If you do not fuse the stereo pictures immediately, chances are that you have the pictures tilted. You wouldn't be tilting the viewer like these boys, would you?

WRONG!

1. If you close one eye and look around, everything will seem flattened out. The size and shape and distance of things will be very hard to judge, and everything will look rather strange.

YOU DON'T LOOK AT THINGS WITH ONE EYE . . .

BUT

THE ORDINARY CAMERA DOES!

2. The ordinary camera with only one lens makes flat pictures without any depth. Size and shape and distance are even harder to judge in a flat picture than they are when the real scene is viewed with one eye.

THAT'S WHY

IT TAKES A TWO-EYED CAMERA TO PRODUCE

REAL DEPTH!

1. What Makes Good Stereo

EDGAR BERGEN

You probably never thought of yourself as a living, breathing stereo camera. Don't be surprised. You are! But you *do* have quite an edge on the camera—you have a *brain*, with a tricky innate ability that not only records pairs of images like the camera, but puts them together and makes them "real." There is a lot of talk these days about machines and "mechanical brains" duplicating the functions of men so efficiently that they may soon replace human effort. While the stereo camera is an optical machine that duplicates human vision, it will never push man off the map. Without the mysterious and wonderful mind of man there would be no stereo sensation. Aside from the optics, stereo is "all in the head."

What Stereo Is

So—you may ask—what is it? To find out, first close one eye. You now have *monocular* vision, and you are also seeing the world like a single-lens camera. Look across the room as far as you can see. With only one eye you'll have a hard time judging the relative distances of the furniture. Of course, common sense and past experience assure you that they actually *are* different distances, and different relative sizes as well. But with only one eye, you tend to see them "flat"—all backed up against each other. (Fig. 1.) A flat photograph made with only one lens illustrates this even better. It shows all the different distances "compressed" in one plane, and its power to suggest distance and size is limited (Fig. 2.)

Now, look in the same direction with *both eyes*. (Fig. 3.) This is *binocular* vision, the same as is built into the two-lens stereo camera. You will recognize an immediate feeling of exact separation between yourself and all the furniture. Each has a definite place in the *space* of the room. There is a specific distance between each object, and each object bulks according to its own size.

Drawings by Roy Doty.

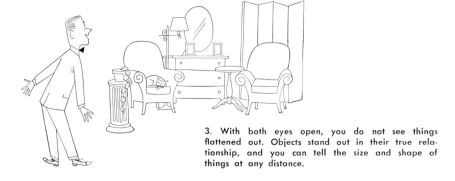

3. With both eyes open, you do not see things flattened out. Objects stand out in their true relationship, and you can tell the size and shape of things at any distance.

In the flat view or the flat photograph, a near-by lamp might look larger than a piano just because it is nearer to you—although again, your common knowledge of pianos would remind you that they are really larger than lamps. But in the *binocular stereo* view you know instantly how big the lamp and piano actually are, and exactly how far they are from each other. *You can compare them in space.* (Fig. 4.)

This binocular stereo vision gives you a direct knowledge of a third dimension—depth—added to the height and width of the one-eyed view or the single-lens picture. Three-dimensional vision (3-D is the popular tag) is a function of anyone with a well coordinated pair of eyes and a brain. It happens because the eyes are separated horizontally and each eye sees a slightly different view of a given subject. The left eye sees a little more on the left side (Fig. 5) and the right eye more on the right (Fig. 6.) These similar but not identical views travel from the eye to the brain, where in an incredible way they blend into one view which the mind interprets in three dimensions. This happens every time two normal

4. The stereo view—made with two lenses spaced about the same distance apart as your eyes—duplicates your stereo vision. In the stereo picture, size and shape and distance are seen with *both* eyes— the same as if you were looking at the scene.

14

5. The *left* eye, or the *left lens* of the stereo camera, sees more on the *left side.* These bottles are all exactly the same distance apart—but this picture, a left-eye view, is only half of the stereo view. With one eye you cannot tell that the bottles are the same distance apart.

eyes and one usable brain are hooked up together. Look at Figure 7 through your Stereo Viewer to see the picture in 3-D. *Next page please!*

The stereo camera duplicates all the circumstances of 3-D vision short of fusing a pair of pictures in a brain. The two lenses of the Realist are the same distance apart as the average adult eyes. They cover about the same angle of view as the average eyes. The color film can—when properly exposed—record just about the same hues and shades as the average eyes; so the camera can set down on film nominally the same pair of images that the eyes see directly—a little more of the right side with the right

6. The *right* eye, or the *right lens* of the stereo camera, sees more on the *right side.* These are the same bottles as in Figure **5,** but in this right-lens picture you see more around the right-hand side of the bottles.

15

7. These are the same left and right pictures shown in Figures 5 and 6. Use the Stereo Viewer to see how they combine into a stereo picture with roundness, space and depth.

lens, and a little more of the left side with the left lens. Later on, when these film images are mounted in the familiar stereo slides, they can be transmitted through a viewer—first to the eyes and then to the brain for blending into a three-dimensional view. It is just that simple! (Fig. 8.)

Starting Out

It is as simple to start taking stereo pictures as it is to understand how they happen. Anyone with a Realist in his hands for the first time wants to rush right out to take "real life" pictures immediately. For the impatient and enthusiastic, here are five quick leads to good pictures on the first try. You can read the rest of the book while you wait for your first pictures to come back. But before you do anything, study the camera instruction book and Chapter 2, *Operating the Stereo Realist Camera*, so that you are familiar with all the working parts. Try out all the camera controls right away. It is always a good idea to know all about your equipment *before* you start thinking about what makes good pictures.

16

8. A pair of stereo pictures is transmitted from the viewer to the eyes to the brain, where they fuse into one three-dimensional scene.

1. GOOD EXPOSURE. *Before anything else* assure yourself of good exposure. The most striking subject or brilliant stereo composition is a total loss without it. For an easy beginning take your camera OUTDOORS on a nice sunny day. Use the average recommended settings for daylight color film: set the shutter speed for 1/50 second and the lens opening to f/6.3—midway between the 5.6 and 8 markings on your camera. Later on you can cope with other conditions, but to avoid beginner's disappointment start out the safe and easy way.

2. ANGLE THE CAMERA AND THE LIGHTING. Don't let the camera or the sun face your subjects square-on. To get good lighting and camera angles:

    A.   Station yourself with the sun directed on the subject from a shallow angle over your shoulder. (Fig. 9.)

    B.   Aim your camera from any angle that looks good to you.

Move around your subject until the camera and sunlight are both looking at it on the slant (Fig. 10). If the subject can be moved, put it where you want it. In the beginning, abandon any situation that won't fit easily into this simple scheme. Remember, you don't *have* to take *every* picture!

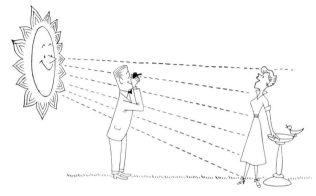

9. Let the sun fall on your subject from a shallow angle over your shoulder.

17

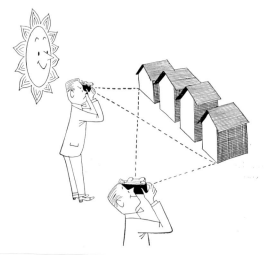

10. Find an interesting camera angle. Here, the fellow in front (right) will have the better picture. The fellow in back will have a flat, head-on picture.

3. LIMIT YOUR SCENES. Don't aim at the whole countryside. Compose your first pictures around one main subject prominent in the foreground, with two or three less important things at various distances in the background. Keep vital subject matter in the "safe" zone between 10 and 25 feet. Omit things closer than 10 feet and avoid large areas of distant background.

4. SHARPNESS. To look "real" your finished pictures should be sharp all over. They will be sharp if you:

Hold the camera steady—or even better, use a tripod.

Avoid fast-moving subjects.

Focus properly.

Your basic settings for good exposure in Step 1 help you here. The 1/50 second shutter speed is fast enough to stop any slight movement of the subject or your own tentative grip on the camera. And the f/6.3 lens opening is small enough to have everything in focus from 10 feet to infinity—*when you set the focusing knob to 20 feet.* Take this 20-foot setting on faith for now. We'll explain later.

5. FAIR WARNING. Always keep your camera *levelled horizontally.* You can tip it up or tip it down. *Do not tip it sideways.* (Fig. 11.)

Altogether, here is a summary of the quick leads to good pictures on the first try:

Outdoors, sunny day, daylight color film

1/50 second shutter speed

f/6.3 lens setting

20-foot distance setting

Simple subjects no closer than 10 feet

Angle the camera and the lighting

11. YOU MUST HOLD

THE CAMERA **LEVEL** ▸

SIDEWAYS, THAT IS . . .

YOU **CAN** POINT IT

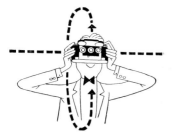

UP

OR

DOWN

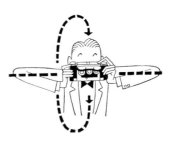

NEVER TILT IT SIDEWAYS . . .

AND NEVER

NEVER

HOLD

IT

SO

▸

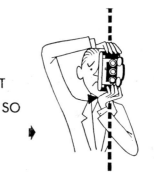

With these suggestions and a roll of film, you can take your first stereo pictures with assurance—and even a touch of swagger that always comes with owning a wonderful new camera.

Avoiding Bad Pictures

Some beginners—under the delusion that stereo alone guarantees a good picture—shoot wildly without thinking. They can be depended on for all the basic errors: washed-out or blacked-out exposures; fuzzy, blurred images; hodge-podge, jumbled scenes that confuse the eyes; head-on views that push you out of the picture instead of drawing you into it; and dozens of other blemishes that distinguish the snapshooter from the sensible, enthusiastic photographer. Don't fall into the trap. Use the simple aids to quick success until you have time to think about the finer points and work out your own approach to good pictures.

Good Pictures

Good stereo pictures always bring out a rash of adjectives. *Exciting! Stupendous! Colossal! Wow!* This time they are not press-agent blurbs! *Excitement* is the key. It's the stereo excitement of *being there—anywhere.* You score a hit every time your picture makes somebody say, "Oh boy, I feel as if I were *there!*" Whenever they just say, "Mmm-hmm," you haven't quite made it!

Now what's the difference between an "Oh boy!" masterpiece and a "Mmm-hmm" flop? First off, it's mastery of technique; and second, the

12. In this stereo picture you can see the actual drop to the floor of Grand Canyon. Stereo by Douglas Morgan.

20

13. An exposure meter is the most accurate way of measuring light intensity. The meter dial gives many different lens-and-shutter combinations for different lighting conditions.

personal viewpoint that finds the special, most striking interest in a scene. Stereo space recreation is more vividly real than any other art, but the crutch of reality is not enough. Nobody wants to look at a dull picture no matter how real it is.

There are no easy rules for making brilliant pictures. Nothing, unfortunately, substitutes for the skill, ingenuity and imagination of a fine photographer. Your own success in recreating things in stereo depends on how you seek out, see and finally photograph. You have to see things in three-dimensional relationships that make exciting and stimulating pictures. Pictures that draw the eyes through the whole scene, detail after detail. The longer people *want* to look at a picture, the more do they mean "Oh boy!" and the better it is. Except for lucky accidents—and don't base a career on them—successful pictures include a mastery of the basic demands of stereo. Let's consider them.

Just-Right Exposure

Everything you do in color stereo photography—from camera adjustments to composition—is governed from the first by exposure. A certain amount of light *must* reach the film to duplicate the scene faithfully. Use any means at your disposal—an exposure meter, an inexpensive calculator like the 25-cent Snapshot Kodaguide, experience or good judgment—but be sure you have some system to guarantee proper exposures. The latest Realist camera has an exposure chart right under the lens cover, and you can use this for all general work.

Color film does not react as quickly to light as black-and-white film. The one right exposure is much more critical. And once you have made a color exposure you can do nothing to correct it if it is wrong. You can't develop it a little longer, or print it a little stronger. You're stuck with it! So take extra care, and be sure that your exposures are good.

Together, the size of the lens opening and the speed of the shutter determine how much light reaches the film. Many different lens-and-shutter combinations will deliver the same amount of light, as you can see from the exposure meter shown above. Sometimes it will not matter which combination you use. More often in stereo it will, as we will soon see.

21

Sharpness and Definition

In real life we *automatically* focus our eyes clearly on everything we look at, from the nearest tree to the farthest horizon. If necessary we get eyeglasses to help. The important thing is that we *do* focus sharply and define clearly everything of interest at any distance. So it is important to be able to focus sharply and see clearly everything in the stereo view. If a scene is not sharp all over the film, the eyes cannot make it sharp in the viewer. Fuzziness and blur are not like real life, and destroy the reality of most stereo pictures. *Don't make fuzzy pictures.*

1. KEEP THE CAMERA STEADY. For speeds 1/25 second or slower, always use a firm support. If you do not have a tripod, brace the camera against something solid—furniture, a tree, a wall, anything. If you can't find a suitable brace, don't take the picture.

For speeds 1/50 second and faster it is usually safe to hold the camera in your hands. Brace it firmly against your face. Take a deep breath, hold it and stay perfectly still. No part of you should move except your finger, which you squeeze gently on the shutter button to make the exposure. *After* releasing the button you can breathe! This is a basic habit to practice without film in the camera.

2. LEARN THE TRICK OF FOCUSING. If you took the suggestion for setting the camera at 1/50 second, f/6.3 and 20 feet—and photographed nothing closer than 10 feet—you must have had good results. However, you probably wondered why you set the distance knob to 20 feet and were still focused sharply for 10 feet and infinity (∞).

14. Interesting camera angles are sometimes ready-made, as in this shot of the Empire State Building TV Tower. Stereo by Dorothy S. Gelatt.

15. With the basic camera settings for an average sunny day—1/50 second, f/6.3, 20 feet —everything is in sharp focus from 10 feet to infinity. Stereo by Willard D. Morgan.

Well, sir. When you focus a lens on any given distance, there is always some area both *fore and aft* of that distance that is also included in sharp focus. This sharp area varies with the size of the lens opening as well as the focus point, and is known as the *depth of field*. Of course the sharpness or depth of field does not start and stop suddenly some place in space. It tapers off gradually from "very sharp" to "less sharp" to "not sharp at all" (fuzzy!). The thing to do in making good stereo pictures is to set the distance—lens opening—shutter speed combination for the maximum sharpness in every scene. The *distance you focus the lens on* and the *size of the lens opening* are the two things that determine the depth of field. But the shutter speed is also important because it governs the amount of light necessary to make a good exposure with any given lens opening.

Now in stereo, at least in the beginning, we always want to make pictures that look sharp from the nearest object to the farthest. That is, we want sufficient depth of field in all pictures to make them sharp and easy to view. How do we manage this? It's easy. Latest Stereo Realist cameras have a Depth of Field Scale mounted around the focusing knob. Earlier cameras have a Hyperfocal Table mounted inside the lens cover. Proper use of either of these will give you the secret of easy focusing. Study the one that applies to your camera. Learn what it means. *Use it* and you will never have poor pictures from faulty focusing, which is the most common mistake in stereo photography.

23

16. Midshipmen and crew standing inspection aboard the USS MIDWAY. Focus at 20 feet, with the lens set to f/6.3, gave ample depth of field throughout. Stereo by Robert S. Quackenbush, Jr.

3. FOCUSING WITH THE DEPTH OF FIELD SCALE. The Depth of Field Scale has a duplicate set of f-numbers (lens openings) ranged around the distance figures on the focusing knob. These figures show the *near* and *far* distances that will be in sharp focus with various lens openings when the focusing knob is set at a given distance. You set the distance scale against the marker that runs through the middle of the Depth of Field Scale. Let's see how it works. Say you want to make an average daylight exposure of 1/50 second at f/6.3. You also want to include subjects from 10 feet to infinity (any distance over about 30 feet). You will find that you can do this by setting the distance scale to 20 feet (which is midway between 15 and 25 feet). This automatically puts the infinity marker at the far f/6.3 spot, and the 10-foot marker at the near f/6.3 spot on the Depth of Field Scale. You now know that at f/6.3 everything from 10 feet to infinity will be sharp. If the lens opening you want is not marked on the scale, just use the space between the two nearest numbers. Thus, f/6.3, which is not marked on the scale, falls between f/5.6 and f/8. The same applies to the distance scale on the focusing knob: 9 feet is between 8 and 10, etc.

Practice making different distance settings with the Depth of Field Scale until you are sure of how it works. For example, with a lens opening at f/5.6, you will have everything in sharp focus from 8 feet to 25 feet by setting the focusing knob at about 12 feet.

4. FOCUSING WITH THE HYPERFOCAL TABLE. The Hyperfocal table tells you—for each lens opening on the camera—where to set the focusing knob

24

for sharpness both at infinity and the closest permissible near-point. Remember that the table always includes infinity (anything over about 30 feet) and some near distance. Unlike the Depth of Field Scale, it does not give you combinations of distances closer than infinity and some near point. (A Depth of Field Scale can be installed on earlier cameras for increased focusing convenience, if desired.)

5. MAKE USE OF THE RANGE FINDER. In stereo we need a special attitude towards the range finder. In flat pictures the range finder is generally used to focus sharply on the main subject. If the rest of the picture is out of focus it doesn't matter—often it even adds to the effect. Forget this for stereo. In stereo you want the picture to be sharp and clear from front to back.

The range finder works with the focusing knob, but the image you see in the range finder window will only look sharp at the distance the knob is focused on. This does not tell you how much will actually be sharp in the picture. (As you already know, the Depth of Field Scale or the Hyperfocal Table will tell you that.) So you really want to use the range finder to measure the distance to the nearest and farthest objects in your picture. When you know that, set the focusing knob as required by the Depth of Field Scale or the Hyperfocal Table.

I like to call this "fore and aft focusing" because when you set the focusing knob on some middle distance you are actually in focus on both sides of that point. Set up a strong habit for this immediately. Practice it until it is as automatic as reaching for the brake in your car. Before long you will know the various settings without consulting the table. If you can learn to judge distances without consulting the range finder, so much the better. In photography every automatic judgment you can make frees your attention for the all-important matter of seeing pictures. The less you have to think about technique the more you can think about the pictures.

6. ANOTHER DEPTH OF FIELD TABLE. There may be times when you want to focus with most critical precision. We have already noticed that there is not enough room on the focusing knob or the Depth of Field Scale to include all the distances and all the lens openings. For this reason, a very precise Depth of Field Table is given on page 56. It will tell you all the distances and lens openings that you are ever likely to need and can also be used as an extra focusing guide with cameras that have the Hyperfocal Table.

All of these focusing aids—the Depth of Field Scale, the Hyperfocal Table, the Depth of Field Table—are a basis for helping you decide what distances you can include for a sharp picture at different lens settings. Be guided by them and compose your pictures so that they will fall within the limits of the depth of field. This may sometimes mean that you will have to move forward or backward; or change your lens setting; or change

17. Pictures with near-by and distant objects should always have an interesting foreground. The sweep of the tree branches in the foreground makes a beautiful "frame" for the distant rock. Stereo by John Meredith.

18. A cut-off foreground and an empty background are things to avoid in stereo pictures that show near-by objects and infinity. Stereo made to show the point by Willard D. Morgan.

your shutter speed; or change your distance setting. Experiment a bit until you get the knack of it.

Always remember that depth of field is a gradual thing—it does not start and stop sharply at some imaginary line in the air. In general, small lens openings will give greater depth of field; and at any lens setting, the depth of field will be greater for distant scenes than for close-ups.

It ought to be clear by now that once you know what you want in stereo you may have to juggle things around to get it. This is all part of the fun and part of the learning that leads to experience. Now, with the mechanics of stereo under your belt, take a deep breath and start thinking about the pictures.

Foregrounds

The stereo view is always strongest close by, which naturally makes the foreground very important. In stereo viewing, as in natural vision, the 3-D feeling of space and distance is most acute in the first 25 feet. We are aware of depth to a lesser degree as far as 300 feet. And after that things are nominally "flat" and tend to look like a painted backdrop in contrast to the near things that show depth.

In average pictures, which include near objects and infinity, a strong foreground is a *must*. It provides a jumping-off spot for the rest of the picture. Look at Figures 17 and 18. They both include near objects and infinity. Figure 18 is not exciting because the near object is a cut-off face and part of a handrail—and the rest of the picture dwindles away to empty infinity, with a rock formation jutting out in the middle.

Figure 17, on the other hand, has a striking arrangement of tree branches in the foreground, framing the distant rocks. The foreground is now important and the contrast with the background is immediately interesting. In this picture the infinity background is kept to a minimum, and the scene is fascinating and *real* because we fill an area where 3-D is strong.

In pictures that reach only to 100 or 200 feet or so there is less need for a strong foreground, especially if the objects are large or visually demanding because of color or lighting. The foreground need not be so important because the rest of the scene will be quite strong in depth. Look at Figure 19, where the stereo interest is in the comparison of a number of things that all stand out very definitely at different distances. There is a strong receding pattern in the curve of the pool and the rest of the scene is well defined in space.

Pictures that stop at 25 to 50 feet include the most concentrated 3-D expanse. Everything looms large and lifelike, and often you will be pleased to have nothing at all in the immediate foreground. If the view is compelling, an empty foreground will seem to leave room for you, the viewer, to step in and look around. This is what happens in Figure 20. And this brings up the question of the "stereo window."

The stereo window relates the observer to the scene. In medium and distant scenes the view always seems to be on the other side of a window hanging before us in space. In near-medium scenes the view is still actually behind the window, but so close that we can mentally put ourselves in the middle of it, as we do in Figure 20. In close-up scenes, which we will discuss in a minute, the subject may even extend through the window and seem to touch us on our side. Chapter 6, on slide mounting, will explain in detail about manipulating this apparent window.

Finally, in considering foregrounds, we come to the close-ups: pictures with most of the view in the 2½ to 10-foot area. These pictures are all foreground, and handling them is up to you. Close-ups are good for shock-appeal, especially close-ups of people. But don't overdo them. You can get just as tired of full close-ups as empty long shots.

The Important Subject

Decide what you want to star in your picture and then think about the best way to show it. Although at all reasonable distances the stereo view will separate your important subject in space from everything else in the picture, you can't rely on this alone. In stereo you don't have the old flat-picture danger of telephone poles growing out of people's heads. But neither have you any guarantee that the poles will be subordinate to the people—unless you make them so. It's your point of view that counts. Move around, or when possible move the subject around until

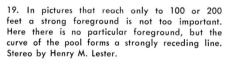

19. In pictures that reach only to 100 or 200 feet a strong foreground is not too important. Here there is no particular foreground, but the curve of the pool forms a strongly receding line. Stereo by Henry M. Lester.

28

20. Pictures that reach only to 25 or 50 feet can have an empty foreground as this one does. At medium distances the stereo sensation is very pronounced and you do not need a strong foreground to increase the three-dimensional interest. Stereo by Dorothy S. Gelatt.

you show it the way you think is most interesting, most revealing, or most striking. Decide for yourself what the scene means to you and photograph it accordingly. Is it people? Texture? Pattern? Vista? Color? Single out what you want to catch the eye and let your ingenuity take it from there. At all costs, have an important subject and avoid a confused, jumbled hodge-podge. Simple, straightforward subjects make the best pictures, both for interest and for composition.

Framing The Important Subject

"Framing" in stereo really means selecting a viewpoint with near-by objects that lead the eye to the important subject. Don't mistake "frame" for a flat picture frame. In stereo it is meant as a point or points of reference leading the eyes on through space. Just to give you an idea, look again at the tree in Figure 18. The tree leads the eye through the picture to the distant rocks. In this picture all the colors were muted desert hues, and the fascinating *shape* of the tree provided the interest, since there was no color contrast. In Figure 20, on the other hand, the girl was dressed in bright red and stood out as a sharp color contrast to the light clothes on the wash line. In this picture the receding laundry lines are the "frame" that leads to the girl, and past her to the background.

Remember that thoughtful "framing" should not only *lead* to the important subject, but make it the center of attention. Color, shape, size and

21. Leading lines make wonderful stereo compositions when there is no depth or bulk to the subject. This picture of bean poles in California is fun to look at because of the long receding perspective. Stereo by Billy Wilder.

interest will determine the best way of "framing" or composing any given picture.

Composing In Planes—And Leading Lines

The foreground framing and the important subject are the basic stuff of most stereo views. But don't stop with one or two static items. In developing a knack with stereo composition, learn to look for an extension of the basic subjects so that your pictures are an arresting total of different planes that all contribute to a seeming movement through the whole scene. Sometimes if you can't "frame" a subject, you can lead into it, or lead through it. Shooting at an angle will automatically do this with buildings, roads, or anything that presents a flat field or head-on view. If a subject doesn't have bulk or distinctive line or separation in space, it can always have perspective. Figure 21, which is all receding lines, relies solely on the perspective of the rows of bean poles.

The Background

There is always a background, although we have only mentioned it indirectly so far. Sometimes it can make or break a picture. In close-ups don't let the background be so busy that it distracts from the main subject. Simplicity is very often a key to great pictures! In medium shots try to make it an integral part of the whole scene. And in distant shots use it sparingly for contrast with strong subjects in the foreground. In any case, never ignore the background. Be aware of it, and make it work for you. Figures 17 and 19 show good handling of distant and not-too-distant backgrounds.

Live Subjects And Action

Anything living (like people and animals) or moving (like water) needs special understanding in stereo where the accent is on reality. It is very disconcerting to see pictures of people "caught in the act." A hand or foot "frozen" in mid-air, or a face contorted in talking, makes a bad impression in a stereo still. Unresolved action is unreal, and the mind won't accept it mixed in with the strong suggestion of reality that we get in 3-D. Learn to photograph actions compatible with the three-dimensional still. You can suggest action more readily with the proper pose than by stopping it midway in the act. Figure 7, Page 100 shows a pleasant portrait of two people just standing at ease. They would not look as natural if they had been snapped with faces twisted and arms waving while talking. Learn to catch action at its completion, not at its peak. This is as good a suggestion for animals and pets as it is for people.

Of course you may sometimes want to catch action on the fly. Figure 23 is a good example, and while it defies gravity it is not unreasonable—

22. Pictures of water and of action are both very tricky for beginners to master in stereo. The danger is in "freezing" the water or action so that they look unnatural. Here the action is "unfrozen" because it is in the direction of the camera. The water and spray have a suggestion of movement which keeps them "unfrozen" too. Stereo by Gilbert Morgan.

31

23. This "frozen" action is not unreasonable because we expect to see tumblers sailing through
the air. When the action suits the subject, a
"frozen" picture is very effective. Stereo by John
Meredith.

24. Still water sometimes looks like glass in stereo.
Here the pool gives a "mirror reflection" and the
result is natural enough. Stereo by Henry M. Lester.

because we *expect* to see tumblers in mid-air. Figure 22 is a more usual action shot, and it holds a useful clue for stereo action. The action is coming *towards* the camera, not crossing in front of it. This is a good way to avoid "frozen" action pictures.

Water is sometimes a problem too. "Frozen" water can look like jelly or glass if you are not careful. The swimming pool in Figure 24 looks like glass. There is no sure way to avoid this. Sometimes a shutter speed just slow enough to allow a suggestion of blur will make the water seem to move in the picture. The water in Figure 25 is more natural; it is a little blurry and the waves look real. The spray kicked up by the horses in Figure 22 looks a little bit like solid quartz rather than liquid water, but there is not enough of it to disturb the picture. Most good pictures of water combine it successfully with the rest of the scene so that it does not stand out and appear brittle like glass or blobby like jelly.

Lighting

As we learned in the very beginning, side lighting lends fullness and depth and front lighting tends to flatten things out. Back lighting can be effective too, and so can top lighting. In Figure 27 there is back light, side light and top light on the various children because of their arrangement in the picture. In this case the light stone terrace reflects some extra light into their faces to soften the shadows. Figure 26 has sharp top lighting and short, hard shadows underneath.

26. Sharp top light casts very short shadows, which you can see next to the toy train. This picture of Walt Disney and some friends has a strong foreground and does not need longer shadows to add to the composition. Stereo by Edgar Bergen.

Even when you are not taking pictures, keep your eyes open for lighting effects. Learn the difference between sharp, direct light and soft, diffuse light—how they separate distances and reveal outlines. The chapter on lighting will help you in detail with lighting effects.

Color

Color may be anything from almost black-and-white to a full rainbow riot. Sometimes a spot of color in an otherwise colorless picture is more effective than a lot of reds, blues and yellows screaming together. It all depends on what you are looking for and what you see, as you must know by now. Again, read the chapters on lighting and color, where you will pick up many more threads to tie into your color pictures. And look at all the color illustrations to see what part color plays in the picture.

Telling A Story

If you can tell the whole story in a single picture, fine. But if it takes more than one, don't stint. A series of pictures is exciting, especially when one leads to the next. A series of stereo stills lends movement to a scene and still leaves you as much time as you want to look through every detail. In this respect stills are more revealing than movies. For lively interest learn to see stereo scenes in series, and develop a continuity that tells the whole story.

34

Roundup

We have now gone *through* the stereo view—from front to back, from people to lighting to color to continuity. A lot of suggestions were made, and a lot of rules laid down. If you take them to heart you will always have "good" pictures. But if you stop here you will never make any discoveries of your own. Ignore the suggestions, break the rules—every time there seems good reason to. Make fuzzy pictures if you have something special in mind. Juggle the exposure. Use filters for surprise color. Shoot up from low spots, or down from high spots. Experiment—explore—do anything that promises GOOD STEREO.

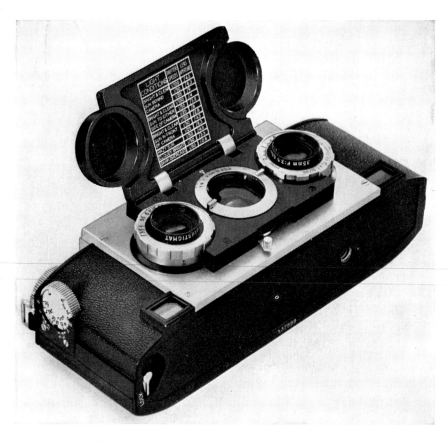

1. STEREO REALIST CAMERA, with the lens cover open, showing the lenses, shutter cocking lever, focusing knob, and view finder and range finder windows. A simple exposure table is mounted inside the lens cover.

2. Operating the Stereo Realist Camera

WILLARD D. MORGAN

The Stereo Realist is more than just a camera; it is a complete system of 3-D photography, fully coordinated from picture taking to viewing. The basic Realist outfit is compact and simple: a 35mm stereo camera; a roll of any standard brand 35mm color film; a stereo hand viewer. All the photographer needs to do is expose a roll of pictures and mail them out to a laboratory for processing and mounting in stereo slides. When they are returned, he can view them in full 3-D in his hand viewer. Realist stereo photography eliminates all drudgery and makes picture taking sheer pleasure — for the first time in the history of stereo.

There have, of course, been stereo cameras available for over 100 years. But only with the introduction of the Stereo Realist and its integrated system of stereo photography has it been possible to make color stereo pictures with such ease, and with a minimum of technical knowledge. A simple system for color pictures is especially important for stereo because, while a black-and-white picture will also have the three-dimensional effect, a stereo color picture is the last word in lifelike realism. But even though the system is simple, for the greatest satisfaction in 3-D picture making the user should be familiar with his equipment and how to use it.

The Stereo Realist is a compact miniature camera using standard 35mm films. Two matched lenses make a pair of pictures on the film at the same instant. When the film is developed and mounted, the two pictures are viewed as a stereo pair either by projection or in a compact hand viewer, recreating the original scene in all its depth and beauty.

Successful results can be obtained from the very first roll of stereo pictures, provided the simple directions for camera operation are observed. It is important, therefore, to read this chapter slowly and carefully so that the operation of the camera can become instinctive, enabling you to concentrate on selecting and composing your pictures.

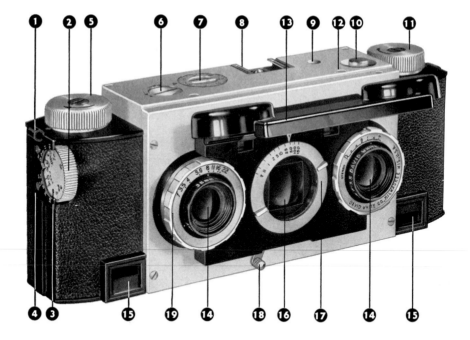

2. PARTS OF THE STEREO REALIST CAMERA. Each part is explained more fully in the text.

1. Neck Strap Lugs
2. Range Finder and Coupled Focusing Knob
3. Distance Scale
4. Depth of Field Scale
5. Film Winding Knob
6. Rewind Disk
7. Automatic Exposure Counter
8. Accessory Attachment Clip and Flash Contact
9. Shutter Trip Indicator
10. Shutter Release Button
11. Film Rewind Knob
12. Cable Release Socket
13. Lens Cover
14. Matched Camera Lenses
15. Range Finder Windows
16. View Finder Lens
17. Shutter Speed Setting Ring and Shutter
18. Shutter Cocking Lever
19. Diaphragm Setting Rings

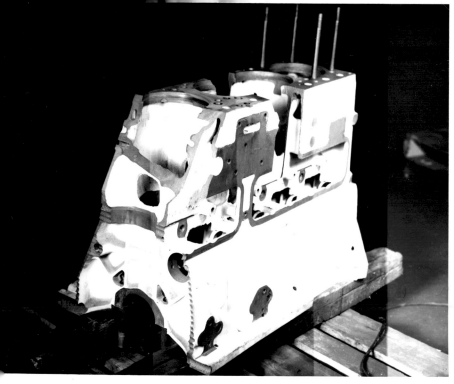

Let's look at the Realist specifications. (See Figures 2 and 4.)

1) NECK STRAP LUGS — Attach the leather neck strap to the two metal lugs on each end of the Realist camera. The special Realist protective leather case attaches to the camera without removing the neck strap. Always use the neck strap to prevent the camera from falling accidentally.

2) RANGE FINDER AND COUPLED FOCUSING KNOB — The knurled focusing knob located at the upper right end of the camera operates the built-in range finder for determining correct distance settings. The split-field coupled range finder has a wide base of 4¾ inches. The closest focusing distance is 2½ feet.

3) DISTANCE SCALE — The figures 2½, 3, 4, 5, 6, 8, 10, 15, 25 and INF. around the focusing knob represent distances in feet. Estimate distance between figures.

4) DEPTH OF FIELD SCALE — This serves as a quick reference for finding the maximum range of sharpness in a picture. It is a plate attached to the camera body surrounding the focusing knob. The plate has two sets of numbers, each duplicating the lens diaphragm stops engraved on the lens setting ring; a center line between the sets of numbers points to the distance (in feet) shown on the focusing knob. Used together, the lens stop numbers and the focusing knob distances show the *near* and *far* distances that will be in sharp focus. (Look at the illustration in Figure 24.) The "near" and "far" sets of numbers marked on the Depth of Field Scale point to the *near* and *far* distances (on the focusing knob) that will be in sharp focus at any selected lens stop and distance setting.

5) FILM WINDING KNOB — After each exposure the film winding knob is turned in the direction of arrow *until it comes to a firm stop.* The film wind release button (20) is pressed in and held down for the first quarter turn of the knob and then released while the winding knob is turned to a firm stop.

6) REWIND DISK — Turn rewind disk in direction of arrow to "R" when film is ready to be wound back into its original cartridge. After film is removed from camera, turn rewind disk back to "A" position for taking pictures again.

7) AUTOMATIC EXPOSURE COUNTER — The disk is calibrated from 1 to 35 and automatically indicates the number of exposures taken. The following 35mm Kodachrome films give 15, 20 and 28 stereo pairs:
K135 and K135A — 20-exposure gives 15 stereo pairs
36-exposure gives 28 stereo pairs
K335 and K335A give 20 stereo pairs returned from Kodak
in stereo mounts.

8) Accessory Attachment Clip — The flash attachment or any other special accessory fits into this clip.

9) Shutter-trip Indicator — As each exposure is taken, a small red disk appears, indicating that the lens shutters have been tripped. The red disk disappears when the film is advanced for the next exposure.

10) Shutter Release Button — When this button is pressed (gently!) the stereo shutters are released together to make both stereo pictures at the same instant.

11) Film Rewind Knob — Used for winding film back into original cartridge after all exposures have been made. Be sure rewind disk (6) is turned to "R" when using the rewind knob.

12) Cable Release Socket — A standard wire cable release is screwed into this socket when taking time exposures or at other times when the camera must remain steady on a tripod or other support.

13) Lens Cover — The hinged lens cover folds down to protect both lenses (with Realist filters in position) when the camera is not in use. When closed it also covers the view finder lens, which automatically prevents you from taking pictures with the lenses covered. The lens cover is flipped up quickly for picture taking. A handy exposure table is found inside the lens cover of latest cameras. Earlier cameras have a hyperfocal table inside the lens cover.

14) Matched Camera Lenses — The Realist Model ST-41 is equipped with two f/3.5, 3-element, matched, color-corrected, coated anastigmat lenses of 35mm focal length. The Model ST-42 is equipped with f/2.8, 4-element matched lenses. Iris diaphragms are mechanically coupled for making identical exposures. The vertical angle of view is 38°, horizontal angle 35°, and the diagonal angle is 50°. The field of view at 6 feet is 6 feet 3½ inches wide and 6 feet 11½ inches high. The short focal length of these lenses is responsible for the great depth in Realist pictures, even at fairly large lens openings.

After careful alignment at the factory the lenses are locked in position on a solid lens board and remain stationary in their original position. This provides good image alignment at all times. Focusing takes place within the camera by moving the film plane.

15) Range Finder Windows — Openings to admit images for the split-field range finder, which is used to determine distances.

16) View Finder Lens — The view finder lens is placed midway between the picture-taking lenses and on the same level with them. This eliminates all parallax problems; there is no danger of cutting off heads or feet in Realist pictures. What you see in the Realist finder you get in the finished pictures.

17) Shutter Speed Setting Ring and the Shutter — The synchronized dual shutters on the Realist operate together to make identical expo-

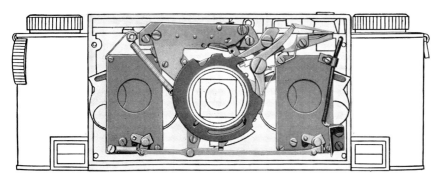

3. Mechanism of the Stereo Realist shutter. The stepped ring in the center moves the various internal levers in the shutter to change speeds and also the mechanism for the "Bulb" setting. The remaining linkage above operates both shutter blades at the same time, and for the same period of exposure, to produce two matched pictures.

sures when the release button is pressed. They are of the rim-set, gear-retarded, cocking type, with speeds of 1, 1/2, 1/5, 1/10, 1/25, 1/50, 1/100 and 1/150 second, plus (T) time and (B) bulb, in the Model ST-41 with f/3.5 lenses. Realist Model ST-42 with f/2.8 lenses has speeds from 1 to 1/200 second plus time and bulb. These shutter speeds appear on the shutter speed setting ring.

Always set the shutter speed *before* cocking the shutter (see 18). And when the camera is not in use, always leave the shutter set on some slow speed, like 1 second; leaving it on a higher speed will put undue strain on the shutter springs, which are pulled taut at the high speed settings.

When set on (B) bulb, the shutter remains open only as long as the release button (10) is held down; it closes when you let go of the button. The (B) setting is convenient for short time exposures of 2 to 5 seconds. For longer time exposures — 10 seconds to several minutes — use (T) time. On (T) the shutter opens and remains open when the release button is pressed and released. A second pressure and release of the button closes the shutter after the exposure is made. With the (T) setting the double exposure control (23) must be pulled out and moved to the side so that it remains out. If this is not done the shutter cannot be closed.

It is advisable to use a cable release on the camera for making (B) bulb, (T) time, or exposures longer than 1/25 second. Screw the cable release into the small threaded opening (12) just in front of the release button. Mount the camera on a rigid tripod for all exposures longer than 1/25 second.

Set the shutter at 1/25 second when using the Realist flash attachment. Electronic flash may be synchronized at any shutter setting.

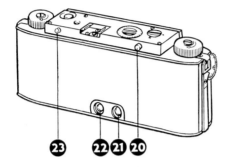

4. Rear view of Realist Camera, showing additional working parts explained in text.

20. Film Wind Release Button

21. Range Finder Eyepiece

22. View Finder Eyepiece

23. Double Exposure Control

18) SHUTTER COCKING LEVER — After setting the shutter speed ring (17), move the cocking lever all the way to the left. This sets the shutter for the exposure.

19) DIAPHRAGM SETTING RINGS — These rings are internally coupled so that both lens diaphragms are always at the same setting when either ring is turned. The f-stops (lens openings) are marked on only one lens.

20) FILM WIND RELEASE BUTTON — After each exposure press and hold this button down for one-quarter turn of the film winding knob (5); then release and continue turning knob to a good firm stop.

21) RANGE FINDER EYEPIECE — Hold the camera close to your eye when looking through this eyepiece and rotate the focusing knob (2) until you see both halves of the split image aligned. The distance scale (3) will indicate the distance in feet to this object.

22) VIEW FINDER EYEPIECE — After using the range finder and focusing knob to set the distance, shift the eye to the view finder eyepiece to compose the picture. What you see through this eyepiece you get on the final stereo picture. The view finder and range finder eyepieces have been placed next to each other for rapid focusing and viewing. Their position at the bottom rear of the camera is both unusual and useful. It permits the camera to be steadied against the forehead to avoid moving it when releasing the shutter. The finder is a direct-vision type giving an erect and unreversed image.

23) DOUBLE EXPOSURE CONTROL — All current Realist cameras have a completely automatic built-in device to prevent double exposures. The double-exposure control button (23) is left in its neutral position for normal picture making. The double exposure control can be installed on older cameras. See page 49 for operating instructions.

The Realist Camera Models ST-41 and ST-42 weight 1¾ pounds. The cameras are 6¾ inches long by 2½ inches high and 2-3/8 inches deep. The die-cast aluminum body furnishes a rugged frame for holding all the external and internal parts of the camera.

Picture Spacing in the Realist

To those who examine a roll of uncut Stereo Realist pictures for the first time, the arrangement of the separate images on the roll may appear somewhat random, and some have thought that a complicated and irregular winding motion is used in the camera to get the pictures in this order. This is not so, however, and a glance at the diagrams on the next page will show how the spacing of the pictures is accomplished with a straightforward, simple, winding mechanism.

The Realist takes two pictures at each exposure; each picture occupies a length of film equal to 5 perforations. Thus, the film must be wound a total distance of 10 sprocket holes each time the knob is turned.

Now, in Figure 5 we see the film just after the first picture has been taken and before the film is wound. Two pictures have been made, and there is space between them for two more.

The film is then wound forward, a distance of 10 sprocket holes. In Figure 6 we see that the right-hand picture 1A has moved two spaces to the right, and so has the left-hand picture 1B. The second picture is now taken, and 2A is made just to the right of 1B, with 2B in the place where 1B was before the film was wound.

In Figure 7, the film has again been wound and another pair of pictures has been taken, called 3A and 3B. Picture 3A has filled up the remaining empty space between 1B and 2B, and a new empty space exists between 2B and 3B. In turn, when the film is again wound, 4A will drop in this empty space between 2B and 3B and a new empty space will exist between 3B and 4B, which will be filled in by 5A and so on.

But we never did fill up the empty space between 1A and 2A, and it remains blank. We can use this space for an identification shot if we wish —see the Realist Film Identifier later in this chapter. Likewise, at the end of the roll, there will be one blank frame between the penultimate and the last B shot. If, for example, we have a 20-exposure roll, there will be a blank between 19B and 20B. Except for these two, there are no blanks throughout the roll, and no film wasted.

Identification Notch

Except for a few early Stereo Realist cameras, there is a notch in the lower edge of the right-hand picture aperture; this produces a visible mark on the upper edge of the "A" picture of each pair. (Remember, of course, that the image in the camera is upside down.)

This notch serves two purposes. First, it identifies the beginning of an uncut roll of film—the first picture has the notch in its upper edge, the last does not. Second, it aids in identifying pictures in case of an accidental mixup—the notched picture goes in the *left* side of the Stereo Realist mask during mounting (emulsion side up) and is the picture which is seen by the *right* eye when the picture is viewed. See Chapter 6 on slide mounting for further information on this point.

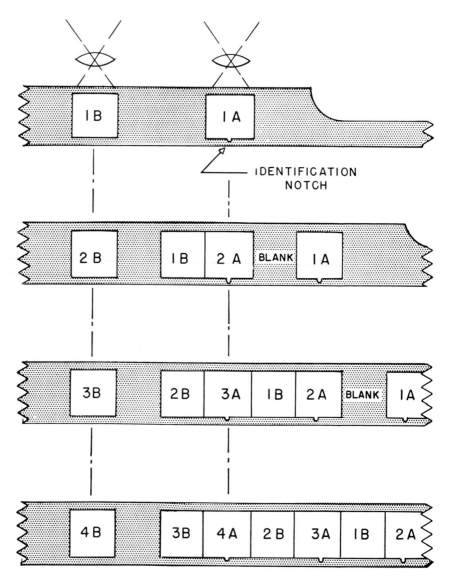

5. Spacing of pictures in the Stereo Realist. First picture pair is taken at the beginning of the roll.

6. Film is wound 10 perforations, and the second pair of pictures is taken.

7. Film is again wound, and the third pair is taken. Picture 3A fills in the empty space between 1B and 2B.

8. Continuing to take pictures, each new A picture drops in between two previous B pictures, while a new space is left for the next A picture.

9. Removing the back of the Realist camera for loading. The right end must be lifted first, and the back swung out, after which it can be removed from the camera completely.

Loading the Stereo Realist Camera

a) Place the camera face down on a table, lens cover closed, with the back of the camera facing you. Press shutter release button to make sure shutter is closed. Release the back plate by turning the lever at the right of the bottom of the camera *away* from *lock* position as far as it will go. Lift the camera back, raising the right end first, and remove from the camera. (Fig. 9.)

b) Note the sprocket wheel (Fig. 10) at the top center of the film track. The teeth of this wheel engage the film perforations to operate the counter and also the automatic stops for each new set of stereo pictures. Turn the sprocket in either direction with your finger tip until it clicks to a stop. Next, hold down the film wind release button with the right thumb and turn the sprocket with the left forefinger until a white dot between the sprocket teeth is positioned opposite the U-slot under the sprocket wheel, as in Fig. 10. (Earlier cameras without the white dot can be marked by following directions given on page 48.)

c) Turn rewind disk on top of the camera (6) to "A" (advance). On some older cameras line up the two dots.

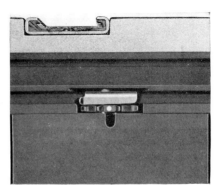

10. Before the film is inserted, the sprocket is turned by a finger tip until the white dot is aligned with the U-slot as shown here.

45

11. The end of the film is then pushed into the slot in the take-up spool. It should be down against the bottom flange of the spool as tightly as possible.

d) Turn winding knob until slot in film take-up spool at right is uppermost. Pull out rewind knob (11) at left as far as it will go to permit film cartridge to be inserted.

e) Remove film *magazine* from its carton. Keep the metal film container with its cap and the film mailing bag for later use. Also save the direction sheet.

f) Hold the film magazine in the left hand and insert the film end into the slot in the take-up spool. See Figure 11. Press the film end firmly into the slot by allowing the finger to overlap on the film and the spool while working the film into the slot. Film will go into the slot about ¼ inch. If you load your own 35mm film from bulk rolls, be sure that the beginning of the film is cut away in the same pattern as seen in Figure 12.

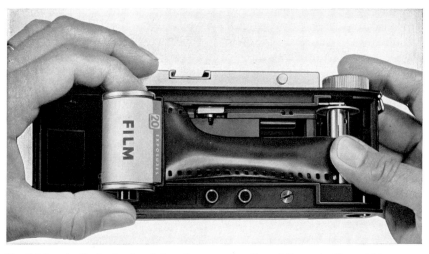

12. Holding the film in the slot of the take-up spool, pull carefully on the film cartridge, so that only enough film unwinds to permit dropping the cartridge in its compartment.

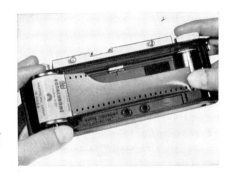

13. Drop cartridge into its compartment, and push down on film rewind knob until it engages with slot in cartridge spool.

g) While holding right thumb on take-up spool with film attached, move film magazine to left end of camera and drop into position, permitting only enough film to unwind to cover the distance across the back of the camera. Press rewind knob (11) back into position to engage its slotted end within the film magazine. *Note:* Do not pull out any more film from the magazine than is necessary or the first picture might be fogged. (Fig. 13.) The film will wind properly with the leader you see in the picture.

h) Do not wind film out to engage sprocket. Unless the camera back is replaced, the film will be exposed and will not advance properly over the sprocket.

i) Replace back on camera by inserting wide hinge of the back into left end of camera (Fig. 14.) The view finder and range finder openings will be at the bottom of the camera. Press the right end of the back into its closed position and turn the lever at the bottom of the camera to the *lock* position. (Fig. 15.) The lock will not hold the back unless the hinge is properly fitted into the back of the camera.

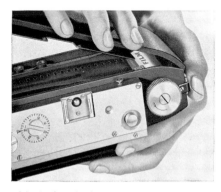

14. Replace back on camera by inserting the wide hinge into the left end of the camera. Then press down to close back.

15. With the back held firmly shut, turn locking lever clockwise to fasten the back tightly in place.

47

16. After winding off the necessary blank exposures at the beginning of the roll, set exposure counter to 1 by turning with the thumb.

j) Turn film winding knob in direction of arrow until knob locks.

k) Wind off three blank exposures as follows: Hold down film wind release button with thumb of left hand and turn film winding knob ¼ turn in direction of arrow. Remove thumb from release button and continue winding the knob until it comes to a firm stop. Repeat this full operation twice more, for a total of three blank exposures. This gives sufficient blank leader for the processing laboratory and prevents light from leaking through the magazine slot onto the first picture. (*Note:* This procedure provides one more blank exposure than called for in the Realist instruction book; but it follows the data sheet supplied by the Eastman Kodak Company with K335 Kodachrome film for stereo cameras. To avoid fogging the beginning of the roll, it is well to follow this procedure with any film used in the Realist.)

Now set the automatic exposure counter (7) to Number 1 on the dial, and the camera is ready for the first stereo picture. (Fig. 16.) Always set the exposure counter as soon as the film is loaded.

The White Dot on Earlier Realist Cameras

Every picture counts on a stereo roll of film. To avoid the possibility of fogging the first picture at the beginning of the roll, be sure that the white dot on the sprocket wheel is centered before loading the film, as shown in Figure 10. Some earlier models do not have this white dot, but a mark can be made as follows:

After the back of the camera is removed, and before the film is inserted, rotate the sprocket in either direction with your finger until it locks. Make sure that the rewind disk is in the advance position with the dot next to the "A" marker, or in some cases two dots together. Press the film release button and turn the sprocket counterclockwise for a distance of 3 teeth. At this point take a sharp blade and scrape the finish between the third and fourth tooth now on either side of the U-shaped slot found in the center edge of the aperture plate. This shiny spot will identify the proper

17. Top view of camera showing: (top) Shutter Trip Button, (center-right) Shutter Trip Signal Indicator, and (bottom) Double Exposure Control Button.

position for the sprocket when a film is loaded. A spot of white lacquer can also be used for marking this position.

Advancing Film for New Pictures

After each exposure the shutter trip signal indicator (9) on top of the camera will show red. See Figure 17. Advance film to the next picture space by repeating directions in *step k* previously given in film loading instructions. Wind off *only one* exposure after each picture.

When the counting dial indicates that you have reached 15, 20 or 28 exposures, depending on which length of film you are using, *stop* and rewind film back into its original magazine. Don't try to force "one extra" exposure on the roll. You might tear the film loose from the magazine spool and not be able to wind it back. Also, it often happens that only a part of one side of the picture is obtained when trying to force an extra exposure.

How to Use the Double Exposure Control

The Double Exposure Control, as shown in Figure 19, prevents any double exposures when using the camera for normal picture making. How-

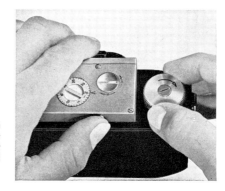

18. To wind film after exposure, press in on film wind release button and start turning the film winding knob. Then let go of button, and continue winding till knob stops turning.

49

19. Using the double exposure control. To recock the shutter, simply pull out on button and let go. For Time exposures, the button must be pulled out and locked to one side.

ever, there are times when this control is not required — as in taking stereo trick pictures or when only one picture of the stereo pair is to be exposed. For normal picture taking, leave the control button *in*. (Fig. 17.) This will prevent double exposures if you have forgotten to advance the film.

When a double exposure is desired proceed as follows:

a) Take first exposure in normal way. Do not wind film.

b) Pull control button out and release back to original position.

c) Recock shutter.

d) Make second exposure.

e) Any number of exposures can be made on the same film area if the control button is pulled out and set slightly off center so that it remains in the extended position.

f) When the shutter is set on time (T) the control button must be pulled out and left in the extended off-center position before operating the shutter.

g) Don't forget to move the control button to its original *in* position after it has served its purpose.

20. At the end of roll, turn rewind disk to "R" with the thumb. This releases the film so it can be wound back into its original cartridge.

To make single exposures, cover one lens with a tight-fitting lens cap; cock the shutter and expose the first picture. Transfer cap to other lens. Without winding film, pull double exposure button out and release. Cock the shutter again and expose the second picture. See the chapter on *Stereolusions* for special effects. The Double Exposure Control can be installed on the earlier Stereo Realist cameras.

Unloading

After exposing 15, 20 or 28 stereo pairs, depending upon the length of film used, turn rewind disk (6) until the dot stops opposite "R," which sets the camera to film rewind position. See Figure 20.

Turn film rewind knob (11) in direction of the arrow and continue turning until all the film is wound back into the original magazine. When the film winding knob at the other end of the camera stops rotating, this indicates that all the exposed film is almost rewound back into the magazine. Keep turning a few more times to make certain that all film is back in the magazine.

Open back of camera. Pull up film rewind knob and remove film magazine. To reload, repeat loading instructions previously given.

Operating and Holding the Realist Camera.

It is always important to hold the camera steady for every exposure. Here are some operating tips:

a) Use a shutter speed of 1/50 second or faster if light permits.

b) Use a sturdy tripod for the ultimate in steadiness.

c) Hold the camera as shown in Figure 21. Note position of thumbs — straight out, supporting the bottom; index fingers on top, with the middle finger operating the focusing knob. All controls are easily operated when the camera is held correctly. *(Note:* People with small hands may find it convenient to keep their thumbs against the camera back, which will allow the index fingers to operate the shutter release button and focusing knob. Use whichever position you find most comfortable, but always be sure to keep the fingers clear of the range finder windows.)

d) Hold camera firmly against forehead while framing scene through view finder. Then prepare to press release button with left middle finger. The range finder and view finder eyepieces are located at the rear and base of the camera, thus permitting the camera to be steadied against the forehead while framing the picture in the finder. Note that the view finder is in the exact center of the camera, thus eliminating any parallax or off-center pictures.

e) Equalize pressure between left thumb and middle finger as you gradually squeeze the release button. Try this once or twice until you develop a smooth, easy pressure on the button.

21. Holding the Stereo Realist camera. With fingers on top and bottom of the camera as shown, the camera can be held firmly, the third finger of the left hand being used for tripping the shutter. Focusing can be done with the tip of the third finger of the right hand. The camera must always be held level as shown.

f) Don't jab release button or final picture may not be sharp. Hands vary in size and coordination, and there will naturally be some individual modifications in holding and operating the camera.

g) Avoid covering the two range finder windows with fingers, so that you always see both halves of the image.

h) The camera must always be held in the *horizontal level* position — never in the vertical position. *This is very important.* Stereo pictures taken when the camera is not level are difficult if not impossible to fuse into a stereo image.

Focusing

A sharp image is essential for the successful stereo picture. Follow these important steps when focusing the camera:

a) Hold the camera against the forehead just above eye level; look at the scene from below the camera to determine the best objects to focus on.

b) Lower the camera so that the range finder window is in front of your eye.

c) Center the object you wish to focus on in the lower, stationary half of the range finder sight.

d) Turn the focusing knob until the top half of the split image lines up with the bottom half in the range finder sight. Note the distance that this setting gives on the focusing knob.

e) Focus as above on the nearest and farthest objects in the scene to be photographed, noting the distances on the focusing knob. Then check the Depth of Field Scale (on late models) or the Hyperfocal Table (on earlier models) to make sure that you choose the proper lens opening to put your whole picture in sharp focus.

Practice with the Controls

Before loading the camera it is wise to go through the operating steps. Turn the focusing knob while looking through the range finder sight. Note the distance in feet after adjusting for some fixed point. Move the lens diaphragm scale to different positions. Set the shutter dial at some position such as 1/50 second. Set the shutter cocking lever by pushing it across to the left, when sighting through the viewer. Hold camera in picture-taking position and frame subject in the view finder. Then press shutter release button gradually to trip shutter. Repeat these operations a few times until you are familiar with the operation of the camera. You will have to pull out and release the double exposure control (23) to be able to continue tripping the shutter in the current models.

Now remove the back of the camera and go through the operations again. Observe that the film plane moves, not the lenses, when the focusing knob (2) is turned. This assures more accurate alignment of the two images. Hold the camera up before a light and note that the two shutters trip at the same moment when the release is pressed. Knowing all about these simple operations will be helpful in obtaining good stereo pictures.

22. Cocking the shutter is done by pulling the small lever over with the thumb and letting it go. The shutter will not trip unless it is cocked before each exposure.

23. Setting the lens diaphragm is done by turning the ring around either lens. A white dot on the inner ring is the index against which lens settings are read.

Making Your First Stereo Picture

a) Load the camera as explained in the directions.

b) Set the shutter speed to 1/50 or any other setting (as indicated by use of an exposure meter or table) which is shown on the shutter speed setting ring. The shutter is now set to operate in synchronization at the selected speed. *Never set the shutter between the marked speeds.*

c) Measure the necessary distances with range finder and focusing knob.

d) Adjust the lens opening as indicated by an exposure table or meter, or as required by focus. The lenses can be set on the marked stops *or* between them. See Figure 23.

e) Hold the camera *level* as shown in the illustration (Fig. 21).

f) Move the shutter cocking lever from right to left (when the lenses are facing away from you). This cocks the shutter for the exposure. It is essential to cock the shutter *after* the speed is set. The shutter has an audible click when being cocked. (Fig. 22.)

g) Hold the camera in picture-taking position with one eye close to the eyepiece of the view finder. You can now compose your picture, ready for the final shutter releasing. What you see in the view finder you get on the film.

h) After all settings have been made and the image is located properly in the view finder, take the exposure by a gradual but firm pressure on the shutter release button. Let your finger rest firmly on the camera body while the finger tip presses down on the release. This will prevent camera movement at the instant of exposure.

i) Advance the film to the next picture, as explained earlier. (Be sure to take your finger off the film wind release after the first ¼ turn of the winding knob; otherwise you will continue winding film and the pictures will not be properly spaced.) You are now ready for the next exposure.

Settings for Average Outdoor Pictures

If you don't want to bother focusing or using an exposure table or meter, you can use the following settings for all average outdoor pictures in daylight.

a) Set shutter speed ring on 50 (marked in red, opposite arrow, on latest cameras).

b) Set focusing knob on 20 feet (marked in red, opposite arrow, on latest cameras). This gives a sharp picture from 10 feet to infinity.

c) Set lens at f/6.3 — midway between f/5.6 and f/8 (marked with red dot on latest cameras).

You will get good pictures all the time at these settings if it is an average sunny day and you keep the sun at your back. If the light is exceptionally bright, as in beach or snow scenes, or if the sky is cloudy, consult an exposure table or meter to adjust the lens setting slightly.

These simple settings have become known as *The Three R's in Outdoor Stereo Photography* ever since they have been marked in red on recent cameras. Anyone can use *The Three R's* for foolproof picture taking outdoors in good weather.

Depth of Field

Maximum sharpness of each image is an important part of every stereo picture. An out-of-focus or blurred object in the foreground or background is always annoying to the eye when seen in the viewer or on the projection screen, especially if the object dominates the scene. There is an easy way to avoid these blurred areas in a picture simply by referring to what is known as the depth of field table or scale. Latest cameras have a convenient scale around the focusing knob, as seen in Figure 24. Earlier cameras have a similar method, a hyperfocal table mounted inside the lens cover. A complete Depth of Field Table is also included in this book on pages 56 and 57.

Depth of field is a term used to express the maximum sharpness in a scene or object photographed, measured from the nearest point of sharpness to the farthest point of sharpness, or infinity. Infinity for the Stereo Realist lenses is considered to be about 100 feet and over. On the focusing knob scale there are no distances marked between 25 feet and 100 feet or infinity (∞). But it is easy to estimate any points desired by dividing the space proportionally. The depth of field varies with the opening of the lens and the distance setting. As the lens diaphragm is reduced to the smaller openings (f-stops), the depth of field increases.

For example — the Depth of Field Table (page 56) shows that when the lens is wide open at f/3.5 and the distance knob is set to 25 feet, the near point of sharpness is at about 14½ feet and the far point of sharpness at approximately 91 feet. Then by closing the lens opening, or diaphragm,

DEPTH OF FIELD TABLE

Based on Focal Length 35.2mm; Circle of Confusion 1/750 inch.

Diaphragm Setting f/	Depth of Field	DISTANCE SETTING OF FOCUSING DIAL									
		INF	25'	15'	10'	8'	6'	5'	4'	3'	2½'
2.8	FROM	43'	15'10"	11'1"	8'1"	6'9"	5'3"	4'6"	3'8"	2'9½"	2'4½"
	TO	INF	60'	23'	13'0"	9'10"	7'0"	5'8"	4'5"	3'2½"	2'7¾"
3.2	FROM	38'	15'	10'8"	7'11"	6'7"	5'2"	4'5"	3'7½"	2'9½"	2'4½"
	TO	INF	75'	25'	13'7"	10'2"	7'1"	5'9"	4'6"	3'3¼"	2'8"
3.5	FROM	34'	14'6"	10'5"	7'9"	6'6"	5'1"	4'4"	3'7"	2'9¼"	2'4¼"
	TO	INF	91'	27'	14'0"	10'5"	7'3"	5'10"	4'6"	3'3½"	2'8½"
4	FROM	30'	13'8"	10'0"	7'6"	6'4"	5'0"	4'4"	3'6½	2'9"	2'3¾"
	TO	INF	147'	30'	14'11"	10'10"	7'6"	6'0"	4'7"	3'3¾"	2'8¾"
4.5	FROM	27'	12'11"	9'7"	7'3"	6'2"	4'11"	4'3"	3'5¾"	2'8¾	2'3½"
	TO	INF	387'	34'	15'11"	11'4"	7'8"	6'2"	4'8"	3'4½	2'9"
5	FROM	24'	12'4"	9'3"	7'1"	6'0"	4'10"	4'2"	3'5¼"	2'8¼"	2'3¼"
	TO	INF	INF	40'	17'0"	11'11"	7'11"	6'3"	4'9"	3'5"	2'9¼"
5.6	FROM	21'5"	11'6"	8'10"	6'10"	5'10"	4'8"	4'1"	3'4¾"	2'7¾"	2'3"
	TO	INF	INF	49'	18'7"	12'8"	8'3"	6'6"	4'11"	3'5¾"	2'9¾"
6.3	FROM	19'	10'10"	8'5"	6'7"	5'8"	4'7"	4'0"	3'3¾"	2'7¼"	2'2¾"
	TO	INF	INF	69'	21'	13'8"	8'8"	6'9"	5'0"	3'6½"	2'10¼
7	FROM	17'1"	10'5"	8'0"	6'4"	5'6"	4'6"	3'10½"	3'3"	2'6¾"	2'2¼"
	TO	INF	INF	115'	24'	14'10"	9'2"	7'0"	5'2"	3'7½"	2'10¾
8	FROM	15'	9'5"	7'6"	6'0"	5'3"	4'4"	3'9¼"	3'2¼"	2'6¼"	2'2"
	TO	INF	INF	INF	29'	16'10"	9'7"	7'5"	5'5"	3'8¾"	2'11¾

9	FROM TO	13'4" INF	8'9" INF	7'1" INF	5'9" 39'	5'0" 19'6"	4'2" 10'9"	3'8" 7'11"	3'1" 5'8"	2'5½" 3'10"	2'1½" 3'½"
10	FROM TO	12' INF	8'2" INF	6'8" INF	5'6" 57'	4'10" 23'	4'0" 11'9"	3'6½" 8'5"	3'¼" 5'11"	2'5" 3'11½	2'1" 3'1½"
11	FROM TO	10'11" INF	7'8" INF	6'4" INF	5'3" 107'	4'8" 29'	3'10¾ 13'0"	3'5½" 9'1"	2'11¾ 6'2"	2'4½" 4'1"	2'½" 3'2½"
12.7	FROM TO	9'5" INF	6'10" INF	5'10" INF	4'10" INF	4'4" 48'	3'8¼" 15'11"	3'3¼" 10'4"	2'9¾" 6'9"	2'3½" 4'4"	1'11¾" 3'4"
14	FROM TO	8'7" INF	6'5" INF	5'6" INF	4'8" INF	4'2" 99'	3'6¾" 19'2"	3'2¼" 11'7"	2'9" 7'4"	2'3" 4'6"	1'11½" 3'5½"
16	FROM TO	7'6" INF	5'9" INF	5'0" INF	4'4" INF	3'10¾ INF	3'4½" 28'	3'¼" 14'4"	2'7¾" 8'3"	2'2" 4'10"	1'10¾" 3'8"
18	FROM TO	6'8" INF	5'3" INF	4'8" INF	4'0" INF	3'8" INF	3'2¼" 51'	2'10½" 18'7"	2'6¼" 9'7"	2'1" 5'3"	1'10¼" 3'10½"
20	FROM TO	6'0" INF	4'10" INF	4'4" INF	3'9½" INF	3'5½" INF	3'0" INF	2'9" 27'	2'5" 11'4"	2'¼" 5'9"	1'9½" 4'2"
22	FROM TO	5'5" INF	4'6" INF	4'0" INF	3'6¾" INF	3'3¼" INF	2'10½ INF	2'7¾" 48'	2'4" 13'11"	1'11¾ 6'5"	1'9" 4'5"

DEPTH OF FIELD TABLE FOR REALIST CAMERAS. While most photographic problems can be solved with greater ease simply by using the depth-of-field scale on the camera focusing knob, the chart above will be useful where greater accuracy is required, or where preliminary planning must be done before the picture is made—for example, in the case of the trick setups mentioned in the chapter on Stereolusions.

To use the chart, simply locate the camera-to-subject distance in the top heading. The lens stop to be used is found in the left-hand column, and the row followed across to the column previously found, in which can be read the nearest and farthest distance in focus. Or, the chart can be used backward. Find the subject distance on top of the chart, then run down the column until a pair of figures is reached corresponding to the near and far distances or depth of field you need. Then, follow the row to the left to find the lens aperture which will produce this depth of field.

24. The Depth of Field Scale on the Focusing Knob. This scale automatically shows the depth of field for any aperture when the lens is focused for any distance. In this example, the lens is set at 3½ feet; depth of field will be from 2½ to 5 feet at f/16, and correspondingly less at other apertures.

to f/8 and setting the distance knob at 25 feet, the near range of sharpness extends from 9½ feet to infinity. This means that everything from 9½ feet to infinity is in sharp focus as far as the average eye can determine.

Using the Depth of Field Scale

The range of sharpness in a picture is easily determined by checking the upper (Far) and lower (Near) numbers on the depth of field scale (4) to be found on the later Realist models. These numbers correspond to the f-stop numbers on the lens flange. Where numbers are not shown, because of space limits, just estimate the location.

Example. Say your main subject to be photographed is 8 feet away, as determined by the range finder, and the f-stop or diaphragm opening selected is f/8. You will note that the 8-foot mark on the focusing knob, on the present Realist cameras, is opposite the center line on the scale. Then the Near point of sharpness will be about 5½ feet, as indicated on the Near part of the scale, and the Far point will be at approximately 16 feet. These are the two sharp distance points between the Near and Far f-numbers, in this case f/8. Of course there is a small margin of safety before the Near and Far points become fuzzy. The zone of sharpness does not drop off abruptly to not being sharp.

Now move the focusing knob so that the 10, 15, and 25-foot marks are opposite the center line. The depth of field range of sharpness keeps getting greater as: 6 to 23 feet, 8 feet to about infinity (∞), and 10 feet to infinity. In the case of the 25-foot setting, note that infinity is opposite the f/5.6 mark while the lens is still at f/8. To get the maximum advantage of the depth of field, move the infinity mark back to f/8 on the Far side and note that the Near sharpness has been changed to about 9 feet.

When photographing in areas such as rooms and streets where the background distance is less than 100 feet, just focus on the principal subject and the acceptable depth of field will take care of itself if the lens opening is around f/5.6 or smaller. For example, when photographing a subject about 13 feet from the camera with a building background not over 25 feet away, the range of depth is around 8 feet on the Near side and over 25 feet for the Far side when the lens is set at f/5.6. This example would cover many typical street scenes when traveling, and you would be taking the maximum advantage of the lens and distance settings.

Depth of Field Table

By this time you will notice that the depth of field becomes less for close objects and greater for more distant ones. To obtain greater depth in the near scenes, it is necessary to use smaller lens openings and usually slower shutter speeds unless there is intense light or a flash is used. For example, when taking a portrait with the main distance set at 4 feet and the lens opening at f/5.6, the Near point of sharpness is only about 3 feet and the Far point is 4 feet 11 inches. Now put the camera on a tripod and stop the lens opening down to f/16; the range of sharpness extends from the Near point of approximately 2 feet 8 inches to a Far point of about 8 feet.

A detailed Depth of Field Table is given on pages 56 and 57 for times when you want especially critical focusing. This table gives many more lens stops and distance settings than space will permit on the camera's Depth of Field Scale. Look it over carefully to acquaint yourself with the information it holds. This table will tell you, for example, the lens stop and distance setting to use if you already know the near and far distances you want to include in sharp focus. (If you want to include a near distance of 4 feet, 8 inches and a far distance of 29 feet, you will find from the table that a lens stop of f/11 and a distance setting of 8 feet will be correct.) On the other hand, the table will tell you what will be in focus if you have already chosen a lens stop and distance setting. (If you have chosen f/6.3 and 10 feet, the table shows that distances from 6 feet, 7 inches to 21 feet will be in focus.) You can also use the table to find out which setting to adjust for specific problems.

The Depth of Field Table will be useful, too, for people whose cameras have a Hyperfocal Table instead of a Depth of Field Scale.

Using the Hyperfocal Table

The Hyperfocal Table, found under the lens cover of earlier Realist cameras, tells you where to set the focusing knob and lens diaphragm for a range of sharpness from infinity to some near point. Infinity is considered to be about 100 feet and over. Simply measure the distance to the nearest object in the picture and then set the focusing knob and lens diaphragm as indicated in the table. Then adjust the shutter speed to give the correct exposure with the lens opening indicated by the Hyperfocal Table. A Depth of Field Scale can be installed on the earlier cameras, if desired, by sending the camera to Realist, Inc., or one of their authorized repair stations.

Realist Flash Attachment

All you need to take good flash pictures with the Realist camera is a Realist Flash Attachment, which fits into the accessory clip on top of the camera (Fig. 25), and some midget flashlamps, such as the No. 5, No. 25, or SM. No connecting wires are required. The built-in flash synchronization is effective when the shutter speed is set to 1/25 second. At this setting the built-in synchronizing switch makes contact and sets off the flash at the moment when the shutters are fully open. If the speed is set faster than 1/25 second, the shutters will open and close before the flashlamp has discharged all of its rated light output. This will make the pictures too blue. The full light output is essential for best results with color film.

Extension flashes or electronic flash units can also be activated by the built-in camera synchronization. They are connected to the camera by a specially designed "foot" which fits into the accessory clip. Chapter 4, *Lighting, Exposure and Color In Stereo*, tells how to use the Realist Flash Attachment and how to take flash pictures.

25. The Stereo Realist Flash Attachment slides into the camera accessory clip and makes contact without wires. Also shown is the accessory Flash Shield.

Flash Guide Rings

To find the proper exposure for pictures to be made with flashlamps a Flash Guide Number is used. You will find Flash Guide Numbers printed on the flashlamp wrappers. Flash Guide Numbers are listed for specific film—shutter speed—flashlamp combinations. You simply divide the Guide Number by the distance (in feet) from camera to subject, and get the proper lens setting for the picture.

Example. The Guide Number is 105 for a G-E No. 5 flashlamp with Kodachrome Film, Type A (indoor film) at 1/25 second. To find the lens setting, you simply divide the Guide Number (105) by the distance (in feet) from camera to subject. If you are 10 feet from the subject, it will be:

$$\frac{(\text{Guide Number}) \quad 105}{(\text{Distance}) \quad 10} = 10.5 \text{ (Lens Setting f/10.5; f/11 is close enough)}$$

To eliminate the mathematics and the nuisance of remembering the correct Guide Numbers, Realist has made two types of Flash Guide Rings. One ring is for use with indoor color film and clear flashlamps; the other is for use with daylight color film and blue flashlamps. These extremely practical rings can be permanently secured around the two lenses of the Realist camera; they do not interfere with the regular operation of the camera. But when you are ready to take flash pictures, their usefulness is quite remarkable. First you focus the camera and note the distance on the focusing knob. You then note that same distance (in feet) for the proper flashlamp on your Flash Guide Ring — and set it next to the nearest white dot. Thus your lenses are automatically adjusted to the correct opening. You can check this by doing the mathematics described above, but it is not necessary.

Installing the Flash Guide Rings

The Flash Guide Rings are supplied by Realist, Inc., or their dealers free of charge on request, and are easily applied to the camera. They are thin metal rings backed with pressure-sensitive adhesive which secures them permanently to the lens mounts.

The set of two Flash Guide Rings have altogether 5 scales for 5 different flashlamps: 3 for clear flashlamps on one ring; 2 for blue flashlamps on the other. The ring with 2 scales should be secured to the lens mount with the lens stops engraved on it. The ring with 3 scales should be secured to the lens mount with no lens stops on it.

To mount the 3-scale ring (for clear flashlamps and indoor color film):

a) Set the camera lenses to f/3.5 (accurately). Note that there are 3 white dots engraved around each of the black lens barrels.

b) Peel the protective paper from the back of the Flash Guide Ring and push out the center disc bearing the identifying imprint. Note that

61

the ring has a pair of black index marks (:) next to the black triangle opposite each of the three scales. (The scales are for No. 5, No. 25 and SM flashlamps.)

c) Align the No. 5 index mark with the white dot on the top of the lens barrel. This will line up the other two index marks with the other two white dots. When carefully aligned, press the ring firmly against the lens mount.

To mount the 2-scale ring (for blue flashlamps and daylight color film):

a) Trim off the unmarked sector of the ring with a sharp scissors.

b) Set the lenses again to f/3.5 and note the white dots on the lens barrel.

c) Align the 5B index mark opposite the lower right-hand white dot engraved on the barrel of the lens with the f-stops. This will line up the other index mark next to the lower left-hand white dot on the lens barrel. When carefully aligned, press the ring firmly against the lens mount. As you will see, the lens diaphragm numbers (f-stops) are left clearly visible in the space that has been trimmed from the ring, and the lenses are set as usual.

Flash Guide Rings are available for earlier models of the Realist camera which have Ilex or Ektar lenses. When requesting this useful accessory you should always mention the type of lenses your camera has.

Remember when using the Flash Guide Rings or any flashlamp Guide Numbers that they apply only to "average" conditions. For light subjects or rooms with light walls, the lenses should always be closed down to ½ lens stop smaller than the ring or the guide number indicates. For dark subjects or rooms with dark walls, the lenses should be opened up to ½ stop larger than the ring or guide number indicates. A little experience will teach you how to modify the guide number settings.

26. The Stereo Realist Film Identifier uses the otherwise unexposed picture between frames 1L and 2L to photograph a small card which may be used for name, date, place or other information needed to identify any particular film roll.

27. The Realist sunshades and adapter rings accept the Realist filters and any standard Series V filter as well. They slip over the lenses of the Stereo Realist camera and are held by friction.

Realist Film Identifier

The Film Identifier is a compact attachment which is easily carried in the camera gadget bag or pocket. There are times when information such as your name, date, place, or film number should be copied right on the stereo roll. This is quickly done by using the Film Identifier as shown in Figure 26. Write out the information on a 1⅜x1⅜ card and slip it into the Identifier, which will be in proper focus when you use the following directions:

a) After loading the camera (as previously explained) replace the back of the camera.

b) Wind the film until the winding mechanism locks.

c) Wind off two blank exposures as explained in *Loading the Stereo Realist Camera, Step k.*

d) At this point place the Film Identifier over the left lens of the camera. This is the lens farthest from the focusing knob. *Set the focusing knob at infinity.* Expose the card with the special information to be copied onto the film. Exposure is judged according to the available light used.

e) Remove the Identifier and wind off the third blank exposure.
You are now ready to take the first picture.

The identification exposure uses the blank frame after the first picture, so that no film is wasted on the roll. When color film is mounted by a laboratory the identification frame will be returned in the box with the other film scraps. You can use the identification frame in your picture filing system, or to identify each roll when a large batch is sent for processing at the same time.

Realist Sunshades

For maximum protection from unwanted reflections, always use the sunshades. These shades are quickly slipped over the lens flanges and do not interfere with the view finder or lens diaphragm settings. The lens flanges are grooved to match the tongues of the sunshades. The sunshades also serve as filter holders and accommodate all Series V filters.

Filters

There are three pairs of identically matched Realist filters, made of coated optical glass, for use with color film. Although most stereo pictures are taken without filters, the following filters will take care of most variations:

a) The Type A, ST 51-1 filter is used with Type A film in daylight.

b) Haze, ST 51-2 is used with Daylight film to cut the excess of ultraviolet light found at high altitudes, over water, and in landscapes with a hazy cast.

c) Flash, ST 51-3 is used with Type A film and wire-filled flashlamps. Cuts excess of blue light which these bulbs produce. Also used with Daylight film when exposed with strobe (electronic flash) or to cut down blue light on overcast days.

Carrying Cases

Your camera and equipment must have constant protection to keep in top working condition. The Ever-Ready case is the best protection for the camera. The neck strap is attached directly to the camera, and the case can be removed separately in two parts. The cover part is removed when taking pictures; the rest of the case is removed only when the camera is to be reloaded. The larger camera and accessory bags are available

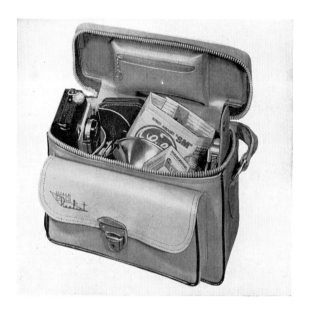

28. One of the Combination Cases for Stereo Realist camera and accessories. This one is of the popular gadget bag type; other luggage style cases are available.

29. The Stereo Realist Ever-Ready Case provides protection for the camera while it is being carried. Front of case snaps off for picture taking; camera need not be removed from case except for loading.

for complete protection from weather, scratching, and hard knocks. There is room in these larger bags to hold the Realist camera plus small accessories, spare film, flashlamps, exposure meter, and other items. The accompanying illustrations show these cases.

Other Realist Equipment

A full line of accessory equipment is available for viewing, mounting and the projection of stereo pictures. This equipment is shown and described in Chapter 6, *Slide Mounting and Projection Equipment,* and Chapter 7, *Viewing and Projection.*

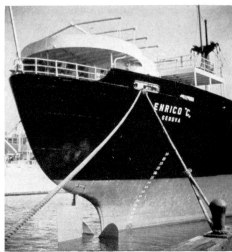

1. Good stereos can be made from the very start outdoors on daylight color film. Have the sun shining full on the subject, set lens to f/6.3 and shutter to 1/50 second. Stereo by John S. Carroll.

3. Color Films for Stereo

JOHN S. CARROLL

The large majority of pictures made with the Stereo Realist Camera are, of course, made in color; the combination of 3-dimensional image and color is accepted as the ultimate in photographic realism. Elsewhere in this book, the subject of stereo-color composition is discussed, while the specific problems of color harmony, lighting for color in 3-D, the emotional aspects of color, etc., are considered in nearly every chapter.

This chapter will concern itself, therefore, with the characteristics of the color films themselves—how they work, and how to get the best results from each type and make of film.

Even the veriest tyro can secure excellent results from the very first roll by following one simple rule:

Have the sun over your shoulder, shining full upon your subject. Set your lens at f/6.3 (halfway between f/5.6 and f/8), your shutter at 1/50 second, and shoot.

This simple rule will produce practically perfect color stereo pictures every time; it is only after one has started to branch out that any more will be needed.

Sooner or later, however, the photographer graduates from the beginner class; he wishes to make pictures in deep shade, on cloudy days, at sunrise, sunset, or indoors. The versatility of the Stereo Realist Camera will enable him to do all of this after he has gained a little practical knowledge of the working of color films.

How Color Films Work

All present-day color films with the exception of Dufaycolor (which is not used to any great extent in the United States) work on the integral tripack principle, which simply means that the film is coated with three layers of emulsion, each layer sensitive to approximately one-third of the visible spectrum. That is, while we can see a large number of individual

colors in the spectrum (whether spread out by a prism, a grating, or by Mother Nature in a rainbow), we can divide the whole into three broad regions of about equal width. One of these sections will be predominantly blue, the next mainly green, and the last will contain the gamut of reds.

To do this, we must consider the nature of photographic emulsions. A plain silver-bromide emulsion is sensitive to blue light only. (We can ignore the ultraviolet, since most of this is absorbed by the glass of the lens.) By adding certain sensitizers to the emulsion during manufacture we can make it sensitive to green light as well as to blue. Other sensitizers make the emulsion sensitive to red as well as to its basic blue. Obviously, by adding both we could make emulsions equally sensitive to red, green and blue light; the "panchromatic" types of black-and-white film are made in this way.

For a color film, however, the sensitizers are used individually. Since all three layers, however, will be sensitive to blue light, means must be provided to avoid this in the layers to be used for the green and red records. This is done in the following manner:

The top layer of emulsion is a normal bromide emulsion: it is sensitive to blue light only. Directly beneath this is coated a thin layer of yellow dye which acts as a filter and removes all the blue light from whatever has passed through the layer above. The next layer has been treated with a green sensitizer; since the blue has been removed from the light beam by the yellow filter layer, it makes the record of the middle third of the spectrum. The remaining layer has been treated with a red sensitizer. It has no green sensitivity, and due to the yellow filter no blue light reaches it; hence it makes the red record.

During development the image in each layer is transformed to a dye which is complementary in color to the sensitivity of the layer. That is, the blue-sensitive layer forms a yellow dye, the green-sensitive layer forms a magenta dye image, and the red-sensitive layer forms a cyan (blue-green) dye image.

Since most natural colors (such as those of flowers, grass, etc.) transmit or reflect light in several parts of the spectrum, it is not difficult to secure acceptable color rendition of such subjects on a three-layer film. However, it should be obvious from this description of how the film works that one couldn't photograph an actual spectrum with a tripack color film, since the emulsions have no way of distinguishing between pure colors which lie within one spectral band.

Thus there are many shades of red lying in the red end of the spectrum; all of these would be rendered by various quantities of the same red color in the final transparency. Many dyestuffs, on the other hand, transmit a good deal of light to which the eye is less sensitive but which affect color films very strongly. Certain blue dyes, for example, have considerable transmission in the far red which is not evident to the eye. When photographed on color film, however, such blue colors appear reddish or violet.

3. Artificial dyes and paint pigments may not always match the spectral characteristics of color films, and test exposures are sometimes needed. Rosita Royce in the film, *Striporama*, directed by Jerald Intrator. Stereo by Dorothy S. Gelatt.

4. Crowd scenes are very successful in color stereo. Colors and shapes that merge into shades of gray in the ordinary flat black-and-white picture are separately defined in the color stereo. Photograph courtesy Realist Inc.

Thus, it is not to be expected that clothing and other artificially dyed objects will appear in their exact shades when photographed on color films. Appreciation of this point will prevent disappointment when color films are used commercially for fashion or advertising purposes.

When certain dyed fabrics or painted walls are used as part of a setting for a color photograph it is essential to make photographic tests to determine the actual shade of color which will be achieved in the final transparency. One must keep in mind at all times that modern color films are capable of producing very pleasing color photographs, but that they are not designed to be used as color-matching or color-measuring media.

When this problem is understood it will not be difficult to appreciate the difficulty in securing adequate duplicates of color transparencies. One must realize that the original transparency does not duplicate the colors of the subject; it approximates them in dyestuffs of very different spectral characteristics. Then a duplicate transparency, in turn, is merely an approximation of the original transparency—a color photograph of a color photograph.

This is not to to say that duplicate transparencies cannot be made; good duplicates are being made regularly on a commercial basis and with very good quality. But their use for fashion photography, advertising, etc., should only be undertaken with the knowledge that color matching will not be, and cannot be expected to be, precise.

Types Of Color Films

In the manufacture of three-layer color films there are two basic approaches. In one, the film contains simply the three layers of differentially sensitized emulsion; the colors in the final transparency are generated by the developers and located in the layers by means of the development process. Kodachrome film is of this type.

The other film, of which Ansco film is a typical representative, contains certain color-forming chemicals in each layer of emulsion. These are designed to react with the developer to form the proper dye image in each layer in a single development process.

Either system is capable of producing excellent results. The only difference between them from the user's standpoint is that processing of the former type must be done by the manufacturer, while the latter film can be processed by the user in his own darkroom, if desired.

In general, Kodachrome film is developed to a fairly high contrast and color saturation; Ansco Color film, with recommended processing, tends to be somewhat softer in contrast and its colors somewhat pastel. This is not inherent in the emulsion, however. Some workers have found that increasing the time of development in the color developer results in more brilliant images and more vivid color. Some adjustment of the time of first development may also be necessary to secure correct color balance as well. For those who do their own processing, a fruitful field for control of color is thus available.

5. Tumblers in a human totem pole. In color stereo they are well separated from the building in the background; in an ordinary picture they would have needed the plain blue sky for background. Stereo by John Meredith.

71

6. Jet fighter approaching the catapult on the flight deck of an aircraft carrier. The plane is sharp and the background blurred for motion effect by panning the camera. Stereo by Henry M. Lester.

Color balance is only slightly affected by processing technique; much more variation in balance is due to differences in color of the exposing light. Manufacturing variations in balance are very small and nearly unnoticeable. However, one major problem lies in the very great spectral difference between daylight and artificial light. All manufacturers of color films, therefore, make two types of color film, one for exposure to daylight, the other for some kind of artificial light source.

It is, of course, possible to adjust the light source to the film, usually by using a filter over the camera lens. This solution is handy when making a long series of pictures alternately indoors and out where film changing would be difficult or impossible. In general, a large loss of film speed occurs when using daylight-type film indoors with a blue filter; the exposure increase is usually of the order of 4X, and this increase comes when ample light is difficult to get at best.

On the other hand, tungsten-type films used outdoors with the reddish correction filter lose little or no speed; the exposure is usually just about the same as for daylight-type film. For this reason, if the photographer wishes to use one type of film only, the best is tungsten-type with the correct conversion filter for use outdoors.

None the less, this cannot be recommended for all-around outdoor use; tungsten-type film and the filter do not always produce the best color rendition. The correction filter has the same effect on the ultraviolet

72

balance as a haze filter. There are times, however, when the bluish haze over distant scenes is desirable to aid in the perspective of the scene, and daylight-type film, used without any filter at all, would be preferable.

It is, of course, essential at all times to use only the proper filter for the given film in use. The Ansco No. 11 Conversion Filter, which adapts Ansco Color Film, Tungsten Type, for use outdoors, is not the same as the Kodak Wratten No. 85 used with Kodachrome Film Type A outdoors. Though the *purpose* of both filters is identical, the transmission of each is adjusted to the particular sensitivities of the films for which they are designed, and they cannot be used interchangeably.

The same caution applies to the use of other filters such as the haze filters, compensating filters for strobe lights, flashlamps, etc. In general, follow the manufacturer's directions for exposure, filters, etc.

For the Stereo Realist camera, Realist Inc. supplies matched pairs of filters for the above purposes. These may be depended upon to perform the required corrections and, in addition, not to cause differences in color balance between the pictures of a stereo pair.

Color Temperature And Illumination

The concept of "color temperature" as applied to practical light sources has been explained at great length throughout the photographic literature. It will not be discussed from a theoretical standpoint here for reasons which will be made evident.

73

Color temperature applies, strictly speaking, to light from an imaginary source which emits light of a given energy distribution and which has no reflecting powers whatever. Such a light source does not exist, though a few approximate these conditions. For example, a 3200°K incandescent lamp does emit light having an energy distribution very close to that of the theoretical non-reflecting radiator, or "blackbody." On the other hand, the light of a "warm-white" fluorescent lamp, sometimes also stated to be 3200°K, actually has no relationship to the light of the 3200°K incandescent lamp except a *visual match;* its energy distribution is entirely different from that of a blackbody radiator at 3200°K. Thus these two light sources will affect color films altogether differently. In the same way, it cannot be said that daylight is 5600°K or 6500°K or any other figure; daylight is simply a mixture of blue skylight, white sunlight, and various amounts of ultraviolet and infrared.

Color temperature as a means of controlling color-film rendition has another serious fault: the same visual difference is not represented by the same number of degrees at various points on the scale. For instance, the eye can detect a difference of 50 degrees in the vicinity of 3200°K. But at daylight temperatures the smallest visible difference is nearly 200°K. A filter which will make the "just-visible" difference, however, will do so at any point of the scale; thus the same filter will raise a 3200°K lamp to 3250, and a 6000°K light source to 6200. It is not possible, therefore, to specify that a given filter will raise or lower color temperature by a given number of degrees except at one particular color temperature.

For this reason it is becoming evident that the entire concept of color temperature will soon have to be abandoned in favor of some system of constant visual differences. Meanwhile, however, since the system exists, the terminology of this chapter will conform to the present usage with the reminder that very often such usage is of very limited accuracy.

This must not be taken to mean that we may be equally inaccurate in the actual handling of color compensation filters and light sources. We must understand, once and for all, that color films are made to match *light sources* and that when the term 3200°K is used in connection with a color film it means that this film is balanced for use with *incandescent lamps* having an equivalent visual color temperature of 3200°K.

In the same way, Kodachrome Type A is designed for use with photoflood lamps, not with any lamp having a visual color temperature of 3400°K — it won't produce satisfactory color rendition with "cool-white" fluorescent lamps which are considered to be 3400°K visually. Likewise, daylight color films are balanced for use in daylight, which is a mixture of sunlight and sky—*not* for an artificial light source having a color temperature of 6500°K.

If this is understood we can appreciate why, when we wish to use a film with some other light source, we must use a compensating filter, and that these filters in turn are specified strictly for use with a given film and a given light source without mention of a color temperature shift. For example, there are the Kodak Light Balancing Filter 81A and the Ansco Filter UV-15. Both of these are designed to permit their

9. In strong sun there is plenty of light for action pictures with short exposures on color film. Here, slight foreground blur lends motion to the young pugilists. Stereo by Gilbert Morgan.

respective films to be exposed by photoflood light (3400°K visually) while the films in question are balanced for 3200°K lamps. Though the apparent correction is 200°K in each case, the two filters look quite different, and in fact *are* quite different. Neither can be said to be a "200°K correction filter" except with the particular film for which each was designed, and in the vicinity of 3200°K; either of these filters will produce a much larger color temperature shift in daylight, though the visual difference will be about equal.

For the greatest simplicity in the use of color film it is best to use a given film with the light source for which it is balanced. Under other conditions the filter recommended by the manufacturer for the film in question is the only one which will produce optimum results. The data sheets at the end of this chapter list the various filters recommended by the film manufacturers for their respective films.

Color Films Outdoors

As mentioned at the beginning of this chapter, outdoor color photography is by far the simplest. The principal light source is daylight, and when using daylight-type film excellent results may be achieved without the use of filters of any kind, particularly with objects which are not very far from the camera. And since near-by subjects make the best stereos, most outdoor stereos can be made with no accessory equipment.

However, where distant scenes are being photographed, or even where background objects are at a considerable distance, the proportion of

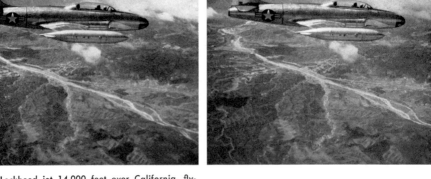

10. Lockheed jet 14,000 feet over California, flying at 500 miles per hour. Daylight color film with haze filter. Compare the effect with Figure 7. Stereo by Alec Milne.

skylight to sunlight on the background is greater, and the farther parts of the scene will be covered with a bluish haze. Normally this increases the apparent depth, even of a flat picture; however, if it is deemed objectionable, or where near-by objects are being photographed in shady spots, the use of a light-balancing filter is recommended. For Kodachrome Film, Daylight Type, the Kodak Skylight Filter is used; for Ansco Color Film, Daylight Type, use an Ansco Color Filter UV-15. If a greater degree of warmth is desired, the Kodak Wratten Filter 2-B or the Ansco UV-16 may be used with their respective films, though foreground objects may be rendered too warm in tone with these filters.

When tungsten-type films must be used in daylight, the conversion filters of the respective manufacturers must be used. (See tables at end of this chapter.) In this case, addition of Skylight or UV filters is unnecessary, since the ultraviolet correction of these filters is automatically accomplished by the conversion filter.

Outdoor Color Photography At Night

A really fascinating field of photography, particularly in stereo, is night photography outdoors. In almost any fair-sized city some section will be found with an array of varicolored neon signs, traffic lights, white street lights, theater marquees, etc. Innumerable patterns can be made with these colored lights, and the effect can be further enhanced by shooting in a light rain or in mist. Reflections from colored lights and signs in wet pavements sometimes take on new, exotic shapes, almost

11. A few flat colors will often make a striking stereo, as with this black and red train against a blue sky. Gold lettering shines on the black engine. Stereo courtesy Realist Inc.

77

abstract and frequently more striking than the signs themselves.

It is difficult to give any directions for estimating exposures under such conditions. In general, tungsten-type color films should be used, both for more accurate rendition of color and because they are often faster than daylight-type films in artificial light. An exposure meter can be used to estimate exposures for a preliminary test; however, a number of additional exposures should be made, both above and below the metered exposure. Where lights are included in the scene a decision must be made as to whether they need be rendered in color; if they are white lights, they may be permitted to burn up while the dimmer neon tubes and colored bulbs are registering. Floodlighted buildings photographed from such angles that no light sources are visible may take exposures running from 1 to 5 seconds with a wide-open lens; often shots may be made of store windows and under theater marquees at about the same exposure.

Where the lighted signs themselves are the picture, and there is no objection to a completely black background, exposures may be considerably less; shots of the illuminated signs in Times Square have been made with shutter speeds of 1/10 to 1/25 second at f/3.5 on Kodachrome Film, Type A.

Brightly lighted store windows may often be photographed in color with a short time exposure. However, the lamps used in store windows usually burn at a lower color temperature than the photographic lamps

78

to which the film is balanced; hence the pictures may be somewhat warm in tone. If this is objectionable, a Kodak Light Balancing Filter such as the 82C may be of assistance. Meter readings will be of some help in estimating the exposure of a store window, but often it will be found that the light level is lower than it appears to the eye, and meter readings are so low as to be unreliable. In such a case, the only solution is to make a series of tests and keep accurate notes of the results.

Artificial-Light Photography

The two principal types of indoor color film available for the Stereo Realist camera are Kodachrome Film, Type A, and Ansco Color Film, Tungsten Type. While both are intended for use with artificial light, their color balance differs somewhat, since they are designed for two different light sources. Kodachrome Film, Type A, is designed for use with photoflood lamps, which are said to have a "color temperature" of 3400°K, while Ansco Color Film, Tungsten Type, is balanced for use with the so-called "3200°K" lamps.

However, in each case correction filters are available so that either type of film may be used with both types of illumination. In the case of Ansco Color Film, the Tungsten Type may be exposed to photoflood light provided a UV-15 filter is used to avoid excessive blueness. Kodachrome Film, Type A, may be used with 3200°K lamps when photofloods are not available, using a pale bluish filter, the Kodak Light Balancing Filter 82A.

13. Snow on the ground is a ready-made reflector for filling in hard shadows in strong sunlight, making a better brightness range for color film. Stereo by R. H. Bills.

Photoflash illumination is considerably colder than either of these two incandescent sources (it is said to have an equivalent visual color temperature of 3800° to 4000°K), and other filters are recommended for flash exposures with tungsten-type films. Recommendations for this and for other special types of illuminants are given in the data pages at the end of this chapter.

Electronic discharge lamps or "strobe" lights give excellent results with color films; they act as if they had a color temperature of about 7000°K, and excellent results are obtained on *daylight-type* color films without any filter at all. Some photographers think the results are slightly cold; they use a Kodak Light Balancing Filter 81B over the lens for slightly warmer rendition. Ansco Color Film, Daylight Type, may be used with an Ansco UV-16 filter for fairly normal rendition.

For a further discussion of lighting techniques and effects in stereo, see Chapter 4.

Storage and Processing of Color Films

UNEXPOSED color film of all makes should be stored in a cool, dry place until used. If extended storage is required, an excellent place is the refrigerator (but NOT in the freezer compartment) *for unopened packages only*. These should be removed from the refrigerator at least 24 hours in advance of use and allowed to warm up to room temperature before using. If the packages are opened in a warm, humid place while they are still chilled, moisture may condense on the film and cause damage.

EXPOSED color film should be rewound immediately into the cartridge, which is then placed in the metal container it came in. For best results exposed color film should be processed immediately after exposure, especially in warm or tropical climates. If this is not feasible, it should be dehydrated if possible and stored in as cool a place as can be found. When film has been exposed in a very humid climate, it should be replaced in the metal container without screwing the cap on tightly—either for storage or mailing to the processing laboratory. Partially exposed films should not be kept in the camera for a long period of time in hot or humid climates. Since temperature or humidity extremes can produce changes in the latent image that will cause inferior color results in the processed pictures, it is wise to finish the roll of film quickly. Sometimes it is even preferable to send a partially exposed roll of film for processing rather than risk spoiling good pictures by waiting until you have a chance to finish the roll.

PROCESSED color transparencies should be kept in closed boxes and protected from light, heat, dust and moisture. Present-day color films are far more stable than in former years, but heat, dampness, turpentine and paint fumes and other chemical vapors can still cause fading. Sealing the finished pictures in glass mounts is still the best method for long-term preservation.

Processing of Kodachrome is done at the processing stations listed on the data sheets packed with the film. Ansco Color film can be processed by the user or any of the independent laboratories offering this service. Condensed instructions for Ansco Color processing are given further on in this chapter.

Information on how to send Kodachrome and Ansco Color stereo films for processing are given in the following discussions of the two films. For any other color film, consult your dealer or the film manufacturer.

Kodachrome Film

Six different packagings of 35mm Kodachrome Film are available for use in the Stereo Realist camera. Two of these packagings are intended especially for stereo:

K335 (Kodachrome Film, Daylight Type).

K335A (Kodachrome Film, Type A, for artificial light).

These films will give 20 stereo pairs of the Realist picture size: 23x24-mm. When exposed in cameras producing stereo pictures 23x24mm, with standard spacing between pictures, these films are processed *and* mounted for hand viewing without additional charge. The Kodaslide Stereo Mount is cardboard with the window located for hand viewing of normal stereo views. Close-up views or pictures intended for projection can be easily removed from the Stereo Mounts and remounted in the required manner. The Kodaslide Stereo Mounts are not available separately.

Kodachrome film packaged for regular 35mm cameras (not stereo) can also be used in the Stereo Realist camera, but the price of the film includes processing only, and an additional charge, on a prepaid basis, is made for mounting. These films are:

K135 20-exposure (Kodachrome Film, Daylight Type). Makes 15 stereo pairs in the Realist.

K135A 20-exposure (Kodachrome Film, Type A, for artificial light.) Makes 15 stereo pairs in the Realist.

K135 36-exposure (Kodachrome Film, Daylight Type.) Makes 28 stereo pairs in the Realist.

K135A 36-exposure (Kodachrome Film, Type A, for artificial light.) Makes 28 stereo pairs in the Realist.

Stereo mounting is now available from the Eastman Kodak Company processing stations in Rochester, Chicago and Hollywood. Kodachrome films used in stereo cameras can be sent *for processing only* (no mounting) to any of the Kodak processing stations throughout the world. A list of these stations will be found on the instruction sheet packed with every roll of film. Stereo films sent for processing only are returned uncut in one strip. To indicate that you want the film back uncut, it is necessary to clip off one corner of the mailing tag attached to the yellow film bag. No charge is made for returning film uncut, nor is any refund made for films that have been returned unmounted.

For quick reference, the table below shows the various packagings of Kodachrome that can be used in the Stereo Realist camera, the number of stereo pairs that can be made, and the way to indicate to the processing station how you want to have the film returned.

KODACHROME FILM FOR STEREO

Film	Number of Stereo Pairs	Stereo Mounting	No Mounting (Processed Film Returned Uncut)
K335 K335A (Stereo packing)	20	Included in price of film.*	Clip corner of mailing tag.† No charge. No refund.
K135 K135A (36 Exp.)	28	Enclose $1.60 (no stamps) in film mailing bag.*	Clip corner of mailing tag.† No charge. No refund.
K135 K135A (20 Exp.)	15	Enclose $1.00 (no stamps) in film mailing bag.*	Clip corner of mailing tag.† No charge. No refund.

*Send only to processing stations in Rochester, Chicago or Hollywood.
†Send to any Kodak processing station.
(See instructions packed with film for addresses of all processing stations.)

Kodachrome Film, Daylight Type

A color film designed for use in miniature cameras; processed by the Eastman Kodak Company and balanced for exposure in sunlight. Kodachrome duplicates, enlargements and prints are available from the Eastman Kodak Company.

EXPOSURE INDEX AND SPEED RATING

WESTON		ASA EXPOSURE INDEX	
Daylight	Tungsten	Daylight	Tungsten
8	3*	10	2.5*

*For emergency use with Kodak Photoflood Filter for Daylight Type Kodak Color Films (Wratten No. 80A).

These settings apply to reflected- or incident-light readings, properly made, of average subjects. Certain reflected-light meters should be tilted downward to minimize the effect of the sky. Still-camera settings of less than 1/50 second between f/8 and f/11 should be questioned because underexposure is likely.

DAYLIGHT EXPOSURE TABLE

| Subject Type | Lens openings below are for shutter speed of 1/50 second | | | | |
| | Clear Sun Falling On: | | Hazy Sun | Cloudy Bright | Open Shade (5) |
	Front of subject	Side or back (4)			
Light (1)	f/8	f/6.3	f/5.6	f/4	f/2.8
Average (2)	f/6.3	f/5.6	f/4.5	f/3.5	f/2.5
Dark (3)	f/5.6	f/4.5	f/4	f/2.8	f/2

1. Distant scenes; near-by people in beach or snow scenes. Light objects predominating.

2. Near-by people, gardens, houses, scenes, not in shade. Light and dark objects in equal proportions. Use this classification if in doubt.

3. People in dark clothing; dark foliage, animals, buildings.

4. With back-lighted objects containing important shadow detail give ½ to 1 stop more exposure than listed. If possible use supplementary flash with side or back lighting.

5. Subject shaded from sun but lighted by a large area of clear unobstructed blue sky. Use larger lens opening with smaller sky area; a slightly smaller lens opening with reflecting clouds.

LIGHT SOURCES. Best color rendering is obtained in clear or hazy sunlight. The light sources listed in the following table can also be used, but in general they do not give as good results, even with the recommended filters.

Light Source	Kodak Filter	Remarks
Bluish daylight	Skylight (Wratten No. 1A)	This filter is recommended primarily for use in shade under a clear blue sky
Photoflood lamps	Photoflood (Wratten No. 80A)	For best results and shorter exposures use of Type A Film is recommended
Blue flashlamps	None	
Daylight fluorescent lamps	CC-20B	

SUPPLEMENTARY FLASH OUTDOORS. In bright sunlight, lighting contrast is frequently excessive, particularly with near-by side- or back-lighted subjects. More pleasing results are obtained by using blue flashlamps to illuminate shadows. With flash fill-in, use the same settings for front, side or back lighting.

LAMP-TO-SUBJECT DISTANCES FOR SUPPLEMENTARY FLASH

Flashlamp	1/25 between f/8 and f/11
5B or 25B lamp	5* to 10 feet
22B or 2B lamp	8* to 15 feet
*At shorter distances, drape a white handkerchief over the flash reflector.	

FLASH EXPOSURE GUIDE NUMBERS. Although intended for supplementing daylight, blue flashlamps can be used in an emergency as the sole light source. The results should not, however, be expected to match the quality of pictures made on either Daylight Type or Type A Film with the source for which it is balanced. Divide the proper guide number by the lamp-to-subject distance in feet to determine the lens opening for average subjects. Use ½ stop larger for dark subjects; ½ stop smaller for light subjects.

GUIDE NUMBERS FOR BLUE FLASH AND KODACHROME FILM, DAYLIGHT TYPE

Flashlamp	Guide Number for 1/25 Shutter Speed
G-E 5B	45
Sylvania 25B	45
G-E 22B	75
Sylvania 2B	75

EDITOR'S NOTE: These values are intended only as guides and are those supplied by the Eastman Kodak Company in their film instructions. With the highly efficient reflectors supplied with the Realist Flash Unit, over-exposure may result in some cases, and the guide number may be increased by 25 per cent to 50 per cent, depending on individual equipment.

CAUTION: Since lamps may shatter when flashed, use of a guard or shield over the reflector is recommended. Do not flash lamps in an explosive atmosphere!

84

Kodachrome Film Type A for Artificial Light

A color film designed for use in miniature still cameras and balanced for exposure with photoflood lamps. Processed by the Eastman Kodak Company, it yields transparencies in full color for viewing and projection. Kodachrome duplicates, enlargements and prints are available from the Eastman Kodak Company.

EXPOSURE INDEX AND FILM SPEED RATING

WESTON		ASA EXPOSURE INDEX	
Daylight	Tungsten	Daylight	Tungsten
8*	12	10*	16

*With Kodak Daylight Filter for Type A Kodak Color Films (No. 85). Certain reflected light meters should be tilted downward to minimize the effect of the sky.

These settings are recommended for meters of either incident or reflected-light type. They also apply to reflected-light meters used to take readings from a gray card of 18 per cent reflectance, held at the subject position facing halfway between the camera and the main light. The Exposure Index should be divided by 2 if the reading is taken from the palm of the hand of the subject's face, or divided by 5 if the reading is taken from a white card of approximately 90 per cent reflectance. In either case, set the meter arrow as for a normal subject.

When using a card, the palm of the hand or an incident-light meter, allow ½ stop more exposure for unusually dark subjects, ½ stop less for unusually light subjects.

LIGHT SOURCES. Best color rendering is obtained with photoflood lamps. The light sources listed in the following table can be used, but in general they do not give as good results even with the recommended filters.

SUPPLEMENTARY LIGHT SOURCES

Light Source	Kodak Filter
Daylight	Daylight (Wratten No. 85)
Flashlamps:	
No. 5, 6, 11, 22, 31, 50	Wratten No. 81C
No. 0, 2, 2A, 3, 25, 26, 40	Wratten No. 81D
SM	None
SF	Wratten No. 81A
3200° K lamps	Wratten No. 82A
Warm-white fluorescent lamps	CC-10Y plus CC-20M
Cool-white fluorescent lamps	CC-40Y plus CC-30M

DAYLIGHT EXPOSURES. With the Kodak Daylight Filter for Type A Kodak Color Films (Wratten No. 85) the effective speed of the film to daylight is the same as that of Kodachrome Film, Daylight Type, and exposure tables given for the latter film may be used in this case as well.

PHOTOFLOOD EXPOSURE TABLE

Two No. 2 Photoflood lamps in Kodak Vari-Beam Reflectors at STILL position. Give ½ stop more exposure for two reflector-type photofloods.				
SHUTTER SPEED	**LAMP-TO-SUBJECT DISTANCE**			
	3½ feet	5 feet	7 feet	10 feet
1/25 sec.	f/4	f/3.5	f/2.8	—
½ second	Between f/11 and f/16	f/11	Between f/8 and f/11	Between f/5.6 and f/8

Both lamps at same distance from subject; fill-in light at camera; main light at 45° angle to camera-subject axis and 2 to 4 feet higher than fill-in light.

NOTE: Do not use more than 3 No. 2 or reflector-type lamps on one fused circuit.

FLASH EXPOSURE GUIDE NUMBERS. Based on the use of the recommended filter. Divide the proper guide number by the lamp-to-subject distance in feet to determine the lens opening for average subjects. Use ½ stop larger for dark subjects; ½ stop smaller for light subjects. These lens openings apply to all surroundings except small white rooms; in such rooms use 1 stop smaller.

GUIDE NUMBERS FOR FLASH AND KODACHROME FILM, TYPE A

	SM* or SF*	No. 5* or No. 25*	No. 11† or No. 40†	No. 22† or No. 2†
Open, 1/25	45	70	95	110

*In 4- to 5-inch polished or satin reflector.
†In 6- to 7-inch polished reflector.

EDITOR'S NOTE: These values are intended only as guides, and are those published by the Eastman Kodak Company for use with Kodachrome film and the lamps listed in average reflectors. With the very efficient reflector supplied with the Realist Flash Unit, overexposure may result in certain cases, and the guide number may be increased by 25 per cent to 50 per cent, depending on individual equipment.

CAUTION: Since lamps may shatter when flashed, use of a flash shield or guard over the reflector is recommended. Do not flash lamps in an explosive atmosphere!

Ansco Color Films

All Ansco Color Film for regular 35mm cameras can be used in the Stereo Realist camera, although the film is not specially packaged for stereo. The following packagings are available:

> 20-exposure Ansco Color Film, Daylight Type.
> (Makes 15 stereo pairs in the Realist.)
> 20-exposure Ansco Color Film, Tungsten Type, for arti-
> ficial light. (Makes 15 stereo pairs in the Realist.)
> Bulk-loading Ansco Color Film, Daylight Type and
> Tungsten Type. (For loading into film cartridges by
> the user.)

Ansco Color Film is intended for processing in standard darkroom equipment by the user. Film processing is also available through local Ansco dealers for those who do not wish to do their own processing, or directly from Ansco, Binghampton, N. Y., when it is inconvenient to send film to the dealer.

A Stereo Mounting Service is available in Binghamton at the Ansco Color Processing Laboratory. The charge for the service is $1.00 per roll, in addition to the regular developing fee. Stereo mounting can be ordered at the same time the film is sent for processing. The service is also available to those who return a processed and *uncut* roll of stereos on 35mm Ansco Color film, and the price is the same—$1.00 per roll for mounting. Rolls which have been cut cannot be mounted by Ansco.

Ansco Color Film, Daylight Type

A color film balanced for exposure by direct sunlight from two hours after sunrise to two hours before sunset. Exposure by other light sources, except blue flashlamps, may yield poor color rendition unless proper correction filters are used.

EXPOSURE INDEX AND SPEED RATING

WESTON		ASA EXPOSURE INDEX	
Daylight	Tungsten	Daylight	Tungsten
8	2*	10	2.5*

*For use with Ansco Conversion Filter No. 10 and No. 2 Photoflood (3400°K) lamps.

These meter settings should be considered only as a guide, and changed if results seem to indicate the necessity for correction. Exposure in color photography is more critical than in black-and-white, and variations in equipment and personal methods may cause appreciable variations in speed and color balance.

EXPOSURE IN DAYLIGHT. Exposures in the following table are suggested for use under average summer conditions in the temperate zones, from two hours after sunrise until two hours before sunset. In winter, use the next larger lens opening (1 full stop), provided there is no snow. With exceptionally brilliant light, as in seascapes, snow scenes, or at high altitudes, the indicated exposures may be halved.

The exposures given in this table are for average subjects. Dark subjects require ½ stop more exposure; light subjects require ½ stop less exposure.

DAYLIGHT EXPOSURE TABLE
ANSCO COLOR FILM, DAYLIGHT TYPE

Shutter Speed	Bright Sunlight			Hazy Sunlight, Soft Shadows	Bright Overcast, No Shadows	Dull Over-cast
	Front Lighted	Side Lighted	Back Lighted			
1/100 sec.	f/4.5	f/3.5	f/2.5	f/3.5	f/2.5	f/1.8
1/50 sec.	f/6.3	f/4.5	f/3.5	f/4.5	f/3.5	f/2.5
1/25 sec.	f/9	f/6.3	f/4.5	f/6.3	f/4.5	f/3.5

FLASH EXPOSURE GUIDE NUMBERS. These guide numbers are for "open flash," Time, Bulb or 1/25 second with lamps in *average* metal reflectors. Dark-colored subjects require ½ stop larger lens opening, and light subjects ½ stop smaller.

To find exposure, locate the guide number for the lamp used. Divide this factor by the distance in feet from lamp to subject to obtain the recommended f-stop to be used. For example, for a G-E 5B the factor is 45. At 10 feet the recommended exposure will then be 45 ÷ 10 = 4.5; thus f/4.5 is the correct exposure.

GUIDE NUMBERS FOR BLUE FLASH AND ANSCO COLOR DAYLIGHT

Flashlamp	Guide Number for 1/25 Shutter Speed
G-E 5B	45
Sylvania 25B	45
G-E 22B	75
Sylvania 2B	75

EDITOR'S NOTE: The guide numbers above are those supplied by Ansco for use with Ansco Color film and are based on their own laboratory tests. Due to the very high efficiency of the Stereo Realist Flash Reflector, it may be found that these factors are too low, and exposures up to 1 stop less may give better color rendering. If first tests indicate overexposure, try adding 25 per cent to 50 per cent to the above guide numbers to secure factors better suited *to this particular equipment*.

These guide numbers are recommended with blue flash as a primary light source for Ansco Color Daylight film used indoors. Care should be taken not to mix the flash illumination with incandescent room lighting, if color fidelity is to be maintained.

Blue bulbs can also be used outdoors for "flash-fill," to break up shadows in daylight. First, determine the normal daylight exposure for the scene—either from the Daylight Exposure Table or an exposure meter. Then the subject-to-flash distance is computed using the setting chosen to give the proper outdoor exposure and the guide numbers given for normal indoor use with blue flash and daylight film. Since these guide numbers are computed to give full exposures with light reflected from the walls and ceiling of the average room, they will give about 1 stop less than the normal exposure when used outdoors with no reflecting surfaces available.

This method gives a ratio of from 1:2 to 1:3 between the key light (sunlight) and the fill-in light (flash) and gives a fine lighting balance in most cases. Use this method as a guide to your own particular equipment. In some cases you may want to change either the flash-to-subject distance or the guide numbers to suit your own requirements.

GUIDE NUMBERS FOR ELECTRONIC FLASHTUBES AND ANSCO COLOR DAYLIGHT WITH UV-16 FILTER

Unit Watt-Second Rating	Guide Numbers for 1/25 Second Shutter Speed
25	12
50	18
100	24
150	32
225	40
400	52
900	80

NOTE: The guide numbers given are based on unit watt-second ratings as indicated, and for lamps in polished studio-type reflectors. Increase exposure ½ lens stop when using shallow press-type reflectors or decrease ½ lens stop with narrow-beam concentrating reflectors. Divide the guide number by the distance in feet from lamp to subject to find the recommended lens opening.

FLOODLAMPS WITH DAYLIGHT FILM. With the Ansco Conversion Filter No. 10, Ansco Color Daylight film can be used for floodlamp (3400°K) pictures indoors. It is preferable, however, to use the Tungsten Type film whenever possible for indoor pictures.

For two No. 2 Photoflood lamps in good reflectors. Average subjects in light-colored rooms. Daylight Film. No. 10 Conversion Filter.

		LAMP-TO-SUBJECT DISTANCE IN FEET			
Main Light		3'	4'	6'	8'
Fill-in Light		4'	6'	8½'	12'
Shutter	1 Sec.	f/11	f/8	f/5.6	f/4
Speed	1/2 Sec.	f/8	f/5.6	f/4	f/2.8
	1/5 Sec.	f/5.6	f/4	f/2.8	f/2

Main light above camera, pointing down; fill light on camera level; both lights on opposite sides of camera.
NOTE: Do not use more than 3 No. 2 or reflector-type lamps on one fused circuit.

Ansco Color Film, Tungsten Type

A color film intended for use indoors, and balanced for exposure with photoflood (3400°K) illumination. If used with other illumination without proper filters, poor color rendering may result.

EXPOSURE INDEX AND SPEED RATING

WESTON		ASA EXPOSURE INDEX	
Tungsten	Daylight	Tungsten	Daylight
10	8*	12	10*
*For use with Ansco Conversion Filter No. 11			

These meter settings should be considered only as a guide, and changed if results seem to indicate the necessity for correction. Exposure in color photography is more critical than in black-and-white, and variations in equipment and personal methods may cause appreciable variations in speed and color balance.

It is also important to remember that photoflood and other lamps have a limited life and should not be used for color photography after they have burned past their peak efficiency. Partially used lamps can be saved from black-and-white photography where color is not as critical.

EXPOSURE WITH PHOTOFLOOD (3400°K). The table following covers average subjects in light-colored interiors. Dark subjects will need ½ stop or more exposure, and light subjects will need about ½ stop less exposure. Reflectors of good quality must be used to realize the full lamp output. With shallow home reflectors it may be necessary to increase the exposure ½ to 1 full stop. Due to differences in reflectors and surroundings, this table is given only as a guide.

PHOTOFLOOD EXPOSURE TABLE

For two No. 2 Photofloods in studio-type reflectors. Give ½ stop more for reflector-type photofloods.					
	LAMP-TO-SUBJECT DISTANCE IN FEET				
Main Light	3'	4'	6'	12'	12'
Fill-in Light	4'	6'	8½'	8'	18'
Shutter 1 Sec.	——	f/16	f/12.5	f/9	f/6.3
Speed 1/5 Sec.	f/11	f/8	f/5.6	f/4.0	f/2.8
1/25 Sec.	f/4.5	f/3.5	f/2.5	f/1.8	—

Main light above camera, pointing down; fill light on camera level; both lights on opposite sides of camera.

NOTE: Do not use more than 3 No. 2 or reflector-type lamps on one fused circuit.

FLASH EXPOSURE GUIDE NUMBERS. These guide numbers are for "open flash," Time, Bulb or 1/25 second with lamps in *average* metal reflectors. Dark-colored subjects require ½ stop larger lens opening, and light subjects ½ stop smaller.

To find exposure, locate the guide number for the lamp used. Divide this factor by the distance in feet from lamp to subject to obtain the recommended f-stop to be used. For example, for a Sylvania Press 40 the factor is 105. At 10 feet the recommended exposure will then be $105 \div 10 = 10.5$; thus f/10.5 is the correct exposure, and f/11 will do nicely.

GUIDE NUMBERS FOR FLASH AND
ANSCO COLOR TUNGSTEN WITH UV-16 FILTER

Flashlamp	Guide Number for 1/25 Shutter Speed
G-E 5	95
Sylvania 25	95
G-E 11	105
Sylvania 40	105
G-E 22	125
Sylvania 2	125

EDITOR'S NOTE: The guide numbers above are those supplied by Ansco for use with Ansco Color film and are based on their own laboratory tests. Due to the very high efficiency of the Stereo Realist Flash Reflector, it may be found that these factors are too low, and exposure up to 1 stop less may give better color rendering. If first tests indicate overexposure, try adding 25 per cent to 50 per cent to the above guide numbers to secure factors better suited *to this particular equipment.*

These guide numbers are recommended with Ansco Color Film, Tungsten Type and the Ansco Color UV-16 Filter, which must always be used when taking pictures with the tungsten film and clear flash. Care should be taken not to mix the flash illumination with incandescent room lighting if color fidelity is to be maintained.

EXPOSURE IN DAYLIGHT. Ansco Color Film, Tungsten Type can be used for photography outdoors, if desired. However, wherever possible it is preferable to use the Daylight Type film, which is intended for outdoor photography and balanced to daylight.

Ansco Color Film, Tungsten Type must always be used with an Ansco Conversion Filter No. 11 for photography in daylight.

Exposures in the following tables are suggested for use under average summer conditions in the temperate zones, from two hours after sunrise until two hours before sunset. In winter, use the next larger lens opening (1 full stop), provided there is no snow. With exceptionally brilliant light, as in seascapes, snow scenes, or at high altitudes, the indicated exposures may be halved.

The exposures given in this table are for average subjects. Dark subjects require ½ stop more exposure; light subjects require ½ stop less exposure.

DAYLIGHT EXPOSURE TABLE
ANSCO COLOR TUNGSTEN WITH No. 11 CONVERSION FILTER

Shutter Speed	Bright Sunlight			Hazy Sunlight, Soft Shadows	Bright Overcast, No Shadows	Dull Overcast
	Front Lighted	Side Lighted	Back Lighted			
1/100 sec.	f/4.5	f/3.5	f/2.5	f/3.5	f/2.5	f/1.8
1/50 sec.	f/6.3	f/4.5	f/3.5	f/4.5	f/3.5	f/2.5
1/25 sec.	f/9	f/6.3	f/4.5	f/6.3	f/4.5	f/3.5

ANSCO COLOR FILTERS. Various special-purpose filters are available for use with Ansco Color films. The Ultra-Violet filters are mainly used outdoors as shown in the table; they are also used for small color-temperature corrections particularly with flashlamps. The Conversion series is used for exposures with light sources differing from that for which the film was manufactured.

ULTRAVIOLET SERIES	
UV-15	Slight haze correction. Exposure of Ansco Color Film, Tungsten Type, by photoflood light.
UV-16	Medium haze correction. Exposure of Ansco Color Film, Tungsten Type, by photoflash light. Exposure of Ansco Color Film, Daylight Type, by strobe light.
UV-17	Greater haze correction than UV-16.

CONVERSION SERIES	
No. 10	For exposing Daylight Type film under tungsten illumination. Requires 4X increase in exposure over normal Tungsten Type film in same illumination.
No. 11	When exposing Tungsten Type film in daylight. Use same exposure as Daylight Type film under same conditions.
No. 13	When exposing Tungsten Type film under white (3500°K) fluorescent illumination. Use twice normal exposure.

THE COLOR COMPENSATING FILTERS. These filters are used for making minor alterations in color balance. While they find their greatest application in making color prints on Ansco Color Printon, they are also useful in photography with Ansco Color film when precise color balance is an important requirement. In photomicrography, for example, the standard microscope light source may not yield transparencies of the desired color balance. Under such circumstances, color compensating filters can be inserted in the optical system to adjust the color quality of the light source so that transparencies with the proper color balance are obtained.

COLOR COMPENSATING SERIES	
Yellow 23 24 25	When a —3 filter (23, 33, 43) is added to the light system, about $\frac{1}{6}$ lens stop exposure increase is necessary. The 24, 34 and 44 filters are approximately twice as dense as the 23, 33 and 43 filters. When any one of the former is added to the light system, about $\frac{1}{3}$ lens stop exposure increase is necessary.
Magenta 33 34 35 36	The 25, 35 and 45 filters are approximately twice as dense as the 24, 34 and 44 filters. The addition of —5 filters to the light system necessitates about a $\frac{2}{3}$ lens stop exposure increase. The magenta 36 filter is approximately twice as dense as the 35 filter and an exposure increase of $1\frac{1}{3}$ lens stop is necessary when it is added to the light system.
Cyan 43 44 45	From the above it is apparent that when a —3 filter in combination with a —4 filter is added to the light system about a $\frac{1}{2}$ lens stop exposure increase is necessary; likewise, when a —4 filter in combination with a —5 filter is added, about 1 lens stop increase in exposure is necessary.

Processing Ansco Color Film

Ansco Color Film 35mm can be processed by the user in ordinary amateur darkroom equipment. Either the wire-type developing reel or the transparent plastic reel of the Ansco Developing Tank may be used; they make it possible to carry out the required reexposure without removing the film from the reel.

Since changes are made from time to time in the processing procedure, the following outline is intended only to familiarize the photographer with the processing steps. The directions packed with the Ansco Color Film Developing Outfit should always be followed exactly.

The film must be agitated thoroughly when first placed in solution and then agitated for 15 seconds during each minute of the remaining time. See special agitation instructions for shortstop and hardener below.

IN TOTAL DARKNESS OR INDIRECT GREEN SAFELIGHT

1. FIRST DEVELOPER. Develop Daylight or Tungsten Type Color Film 19 minutes at 68°F (20°C).
2. SHORTSTOP. 1 minute at 68°F (20°C). Agitate continuously for 30 seconds.
3. HARDENER. 4 minutes at 68°F (20°C). Agitate continuously for first minute.

ROOM LIGHTS MAY BE TURNED ON AND LEFT ON FOR REMAINDER OF PROCESSING

4. WASH. 3 minutes in running water at 60°-75°F (16°-24°C).
5. SECOND EXPOSURE. Expose film to light from a No. 2 floodlamp at a distance of 3 feet for 3 minutes, 1½ minutes on each side.
6. COLOR DEVELOPER. Develop Daylight and Tungsten Type Ansco Color Film 16 minutes in Color Developer at 68°F (20°C).
7. SHORTSTOP. 1 minute at 68°F (20°C). (Use same solution as after First Developer.) Agitate continuously for first 30 seconds.
8. HARDENER. 4 minutes at 68°F (20°C). (Use same solution as after First Developer.) Agitate continuously for first minute.
9. WASH. 5 minutes in running water at 60°-75°F (16°-24°C).
10. BLEACH. 5 minutes at 68°F (20°C).
11. WASH. 3 minutes in running water at 60°-75°F (16°-24°C).
12. FIXER. 4 minutes at 68°F (20°C) with agitation.
13. WASH. 10 minutes in running water at 60°-75°F (16°-24°C). If the water is below 60°F, the washing time should be increased to 15 minutes.
14. DRYING. Wipe gently with clean damp chamois or viscose sponge and hang to dry in a cool, dust-free place. For more even and rapid drying, dip film into a 0.1 per cent detergent solution for 10 seconds. The film may then be hung up to dry without wiping with a chamois or sponge.

Partially Processing Ansco Color Film

If it is necessary to store exposed color films for a considerable period of time or under unfavorable conditions of heat and humidity before they can be completely processed or returned to the Ansco Color Laboratory for processing, users should partially process the film. Follow the instructions for First Developer and Shortstop, and eliminate the Hardener, washing in cool running water (60-75°F) for 10 minutes. The film can then be dried in the normal way. Resume processing with "Second Exposure"—Step 5.

If the films are returned to Binghamton for completion of the processing, the package must be clearly marked "Films partially processed—development should start with color developing." Films not so marked will be given complete processing and irretrievably spoiled.

Color Stereos 1

1. Girl On Beach. Basically a three-color picture, with the tans of the sand and rocks echoing the red and yellow in the girl and props. Sky provides the one blue accent completing the color sequence. *John Meredith.*

2. Drying Dyed Cloth. The most treasured travel stereos show unposed people going about their usual work or play. These men are drying their hand-dyed cloth on the roof of a bazaar in Ispahan, Iran. *Julien Bryan.*

3. High Up. Golden Gate Bridge in San Francisco, photographed from a precarious perch on the bridge tower. The striking red and blue color combination and the even more striking angle make this stereo at its best. *Harold Lloyd.*

4. Soft Drink Man. Top light throws the shadows directly under the subject where they do not disturb the composition. Pictures like this are best taken between 11 A.M. and 1 P.M. in most places. This picture was made in New York City. *Dorothy S. Gelatt.*

5. The Chief. The strong lighting in this portrait is particularly appropriate for the strong, weathered face of the subject. Generally stereo portraits are best with softer lighting. An observant photographer will always match the quality of the light to the character of the subject. *Harold Lloyd.*

6. Washday In Singapore. Every day is washday in Singapore's Chinatown, where the clothes decorate the streets like festival banners, in a long succession of planes. *Dick McGraw.*

7. Douglas And Maureen. Stereo portraits generally are most appealing when the pose is relaxed and the lighting is soft. *Willard D. Morgan.*

8. Singapore Food Vendor. Bread, jam, jelly and rolls are all spread out in the crowded open-air market, where the food is often prepared right on the sidewalk. A blue flashlamp with daylight color film was used to lighten the deep shade in this scene. *Dick McGraw.*

9. A New Doll. With a plain background there is no distraction in this simple, enchanting picture of the small girl absorbed in wonder over the exciting new doll. *R. H. Bills.*

10. A New Pet. It isn't every day that a little girl gets a live leopard cub for a pet. But when she does, the Realist Camera and Flash Attachment preserve the happy moment. *James H. Calder.*

11. Magnolias At Night. The black night sky is a wonderful background for stereo flash pictures of delicate flowers that would be lost in the shuffle in daylight pictures. *Dorothy S. Gelatt.*

12. Montmartre. Dulled colors on an overcast day sustain the old-world mood of this picture taken in the famed Montmartre section of Paris. *Harold Lloyd.*

13. Edward Weston. A candid stereo made by daylight coming through a large skylight while Mr. Weston autographed his book, "My Camera on Point Lobos." *Dick McGraw.*

14. Jean Carmen. Taken on a movie set already lighted for a color production, good color balance was automatically assured. From "Striporama," a Venus Production directed by Jerald Intrator. *Dorothy S. Gelatt.*

15. Mirror Room. A multiple flash picture with direct light on foreground and indirect light on the rest of the room reflected in the antique mirror. Interior by Leonora Pierotti. *Dorothy S. Gelatt.*

96

1. GIRL ON BEACH   John Meredith

2. DRYING DYED CLOTH   Julien Bryan

97

3. HIGH UP   Harold Lloyd

4. SOFT DRINK MAN   Dorothy S. Gelatt

5. THE CHIEF   Harold Lloyd

6. WASHDAY IN SINGAPORE   Dick McGraw

7. DOUGLAS AND MAUREEN   W. D. Morgan

8. SINGAPORE FOOD VENDOR   Dick McGraw

9. A NEW DOLL   R. H. Bills

10. A NEW PET   James H. Calder

11. MAGNOLIAS AT NIGHT Dorothy S. Gelatt

12. MONTMARTRE   Harold Lloyd

13. EDWARD WESTON   Dick McGraw

14. JEAN CARMEN   Dorothy S. Gelatt

15. MIRROR ROOM   Dorothy S. Gelatt

4. Lighting, Exposure and Color in Stereo

DOROTHY S. GELATT

There is always a fresh fascination and a certain amazement in the surprising realism of every good color stereo. On the face of it, there seems to be no more logic in the reality of the three-dimensional view that emerges from the fusion of two flat pictures than there is in the flight of an airplane. It's plain to see that there is no depth in flat pieces of film; and airplanes are certainly too heavy to rise in the air! Yet, planes *do* fly; and two flat pieces of film *do* make a scene with all the depth and shape and color of the real world.

Duplicating natural phenomena by some artificial means is one of the particular pleasures of man, who likes to climb up in front with nature, but sometimes wonders in amazement how he got there. Taking off in an airplane is always somewhat unbelievable, no matter how many flights you have made. And the reality of the depth and shape and color in a good stereo is equally incredible—and delightful—no matter how many stereos you have seen.

The fact that this seeming reality is only an illusion, produced by the fusion of two flat photographic images, leaves you considerable leeway in either enhancing or stifling the total effect. Three things contribute to your final color stereo: *camera, film and light.*

The camera produces the two images of the stereo pair in the correct geometric relationship and with a high degree of perfection. The film records the images—and modern color film performs its function with remarkable fidelity. But the major control over the appearance and quality of your stereos is in your handling of the third element, *light.*

For the two pictures of a stereo pair to merge into a complete three-dimensional view, they must be not only sharp in detail, but *well-lighted and correctly exposed* as well. Depth perception suffers in a stereo where detail is dim because of underexposure, or washed out by overexposure. A stereo that is overexposed to the point that it looks like faded laundry

1. Christmas lights at Rockefeller Center in New York. Halo surrounds candle lights from long exposure — 1 second at f/11, for depth of field. Stereo by Dorothy S. Gelatt.

may have depth, but it will not look natural; it is only a semi-picture. Dark, gloomy effects may be all right if you are photographing in a coal mine, but they are all wrong when they are the result of underexposing an ordinary sunny scene.

Most of all, since practically all Stereo Realist pictures are made on color film, faithful color rendition is quite as important as tonal fidelity. Of course, an imaginative photographer who has a lot of experience with color film can work for deliberately unnatural and fantastic effects. The important thing about stereo color photography is that you are creating an illusion, and you can create it any way you like if you know how to control it.

Things That Control Color

Since exposure and lighting contribute to the overall result—a good stereo—let us consider first the things that control color reproduction on color films. There are four of these:

> Film type
> Color and intensity of light
> Filters
> Exposure

FILM TYPE. Complete data on the various color films available to the Stereo Realist user are given in the previous chapter. Here we need

106

consider only the basic fact that all color films come in two types, one to be used outdoors in daylight (occasionally in daylighted interiors) and the other to be used with artificial illumination. Two types are needed because there is considerable difference in the color of daylight and artificial light (we're accustomed to calling artificial light "yellowish"). However, the eye is capable of making a rather large adjustment in its color sensitivity within a minute or so after coming indoors, or going out. Thus flesh tone is flesh tone in any light.* But the film cannot adjust itself similarly, and flesh tone would either be too yellow in artificial light, or too blue outdoors if a single film type were attempted.

So there are two basic types of color film, and while it is possible to correct either type with a filter to more or less match the other, the results are often not as good as if the correct film type had been used. Therefore, for optimum control of color, start with the correct type of film.

COLOR AND INTENSITY OF LIGHT. We have already mentioned the difference in color quality between daylight and artificial light. Each type of light, moreover, varies. Daylight changes from the pale blue-gray of dawn to noonday sun to the red glow of sunset. It is bluer on overcast days, warmer on sunny ones. Daylight changes with the time of day, with the season, with the altitude. It is different in the city and in the country.

Artificial light is no more uniform. Ordinary room lamps are quite yellowish by comparison with the specially made photofloods used for color photography. The light from flashlamps is bluer than that of a photoflood, and electronic flash is bluer yet—so much so that it very closely matches daylight rather than artificial light and is usually used with daylight type color films. Even when you use the proper bulb with the type of color film recommended, there are sometimes variations—old, darkened bulbs make redder pictures than new ones, and voltage variations affect the color of the light, too.

The picture is made, of course, not by the light falling on the subject, but by the light which the subject reflects to the camera and film. It is not easy to realize, however, that the subject reflects light not only to the camera, but in all directions; and also that surrounding objects reflect light not only to the camera but to the subject as well. Thus, we have to take reflected light into account when composing a picture. A subject standing against a brick wall will have some additional red light reflected into his face by the bricks; if the wall itself does not appear in the picture, the red reflection may appear only as a mysterious red cast in the face, or on the clothing.

FILTERS. If you need to, you can adjust the quality of the light with a filter. Sometimes it is necessary, sometimes it is optional, sometimes it is

---

*The reason clothing buyers usually match fabric samples in daylight is not because the eye does not compensate, but because certain dyestuffs are dichroic—that is, they change color in different lights. Natural colors (flesh, flowers, etc.) generally do not.

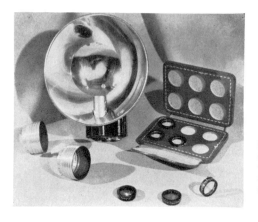

2. Realist Flash Attachment, Sunshades and Realist Filter Kit, including filters for: flashlamps indoors, haze correction outdoors, Type A film in daylight. The sunshades are also filter holders.

unwise. The tables in Chapter 3 list recommended filters for the various color films and suggest uses for them. Mainly you will find that these filters are designed to correct the color of certain light sources to match the more or less fixed character of the color film.

When you know what you are doing you can often use these filters for other purposes, such as special effects, weird colors, or "moonlight" pictures. Until then, it is better to stick to the manufacturer's recommendations. In any case, don't just use filters at random. Get the filters you need as you need them. Probably the first purchase should be a haze filter ("Skylight" for Kodachrome; UV-15 or UV-16 for Ansco Color). The warmer filters used to correct flashlamp illumination to match floodlight can also be used outdoors (with discretion) for a sunny effect. Such uses are a matter of personal taste and experience, and it is wise to use up a few rolls of film on experiments if your fancy leads you in that direction.

In the beginning you need very few filters, and the ones contained in the Realist Filter Kit will answer the needs of most photographers adequately.

Exposure. Exposure has an influence on color rendition, too. Even with the right light source, you will find the color balance of your pictures varies to a considerable degree when the picture is exposed more or less than normal. This is another means of control for the experienced photographer. But it can come only after one has learned how to expose correctly. The correct exposure can be considered the jumping-off point for individual taste and experiment; without this stable foundation, though, experiment is mere tinkering.

Being Aware of Light and Color

Good photographers are always making notes—mentally, on paper, or with the camera—of how things look in different lights and of the manifold variation in light under different conditions. Through long experience, this becomes a "feeling"—the photographer will simply say that a given light is "right" or "wrong" for the picture he has in mind, without specifying just what there is about the light condition that pleases or displeases him. The beginner, on the other hand, takes the light as he finds it, and it is often the final picture that displeases him, without his being able to say why. The only advice that can be given is to study the light before a picture is taken, and then study the resulting picture. Even when you don't have a camera with you, observe light conditions wherever you go—outdoors, indoors, even in the subway!

Notice how different the same subject can look in different lights; how the light can look warm or cold; how it can make things appear opulent or dingy, beautiful or ugly—even happy or sad. Notice how changing light seems to change the color of things: a red brick house will look red in clear daylight, orange from the glow of a sunset and purple ten minutes later in the twilight.

See how the angle of the light can change the whole mood of a place, or how the mood shifts just with a change in the weather. Just for fun, take a walk around your own house at different times of day and different seasons. Stand outside and look around; stoop down and look up; go inside and look out, from downstairs and upstairs. In five minutes you will see a dozen different lighting effects. In a year you will have seen

3. Fine stereos can be made in movie studios, especially if the set is lighted for a color production. Stereo by Sam Clark. Warner Brothers film, *House of Wax*.

109

5. Exposure meter for both incident- and reflected-light readings. G.E. Type PR-1 meter, with incident-light attachment in place (top) over photoelectric cell.

4. A simple exposure meter for reflected-light readings only, and calibrated for shutter speeds and films most often used. G. E., Type PR-30, "The Mascot."

hundreds! Think about them as often as you feel like it, and keep them in mind for pictures.

The light and the color in a scene will contribute as much to your picture as the composition. Learn to think of all three together: they are really inseparable anyhow! In stereo your composition is spread out in space, and so is your light. Observe how the light and the color can make things look more, or less, important; how a big, dark object in the foreground can be less noticeable than a smaller, bright one off in the distance.

Notice how people look in different light. How soft light smooths out wrinkles. How backlight makes even a little tomboy look like the angel she isn't. How strong sunlight makes people squint. How hazy sunlight is sometimes very flattering. How harsh side light or top light can cast hard shadows on deep-set faces.

Things that Control Exposure

Exposure is controlled by two basic factors:

1. The speed or sensitivity of the film.
2. The amount of light that reaches the film.

Of these two things, only one is under the immediate control of the photographer: the amount of light reaching the film. The speed of the film itself is built into it by the manufacturer, and there is nothing you can do to change it. Beware of quack nostrums occasionally advertised which claim to increase the speed of color film—generally they either

110

don't work, or they ruin the color rendition to gain a small amount of image detail. By and large, film speed is a matter of importance to you only in setting your exposure meter and calculating your exposure.

FILM SPEED RATINGS. There are various systems of film speed ratings used in different countries, but the trend is toward a single unified system already adopted by the major American producers as well as the principal European sources of supply; this system is known as the ASA (American Standards Association) Exposure Indexes.

It has been adopted in Great Britain as the BSI (British Standards Institution) in two forms. BSI Arithmetic uses a series of Exposure Index numbers corresponding to the ASA Exposure Indexes; they are completely interchangeable with the ASA numbers. BSI Logarithmic presents the same data in a series of numbers in which every third number represents a doubling of speed. These ratings are distinguished from the Arithmetic series by having a degree sign ($°$) placed after each; thus a given film may be rated in the Arithmetic scale as having a speed of 32; in the Logarithmic scale as 26°. A film of twice this speed would be represented by the Arithmetic value 64, or Logarithmic 29°.

The film speed number, or Exposure Index, tells you how quickly a given film reacts to light as compared with other films. A film with an Exposure Index of 100 will react 10 times faster to light than a film with an Exposure Index of 10.

Color films react relatively slowly to light. For example, Kodachrome or Ansco Color films for daylight have an Exposure Index of 10. The color films for artificial light are slightly faster. Black-and-white films are very much faster.

The practical use of the film speed is in setting the exposure meter, and most meters are calibrated in ASA Exposure Indexes. A notable exception, however, is the Weston meter, which is differently calibrated

6. An easy, direct-reading exposure meter for reflected light. Gives lens settings directly for 1/50 second; other settings from table. Weston D/R Meter.

7. Reflected-light meter with incident-light attachment. The Weston "Master II" meter.

111

and requires the special film speed ratings issued by the Weston Electrical Instrument Co.

AMOUNT OF LIGHT. For any given film there is a specific total amount of light necessary for a good exposure. This total amount is determined by the *brightness* of the light *and* the length of *time* it is allowed to act upon the film. Brightness is controlled by the size of the lens opening, and time by the speed of the shutter.

Brightness and time are directly proportional, so that if you have twice the brightness you need only half the exposure time. And the other way around—if you double the time you need only half the brightness. This is the basis for all exposure adjustments.

Lens Apertures or F-Stops

The numbers engraved on one of the Stereo Realist lens mounts are called lens apertures, or f-stops. As you turn the lens mount the lens diaphragm opening becomes larger or smaller, depending on which way you turn the mount. To see how this works, set the shutter on "time" (T) and press the release to open the shutter. Remove the back from the camera and look through the lenses while you are turning the lens mount. The lens opening will be very large at the 3.5 or 2.8 setting, and it will grow smaller and smaller as you turn it toward 22. Like this:

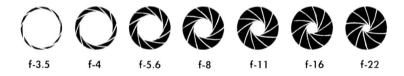

f-3.5   f-4   f-5.6   f-8   f-11   f-16   f-22

This series of numbers—some of them even decimal numbers—may not seem very reasonable to you. Actually, they are arranged in a very orderly manner. Except for the first one, each number lets in half as much light as the one before it. The only other thing you need to know about the numbers is that they are called f-numbers or f-stops. (The f/ stands for the ratio between the size of the opening and the focal length of the lens, and you can read all about it in any standard text if you are really interested.) For practical photography just remember that the f-number is the size of the lens opening. As you can see from the illustration above, the higher the number the smaller the opening. Thus:

f/22 (high number—small opening): lets in very little light.

f/3.5 (low number—large opening): lets in a lot of light.

The lens can be set on any of the numbers, and also between the numbers.

You can already guess that on a day when the light is dim you will want a larger lens opening than on a day when the light is bright. This is just the way our eyes act. In bright light the eye pupils close down to a small opening; in dim light the eye pupils open up. They change automatically for different lighting conditions. The only difference between our eyes and the camera is that the eyes are self-adjusting, but we have to set the camera by hand.

The Shutter Speed Settings

The shutter speed ring between the Realist lenses has this series of numbers:

$$1 \quad 2 \quad 5 \quad 10 \quad 25 \quad 50 \quad 100 \quad 150$$

In this series "1" means 1 full second and the rest of the numbers mean fractions of a second, as follows:

$$1 \quad 1/2 \quad 1/5 \quad 1/10 \quad 1/25 \quad 1/50 \quad 1/100 \quad 1/150$$

This series of shutter speeds is roughly similar to the series of lens openings in that each speed lets in about half as much light as the speed before it. In this series, the larger the number the shorter the exposure,

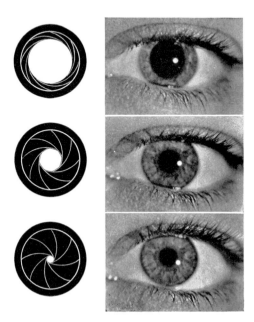

8. The eye adjusts automatically for different light intensities. In dim light the eye pupil opens wide (above). In bright light the pupil closes down (below). The camera lens must be adjusted the same way.

9. An exposure meter dial shows many different lens and shutter combinations that will allow the same total amount of light to reach the film. The meter must always be set for the proper film speed before the reading is taken.

so that less light is admitted to the film with each larger number. This should cause no confusion at all if you remember that the numbers stand for fractions of a second, as indicated above. Thus:

Speed setting 150 (1/150 second) (high number—fast speed): lets in very little light.

Speed setting 2 (1/2 second) (low number—slow speed): lets in a lot of light.

The shutter speeds *cannot* be set between numbers; they *must* be used as marked. And in passing, remember that the speed should always be set before the shutter is cocked. The shutter works on delicate springs, and it puts extra strain on them to change the setting after the cocking lever has been engaged.

Finding the Right Exposure Settings

Any number of different lens and shutter settings will admit the same total amount of light to the film for a good exposure. The basic setting for daylight color film outdoors with average subjects on a sunny day is:

f/6.3 and 1/50 second

Other combinations will give the same total amount of exposure. Here is a typical range of lens and shutter combinations, all of which will allow the same total amount of light to reach the film:

f/14 and 1/10 second
f/9 and 1/25 second
f/6.3 and 1/50 second
f/4.5 and 1/100 second
f/3.5 and 1/150 second

Which to choose? If you want to stop action, choose a fast shutter speed like 1/100 second and set the lens to f/4.5 (halfway between 4 and 5.6). If you want considerable depth of field (sharpness over a large distance), choose a small lens opening like f/9 (halfway between 8 and

114

11) and set the shutter to 1/25 second. Notice that of the lens stops above only f/3.5 is marked on the Realist. However, if for f/9 you set the diaphragm halfway between 8 and 11 it will be accurate enough, and the same is the case for all the other odd numbers given. You can set the lens stops between markings any time but *never* set the shutter speeds between markings.

Although the Realist camera has shutter speeds to 1/150 second, action pictures are not often made in stereo. For certain reasons mentioned farther along, they are not too satisfactory esthetically and are often quite disturbing to some viewers. So most stereo exposures will be calculated on the basis of depth of field requirements.

In this case, having focused on the subject and decided also how far in front and behind the subject we want to focus sharply, we can consult the depth of field charts or the scale on the focusing knob of the camera and determine directly what f-stop to use. Once this has been determined, the shutter speed controls the exposure according to the light conditions.

For example, if the depth of field chart indicates that f/14 is needed to secure the desired depth of field, then in bright sunlight the exposure will have to be 1/10 second, and you will need to use a tripod to avoid camera vibration. If you can't use a tripod, you'll have to open up to f/9 and use 1/25 second at the sacrifice of some depth.

The above discussion has concerned itself with one combination of lens stop and shutter speed—f/6.3 at 1/50 second—and its variations.

10. Late afternoon sunlight, low in the sky, can be used as front light when the camera and subject are both in line with the sun. This is a good way to avoid hard shadows. Front light is flattering for portraits. Stereo by Dorothy S. Gelatt.

11. Shooting from a high angle when the sun is high gives a good stereo effect with front lighting. This picture of a country fair ground was made from the top of a Ferris wheel (see shadow on tent.) Stereo by Dorothy S. Gelatt.

This is correct for an average scene in bright sunlight. It is not, of course, right under many other conditions, and we should know how to determine the amount of light available in all cases so that we can establish a starting point exposure. There are simple exposure guides which work quite well outdoors, in most instances. For extreme cases outdoors, and practically all indoor photography, the exposure meter is the only practical solution. It won't, of course, give you the perfect exposure setting, instantly and without thought; it wasn't designed to perform miracles. It is a tool, like the camera, and should be used with some judgment and skill.

Using an Exposure Meter Outdoors

With a little experience, the exposure meter will produce reliable exposure indications under all kinds of lighting conditions and for all kinds of subject matter—dark or bright, contrasty or soft. And—very important—it will indicate when you should take no picture at all! Sometimes there is just not enough light for color film. Your eye might not tell you so, but a meter will.

Then too, color films have a very narrow latitude for error in exposure. The range of brightness that most color films can record is about 4:1. This means that for accurate color rendition the brightest object in your picture should be not more than 4 times as bright as the darkest part of your picture. If the range is more than 4:1, the overbright part will look

116

"burned out" and the underbright part will be too dark to show much. An exposure meter will tell you what the range of any particular scene is and will point out brightnesses too extreme for the film to handle.

The two basic types of meter are the *reflected-light* meter, such as the Weston, G-E, DeJur, etc., and the *incident-light* meter, such as the Norwood. These classifications are not rigid, however, since incident-light attachments are available for most reflected-light types, while the Norwood is supplied with the Photogrid for reflected-light measurements. Under normal circumstances either type of meter is satisfactory if used sensibly.

THE REFLECTED-LIGHT METER is pointed *at* the subject and measures the light reflected *from* the subject. In doing this it automatically takes into account the fact that the subject may be a very dark or a very light one, and it will therefore naturally indicate that more exposure should be given dark subjects, less to light ones. One would think, therefore, that such a meter would automatically produce 100 per cent perfect results regardless of light conditions or subject matter.

Much of the time this is true; however, there are certain cases where such a method of light measurement can lead to error. For example, take a small black kitten sitting on a flight of whitewashed steps; due to its small size the black area will affect the meter only slightly, and the exposure would be indicated as if the subject were entirely white. This often results in underexposure of the darkest objects, like the black kitten

12. At ground level you will have front light from a high sun angle if you can shoot down on a sloping landscape, as was done in this hillside picture. Stereo by Nina Bourne.

13. Stereos need not always be made in bright sunlight. Soft, diffused light filtering through trees can be used for beautiful, luminous effects. Stereo by Dorothy S. Gelatt.

in this case. One can just as easily imagine the opposite situation: for instance, a white kitten on a deep red plush rug. Due to the low reflectance and large area of the rug, a heavy exposure would be indicated and the kitten would be washed out.

In all such cases, some compensation must be made for the fact that the subject matter differs from the average. One method of compensation is to take separate readings of the darkest and lightest objects in the scene and set the arrow of the meter midway between the two readings. Where the difference is very great this method may not be entirely satisfactory; both ends of the scale would be lost in such a case. Here, one may favor the more important object in choosing the exposure between the limits given by the meter—or it may be possible to add some light to the darkest areas or shade the bright parts to limit the brightness range to one which the film can handle.

For close-ups, point the reflected-light meter only at the subject you are photographing. If you want a close-up of a monkey, point the meter at the monkey, not at the whole zoo. In close-up readings be sure not to cast a shadow on the subject with your hand and the meter: you would then be measuring the shadow and your exposure would be too long.

For general scenes and long shots you want to measure the light reflected from the whole scene. So, aim the meter at the scene. In measuring landscapes tilt the meter down, aiming it at a point midway between your feet and the horizon. This will give a good general reading for the whole scene, including the sky.

118

Whenever there are people in your scene, give them the lion's share of attention in meter readings. In stereo pictures flesh tones should be reproduced naturally or the people will look like waxworks or ghosts. It is best to take exposure readings close up to people. When they are too far away, take a substitute reading from the back of your own hand, with the light falling on your hand at the same angle that it falls on the people in the scene.

The brightness range of most general scenes and subjects can be measured with the reflected-light meter. Simply point the meter at different parts of the scene and watch the needle or exposure indicator. If it shows that the darkest part of the scene needs more than 4 times the exposure of the brightest part of the scene, you will know that the scene exceeds the exposure limits of the film. There are several things you can do about this. If the dark parts are unimportant you can ignore them and expose for the bright parts. (It is unwise to expose for the dark parts because the bright ones will be washed out, which is quite unattractive in color stereo.) You can also try moving yourself or the subject until the brightness range is more within reason. If this isn't feasible, you can sometimes balance the light with reflectors, large sheets of newspaper or blue flash. If the range is still too great, try to refrain from taking the picture. Look for something better!

It is sometimes recommended, where scenes have unusual distributions of light and dark objects, that the reading be taken from a gray card

14. Always use an exposure meter for scenes with heavy contrast. Expose for the bright parts and let the rest of the scene go dark when there is great contrast. Stereo by Dorothy S. Gelatt.

substituted for the subject. This will place the exposure approximately in the middle of the film range and avoid the necessity for taking multiple readings and averaging, provided the card has approximately 18 per cent reflectance (like the Kodak Neutral Gray Test Card). It should be evident that if we are substituting a standard gray card for our subject, what we are actually doing is measuring the incident light, since this card always reflects the same 18 per cent of the incident light. This method is frequently used when an incident-light meter is not available.

As previously mentioned, you can take a substitution reading from the back of your hand. However, average skin reflects about 35 per cent of the light falling on it. Thus, the meter will give a reading about double that secured from the gray card. Therefore, if you use this method, give twice the indicated exposure; otherwise underexposure may result.

THE INCIDENT-LIGHT METER measures the light *falling upon the subject*, and it is held at subject position facing the camera. It would seem that in this case errors like the ones described for reflected-light meters could not occur, since the same reading would be obtained regardless of the subject brightness and distribution of highlight and shadow. Thus dark objects would photograph dark, and light objects would photograph light. Actually, an error is possible here, too, in the opposite direction from the error produced by the reflected-light meter. Due to the fact that the latitude of color films is somewhat limited, very light scenes will be overexposed, if incident-light measurements are made, and scenes which are predominantly dark will be underexposed. Thus, in the case of the two cats mentioned before, if the incident-light meter were used the white background would be overexposed, while the red plush background would be underexposed.

When using an incident-light meter, therefore, some compensation must be made for subject matter. If a subject is made up predominantly of dark tones, with no pure whites, it is usually well to give from ½ stop to 1 full stop more exposure than the meter indicates. And if the subject is predominantly light, with few very dark areas, it is well to give from ½ to 1 full stop less exposure than indicated by the meter.

Regardless of what meter you use, it should be thoroughly checked and correlated with your own way of working. If with a given meter your results are consistently darker than you desire, the simplest way of making a permanent correction for that meter, camera and film is to adopt a new, lower film-speed rating for that particular film. For example, one may find that a setting of ASA 8 for a given color film produces better transparencies than the recommended rating of 10. This does not mean that the recommended rating is wrong; it merely indicates that your camera may have a slightly fast shutter, your meter is reading slightly high, or that you personally prefer a slightly lighter transparency than that considered "normal" by others. The same, of course, is true if your transparencies are consistently lighter than you prefer; simply set your meter to a somewhat higher Exposure Index or film speed than the recommended rating.

You must remember at all times that this altered rating holds true only for that one exposure meter, camera and film. Any one brand of film varies very little from one roll to another, but you may find it desirable to make an Exposure Index correction for one brand of color film, and not for another—or for one camera and not for another. It pays, in any case, to recheck this correction at intervals, since changes *do* take place in the sensitivity of the meter or the speed of a shutter with age and usage.

It pays, also, to be as careful with your meter as you are with your camera. Hard knocks, a dip in the lake, or parking the meter on a radiator all will damage it or reduce its accuracy. If you have reason to suspect that your meter is not reading accurately, try it out on an "average" scene to see if it indicates the average 1/50 second at f/6.3 for color film. If it does not, send it off for checking and repair. In any case, always suspect very high readings, like 1/50 at f/16 or higher, or very low readings when the light is good.

Whatever meter you use, read the instruction book first and make sure that you know what it is all about. Different meters have different

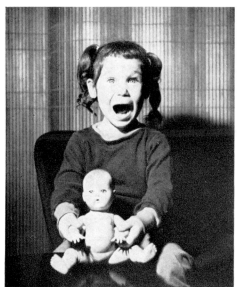

15. Strobe light exposures are so brief that they can make people look "frozen" in stereo, unless the subject is just right — as it is here, where the action is natural. Stereo by Arthur Rothstein.

16. Even where there is no color, bright sunlight will make a picture sparkle. The original of this picture is all gray rocks, the same as this reproduction, with only a touch of color in the skin tone and a box the boy carries. Even gray can be lively! Stereo by Dorothy S. Gelatt.

controls and adjustments even though they all accomplish the same basic things. Some meters have a greater range than others; some are calibrated for still cameras and movie cameras too; some can be used for both incident and reflected light. The choice of a meter is largely a matter of price and personal preference. Any meter designed for still cameras can be used with the Stereo Realist camera.

Using an Exposure Meter Indoors

An exposure meter is most valuable for adjusting the level of artificial lighting units either in the studio or in the home. It is also useful just for measuring the existing light around the house if you are not using any special lighting equipment.

You will find the incident-light meter or incident-light attachment very useful indoors with artificial light. Since it measures the light falling on the subject, and since you can control artificial light much more readily than daylight, the meter can be used as a guide to placing your lights. (This is only for flood and spotlights, of course. You do not use an exposure meter for flashlamps.)

After your subject and lights have been set up, hold the incident-light meter at subject position, facing the camera, and take a reading. Then, with the meter still at subject position, turn it and take readings facing each of the light sources. If the readings vary more than 4:1, move the

122

necessary lights closer or farther away until you have the proper lighting balance. The same kind of readings should be taken throughout the scene to be sure that the light carries to the farthest point you want to photograph. If the meter readings at the background are too low, add extra lights to build them up.

Always be sure that you are not standing between the light and the subject when you take the readings. The same thing will happen here that happens with outdoor close-ups: you will be measuring your own shadow. Also, if the subject is very dark, or very bright, adjust the meter reading—½ to 1 stop more exposure for dark subjects; ½ to 1 stop less for bright subjects.

One last suggestion on using meters for color film. Even though we started out by talking about a black cat on white steps, black and white usually do not count in measuring the exposure for most scenes. You should measure the other colors in the scene, and the blacks and whites will take care of themselves. A good example of this is the fashion picture on Page 239, Figure 12. Here the only real color is in the skin tones of the people, since the clothes and setting are all black and white. Accordingly, the exposure was measured for the skin tones; the blacks and whites, which are far beyond the limits of the film, simply turned out black and white! Although this example is an indoor picture, the same applies outdoors.

Outdoor Lighting

Now, assuming that we have a camera and an exposure meter, we're ready to take some pictures. Most likely, we'll take the majority of our pictures outdoors—that is, in daylight.

Daylight is by no means a fixed entity, as we have already seen. There is a lot of variety in daylight, and while we can't often change it, if the mountain won't come to Mahomet, then Mahomet will go to the mountain. In other words, if the light isn't the way you want it at the moment, it very likely will be some other time. So the thing to do is just wait, at least in the case of immovable subjects.

Otherwise, the subject can be moved or the photographer can move; occasionally a little nature-faking can be done by shading part of the subject from direct light or bouncing a little daylight into a dark shadow with some sort of reflector—even a newspaper will do in a pinch. Dull-day pictures can be brightened up by a judiciously placed flashlamp. In short, there are lots of things you can do with daylight, and even more when you combine it with a flashbulb.

Direction of the Light

FRONT LIGHTING. When the light comes directly from the front, shadows are at a minimum—actually they fall directly behind the subject and aren't seen by the camera. Contrast is low with flat front light, which

17. People look best in stereo when they are re-laxed, not "caught in the act." Here the bright sand reflects light to soften the shadows on the face. Stereo by Willard D. Morgan.

is good for color film but doesn't do anything much to help out stereo-scopically. Without shadows for modeling, all of the burden of pro-ducing depth is thrown on the composition. A good way to get con-siderable depth in a flatly lighted shot is to photograph from a high vantage point. Looking down always accentuates the stereo effect, and the receding planes enhance the effect of depth even with flat light. Figure 11, a panorama of a country fair, was taken from the top of a Ferris wheel. The camera faced the scene at the same angle as the sun, so the lighting is flat. Photographed from above, the scene still recedes nicely in depth, and the straightforward lighting gives a pleasant, sunny feeling to a pleasant, sunny scene.

You needn't always get up in the air, however, to use front light. In Figure 12 the photographer was on a hillside and took advantage of the natural drop in the landscape. Figure 10 is also front-lighted, but this time by a late afternoon sun. When the sun is low in the sky—both in the early morning and late afternoon—it is at a low enough angle to be a front light for things photographed at ground level.

TOP LIGHT. Although all sunlight comes from overhead, it is usually called top light when it is at the highest point in the sky and casts the shortest shadows on the ground. It covers everything more or less equally with light. In most parts of the world the sun is at its highest for a couple of hours around noon during the late spring and the summer months, and that is when you get the sharpest overhead light. Figure 4, Page 98 was photographed in New York in early afternoon summer light. It was a good, clean light for this kind of picture and gave full color saturation from the bright red and yellow of the soft-drink cart to the grayed-down tones of the background. If the same picture had been taken later in the day there would have been long shadows, which in this case would have added nothing.

SIDE LIGHT. In ordinary photography you usually count heavily on side light to add the shadows that separate one part of the picture from another. When you are photographing people, the side light is called modeling light because its shadows add the impression of roundness to face and figure contours. In stereo you don't need the side light as much as you do in flat photography. In fact, you should be careful to avoid hard inky pools of shadow unless they definitely add something to the picture. Figure 18 uses hard side light deliberately to cast an interesting shadow of the tree through an empty part of the picture and lead the eye on through the scene. This picture also shows how the direction of the light is strictly relative to the different parts of the scene. The sun is side-lighting the tree in the foreground; it is front-lighting the woods in the background.

BACK LIGHT. Light that comes *toward* the camera hits the *back* of the subject and has two main effects, depending on the nature of the scene and the strength of the light. Soft back light can give a very luminous effect when it is shining through hair or transparent objects.

18. Hard side light can often be used to cast long shadow patterns that will lead the eye through the empty part of a picture for more interest. Stereo by Dorothy S. Gelatt.

125

Figure 19 is completely radiant with back light: the children are rimmed with soft light and the kites are luminous and transparent. In Figure 20 the back light is hard, and it silhouettes the children against the bright ocean.

Always use sunshades on the lenses when you have light coming toward the camera; they will shield the film from stray light and reflections. (It's a good idea to have sunshades on the camera all the time. You never know when you may need them.)

Quality of the Light

While the direction of the light generally influences the composition of the picture, it is the quality of the light that most often sets its mood. Bright sunlight usually adds cheer and liveliness to a scene. Soft sunlight can make things look restful. Hazy fog can make things look gloomy. Flat overcast can make things look very quiet. Although you are most likely to get a well-exposed picture in good sunlight, you won't have much variety of mood if you don't shoot in a variety of lights. With ordinary care in measuring exposures you can take pictures in all kinds of light and have any mood you want in a picture.

BRIGHT SUNLIGHT. All the pictures we've talked about so far in examining the *direction* of the light were made in bright sunlight. And they all have one quality in common: they are all cheerful. This doesn't mean, of course, that every picture you ever take in bright sunlight will be gay and lively. It's just a clue to how sunlight affects the mood. The

19. Soft, diffuse back light has a beautiful, luminous effect, especially on blonde hair and translucent fabrics like the children's kites in this picture. Stereo by R. H. Bills.

126

sharp quality of the light gives brilliance to the colors, and this in itself is generally more lively than dull.

Bright sunlight can make a lively picture even when there is practically no color in the scene. In Figure 16 the only real color is in the boy's skin and a small yellow box in his left hand. The greatest part of the picture was gray rocks. You might think that gray would be too dull for a cheerful picture. It isn't—the sun makes it sparkle.

SOFT SUNLIGHT. Sunlight that is softly diffused, either by very thin clouds, a very light haze, or by filtering through foliage, has quite a different mood from bright sunlight. Figure 13 was made in soft, diffused sunlight which added to the warm, tender mood of the scene. The colors in the original picture are the red, gold and brown of autumn; the soft light made them gently pastel. If the light had been sharper the colors would have been sharper, too, and the mood completely changed.

The bridal picture in Figure 13, Page 240, was also made with sunlight coming through foliage. Here the sun was bright, but the foliage softened it considerably so that the white wedding dress does not shine like a sheet in the wind.

HAZE AND FOG. Although there are filters to minimize the effect of haze on color film, they aren't always necessary or even desirable. For instance, Figure 22 is frankly a Blue Monday Morning picture. The fog adds an overall blue gloom to the monotony, so no attempt was made to filter it away. You can make all sorts of mood pictures in haze and fog. Try it sometime.

20. Hard back light on the subject (light coming *toward* the camera) makes interesting stereo silhouettes. They are best when background is bright. Stereo by Dorothy S. Gelatt.

127

HARD CONTRAST. Often a scene will have very dark *and* very bright areas that you would like to have in the picture for contrast. Figure 14 is such a picture: the foreground has very heavy shade in contrast to the dazzling bright flowers in the background. In the stereo picture, as in real life, the brilliance of the flowers is enhanced by contrast with the dark foreground. Here the contrast is in both light quality and color. If the picture had been all bright flowers and no dark eye relief in the foreground, it would have been "too much of a good thing." In hard-contrast pictures like this, expose for the brightest part and let the rest of the picture go dark. This is the way the eye would adjust in viewing the real scene, and your picture should be adjusted the same way.

NO CONTRAST. Lighting from an overcast sky (no sunlight at all) gives no contrast and no shadows. You might call it neutral lighting. Some photographers prefer this kind of light for portraits of people; it creates no hard shadow problems.

Flat, no-contrast light is peaceful and won't add a jarring note to an otherwise placid scene. In Figure 21 the flat lighting is very suitable—a country churchyard is supposed to look placid.

One thing to remember about flat lighting is that it has no contrast or shadows to increase the stereo depth. In Figure 21 no stereo help is needed from the lighting: the rows of stone markers start out close by where the stereo effect is strong, and they recede in a strong linear pattern.

128

Lighting People Outdoors

It is easy to take good pictures of people, but none the less they account for more disappointments in stereo than almost any other picture category. The reason is simple: it is mainly a matter of the difference between a stereo picture and everyday experience. The stereo picture snatches an instant in life and holds it *motionless* on film. In real life people are continually *moving*. Even when they are sitting still or sleeping, there is a quality of movement about them. Blinking eyes and breathing keep them in constant motion, though it is sometimes almost imperceptible. People are a restless lot and they seldom stand stock-still unless they are shocked with terror. "He was frozen with fear" is the usual expression. "He was just plain frozen" is the common complaint about a lot of stereos of people! There are other words to describe the symptom: "waxworks," "statues," "cut-outs," etc. They all mean one thing—arrested action, which the mind rejects in a stereo picture because it is unlike real life. The three dimensions look real enough in a stereo picture, and if the people don't look equally real, the illusion is disturbed. This is the problem. Now, how do we solve it? Lighting and exposure play a big part. So does your own observation and finger control on the shutter release. Let's consider the last two first.

Even the most casual observation of people will show you that their pace is constantly changing. Every movement they make has a beginning, a middle and an end. The fault with most "frozen" stereo people is that

22. Hazy light or fog need not be altered by filters when part of the mood of a scene. This Blue Monday picture was made in early morning fog. Stereo by Dorothy S. Gelatt.

23. Natural reflectors like the water here, or the sand in Figure 17, will fill in shadows from strong overhead sunlight. Stereo by Dorothy S. Gelatt.

they are photographed somewhere in the *middle* of the action, So, your first clue for making natural-looking stereos of people is to avoid "taking your half out of the middle." It's bad manners with cake, and it's bad pictures with stereo. Learn to judge action so that your finger trips the shutter when an action is completed, or just before it starts.

There's an easy way to visualize a finished stereo. Find some people who are busy doing things. Watch them for a while to see how they move. Then close your eyes tight and blink them open briefly now and then. The brief glimpse you see when your eyes are open will be just like an average exposure with the camera. You will see the action stopped the way the camera stops it. After a little bit of practice like this, you won't ever take a "frozen" picture again. You will know how to time your pictures for the action.

Now let's see how good lighting and proper exposure can improve your pictures of people. First of all, skin tones are very important. If they are overexposed and washed out, the people will look ghostly. Exposure should be "on the button," especially for people with very pale and delicate complexions.

In general, it's better not to have heavy shadows on faces. The shadows may look heavier on the film than they are in real life, and they will detract from the naturalness of the people. This would seem to indicate some kind of direct, or flat lighting, and for close-ups it generally does.

130

Shadows on people at some distance from the camera will not be as disturbing in the picture as shadows on people close by.

Close-ups of people are often very successful in the flat light of an overcast day. Sometimes you can simulate that light in a shaded area on a sunny day. Be careful of shaded areas, though; they are often full of blue light that will cast a pallor on the people.

Direct sunlight is, of course, your most constant light source. The angle and quality of the light should both be used judiciously for good pictures of people. If the sun is throwing hard shadows, find some way to avoid them. If necessary move the subject, or have him lift or lower his head till the lighting is better. If this won't work, try a higher or lower camera angle. Sometimes just standing on a fence and shooting down is all you need. If the light isn't right for the kind of picture you want, wait until it changes—or come back another time.

Another thing you can do is "fill in the shadows." This means adding light in one way or another. Light walls, concrete pavements, sand or any other reflecting surface will do the trick. If nothing like that is available you can spread some large sheets of newspaper to reflect light into the shadows. Another way is to use blue flashlamps for "fill" light. We'll talk about them in the flash section.

Now let's look at a few pictures of people taken in ordinary light conditions. They all have two things in common: acceptable action and no annoying shadows. In Figure 23 the little boy is fishing very happily, and action is suggested by the slight blur of the fishing line. The shutter

24. Flat light from an overcast sky is very pleasant for portraits, and prevents eye squint. This lovely portrait of actress Doris Day was made by Marty Melcher.

131

speed was 1/25 second to allow a little movement. If the boy had moved during the exposure he would have been blurred, and the picture a disappointment. Although the lighting was from overhead, the surface of the water reflected enough fill light to his face to avoid heavy shadows. The boy on the sand in Figure 17 is a perfect example of a relaxed subject. The lighting is flat, and while there is nothing but air between the boy and the far mountains, it's a good stereo shot anyway. (Notice the difference between the flat picture and the stereo picture you see with your viewer.)

Flat light with no sun (usually called "cloudy-dull" in exposure tables) is often pleasant for pictures of people. Look at the picture of the movie star in Figure 24. This picture of Doris Day by the sea is quiet, informal and just a little pensive. Being an actress, she knows how to pose gracefully and at ease. (Most ordinary citizens do not know how to pose, and if you try to "stage" a picture it will usually end up looking grim and determined!)

The various pictures of people outdoors shown in the two color sections of this book are valuable to examine for lighting and color. Look carefully to see how the different suggestions made here apply to the various pictures. The portrait of the young couple in Figure 7, Page 100 has quiet lighting and a relaxed pose. The picture of the Indian Chief, Figure 5, Page 99, has strong lighting, quite in character with the subject. Ordinarily this kind of hard lighting would make most people look

25. Light patterns make interesting stereo abstractions, with contrast in shapes as well as tones. Stone railing stereo abstraction by John S. Carroll.

like "waxworks," but for the weathered face of the Chief it is very success-ful. The picture of Edward Weston in Figure 13, Page 103 is a very good example of how daylight can be used for an indoor portrait. When you try this sort of thing, be sure you have a large enough window or skylight.

Patterns In Daylight

By watching lighting effects and contrast you can make very inter-esting and exciting stereos that are more like three-dimensional abstrac-tions than three-dimensional real life. Figure 25 is just a stone railing and its shadows, but it has a very pleasing abstract quality. This particular shot is nice as a flat picture, but the pattern would be only light versus dark. In stereo the pattern is also *flat versus round*. And shown as it is, completely isolated from the surroundings, it might lead any place, and it might be any size. Figure 26 is just a scattering of beach grass. It's nothing special, but fun to look at. You will find things like these all the time if you look for them. Other ways of achieving abstract effects are explained in Chapter 5.

Patterns in space need not always be abstract. Sometimes a scene or an object will have an inherent design quality by reason of distance or lighting contrast, or both. Look at Figure 27, which has the same effect in color as in this black-and-white reproduction. The foreground trees are in heavy black shadow and the summerhouse on the lake is brilliantly lighted: the dock farther off in the distance is also in bright sunlight. This

26. A stereo pattern in space can be made from the most simple subjects. This one is just a scatter-ing of beach grass. Stereo by Dorothy S. Gelatt.

133

27. Space patterns need not always be abstract. Many natural scenes have a quality of design in contrast, shape and distance, color and lighting. Stereo by Dorothy S. Gelatt.

makes quite a striking space pattern, with bright spots at various distances framed by openings in the dark foliage. In a picture like this you needn't worry about sharpness in the foreground; even though it is very close, it is so dark that detail won't matter and you can both focus and expose for the bright objects in the distance.

Because of the contrast, the bright summerhouse is the most important thing in this picture, even though it is quite far away. Just for comparison, look at another picture of the same summerhouse in Figure 28. Here it is in close-up, and not especially interesting, even though it has a lot of depth.

Indoor Lighting

There are three basic kinds of light for taking color stereos indoors:

Flashlamps—{clear lamps for indoor color film / blue lamps for daylight color film
Strobe—photofloods, photospots for indoor color film
Incandescent—electronic flash for daylight color film

Chapter 3 explains in detail about the action of different light sources on different color films, and why it is best to use the light sources recommended for specific films. In Chapter 3 you will also find all the data for using various light sources with various color films: there are tables of light sources and filter recommendations; tables of flashlamp guide numbers; and tables for electronic flash. This is the data to consult when you are choosing film, light source and filters. We will not repeat it here: we simply urge you to read it as "technical background" for color photography with artificial light. Read about *color temperature*, too, if you want to understand why color films react as they do.

One thing to understand from the very beginning about artificial light is that, because artificial light sources are relatively small, their light doesn't spread out endlessly like sunlight. The carrying power of an artificial light source depends on the design of its reflector, which determines just how wide an angle a given light source will cover. The strength of the light, within this angle, depends roughly on the so-called "Inverse Square Law." This law states, in its original form, that the intensity of the light varies inversely as the square of the distance. In plain English, it means that as you get farther from the light source, less light reaches you, and that the amount by which the light diminishes is not simply in proportion to the distance, but much more—that is, in proportion to the distance multiplied by itself.

A practical example: if we are 4 feet from the light and our exposure meter reads 100, then at 8 feet from the light it will not read 50, but 25. When we doubled the distance, the light dropped not to half but to one-quarter.

In general, as long as you use an exposure meter you don't have to worry about the Inverse Square Law—the meter will always show you how much more exposure you need when you move light away from or

28. This near-by view of the summerhouse in Figure 27 shows the difference between an ordinary close-up and a subject design-in-space. Stereo by Dorothy S. Gelatt.

29. The Realist Flash Attachment fits into the camera accessory clip for instant use. Realist Flash Guide Rings on lens mounts set the lenses directly for the flash exposure.

toward your subject. On the other hand, it will explain why a background only a foot or two beyond the lighted subject appears so dark, and why if we point a light fairly high on a standing figure the feet and the lower part of the clothing are often underexposed.

Remember the Inverse Square Law too, when you're shooting flash: it explains why a slight error in measuring distance from lamp to subject can cause a much larger error in exposure. It also explains why you can't illuminate a whole room with one flashlamp, no matter how big the lamp (the more power used to reach the far end, the more the nearer objects will be overexposed—the ratio will be the same, no matter how big the bulb). So if you are using only one lamp, keep your subject near the background—or keep darker objects near the camera, lighter ones in the distance.

Probably more indoor stereos are made with flash than with any other light source, mainly because flash is convenient and doesn't need any source of electric current outside of the tiny batteries in the unit. You need a lot of current for incandescent lamps, and the average household lines are not heavy enough to carry it.

Using the Realist Flash Attachment

The easiest way to make color pictures indoors is to use the Realist Flash Attachment and midget flashlamps. The Flash Attachment is compact, easy to carry, and instantly ready for pictures when you slide it into the accessory clip on top of the camera. A contact point in the accessory clip completes the connection between the flash gun and the built-in synchronization mechanism in the camera. Three tiny batteries in the flash unit supply the power for the flashlamps. Always be sure that your batteries are fresh; worn-out batteries won't supply enough current to fire the flashlamps. You can get a small test light to try out the circuit if you are in doubt about the batteries. To use the test light, simply fit it in the flashlamp socket after the flash unit is attached to the camera; close the camera lens cover and press the shutter release button. If the test lamp lights up for an instant when you trip the shutter, the batteries are in good shape. If the lamp doesn't light up, you need new batteries. (Do not advance the film if you have covered the lenses when using the test light; the film will not be fogged, and you can use it to make a picture.) It is always wise to remove the batteries from the flash unit if you are not going to use it for some time. Batteries corrode with disuse, and the corrosion will spoil your flash gun.

The easiest way to find the right exposure for the Realist Flash Attachment is to use the Flash Guide Rings described in Chapter 2, where you will also find complete instructions for using them. They make flash photography practically automatic and eliminate the use of Flash Guide Numbers, which are generally employed to calculate flash exposures. Chapter 2 also explains how to use the Flash Guide Numbers—which you will find printed on every package of flashlamps, and also in Chapter 3. Regardless of which method you use for exposure calculation:

Always set the Realist shutter to 1/25 for flash!

The camera synchronization is designed to utilize the entire output of most flashlamps when the shutter is set to 1/25 second.

Now, all you need is the lens setting, which is determined by the distance from flashlamp to subject. To find the lens setting you simply

30. For good flash lighting balance put darkest objects nearest the flash and lighter ones farther away. Realist Flash stereo by Dorothy S. Gelatt.

31. A simple flash close-up with one layer of white handkerchief over the lamp to soften the light, so that skin tones are not "burned up." Realist Flash on camera; model looks to side, which avoids "pink eye" reflection. Stereo by Dorothy S. Gelatt.

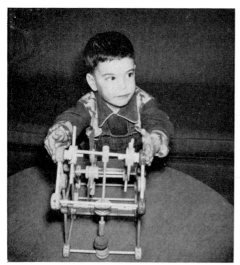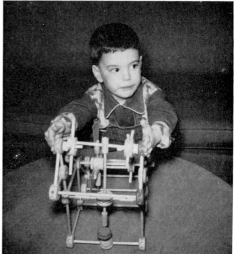

divide the Guide Number (for the type of film and flashlamp you are using) by the distance from flashlamp to subject. For example:

Kodachrome, Type A and No. 5 flashlamp—Guide No. 70

Distance from flashlamp to subject—10 feet

$$\frac{\text{Guide Number}}{\text{Distance}} \quad \frac{70}{10} = 7 \ (f/7)$$

The Flash Guide Rings do this calculation for you automatically. You just focus on the subject, then turn the lens rim until the subject distance on the correct Guide Ring Scale is opposite the white dot on the lens mount. The aperture is now correct for that flashlamp and distance.

Guide Numbers or the Flash Guide Ring give you suggested settings only for "average subjects in average rooms." Light-colored subjects in light-colored rooms will need *less* than the average exposure. Darker subjects in darker rooms will need *more* than the average exposure. The "average exposure" recommendations are intended mainly as a starting point. A little experience will teach you how to alter them for any variations in your own equipment or in the subject matter.

The most common mistake of beginners with flash is "burning up the foreground." Most often, too, there are people in the foreground; the overexposure makes them look pasty and ghostlike. One way to cut down

138

on exposure, of course, is to use a smaller lens stop. Another way is to use a less powerful flashlamp. The easiest way is to hold back some of the light from the subject. This is done by covering the flashlamp with some translucent material like a handkerchief or the diffusion disk that fits in the Realist Flashguard. The diffusion disk will cut down the exposure by about ½ stop. One layer of a man's white handkerchief will do about the same. Two layers of handkerchief can cut down the exposure by a full stop, which is sometimes necessary when you are shooting very light subjects close up. Even if you don't need to cut down the light, it's a good idea to keep the flashlamp covered with a clear plastic Flashguard whenever you are shooting very close to people. Flashlamps have been known to explode on firing, and while this rarely happens nowadays it is always well to take precautions.

With your Realist Flash Attachment right on top of the camera, you don't have to worry about hard shadows; the lighting will be straight from the front. There is one disturbing effect to avoid, however, and that is "pink eye," a reflection from the inner eye when a light shines straight into it from the camera axis. Just watch to be sure that your subjects are not looking straight at the camera and the flashlamp.

The Realist Flash Attachment is ideal for pictures of individuals and small groups. Figures 30 and 31 were both made with the Realist Flash and are average indoor pictures. Figure 30 was made on Daylight Kodachrome with a G.E. No. 5B (blue) flashlamp to balance with the daylight coming through the windows. The family needed a moment's arranging to seat the young man in the dark shirt closest to the camera, since he would receive the most light. The girl in the light blouse was seated farther away so that she wouldn't be a bright glare in the foreground. The overhead house lights in this picture were not strong enough to change the color balance of the scene and were left on to add a little glow. The picture of the little boy in Figure 31 was made on Kodachrome, Type A, with 81C filters and a G.E. No. 5 (clear) flashlamp.

Other Flash Lighting

Sometimes you may need more light than just the flash on the camera; or you may want your light to come from some other position. Off-camera units of any desired type can be synchronized to the camera through the flash accessory clip. A "shoe" that fits into the clip can be attached to the cable of any off-camera unit. Any number of such units can be connected together and all of them set off by the one flash contact in the camera. There are also "slave" flash units like the Heiland Fotoeye which need no wiring connections to the camera flash unit; they are tripped when the light from another flash strikes a photocell in the "slave" unit.

You can get along without elaborate equipment, however, and still take complicated flash pictures if you are willing to spend a little time and energy on them. The mirror-room interior in Figure 15, Page 104 is

an example of the most complicated sort of setup you are likely to find around a house. Still it was made with just a Realist Flash on the camera and an extra flashgun hand-held and hand-fired. The system used for this picture is good for illuminating any large room, and it's a lot easier when you don't have a wall of mirrors to contend with.

The mirror room was photographed on Kodachrome, Type A with an 81C filter. One G.E. No. 5 flashlamp was fired on the camera, and five G.E. No. 22 flashlamps were fired successively from the extra gun. The small flashlamp on the camera lighted the fireplace and the table and chairs in the foreground. It is the only direct lighting in the picture. The rest of the light is all an image in the mirror. To photograph objects reflected in a mirror, light the objects, *not* the mirror. In this case, the object is a whole room reflected in the mirror. So the whole room must be lighted. This is done by blocking out the room into imaginary sections and lighting each of them with a separate flashlamp. Large No. 22 flashlamps were used for the large sections of the room, to equal the effect of the small No. 5 flashlamp on the camera. The No. 22 flashlamps are about four times as strong as the No. 5, and since the distance they had to cover was about twice as great, the light balanced nicely (remember the Inverse Square Law?).

For multiple exposures like this, the camera is used on a rigid tripod and the shutter is opened each time a flashlamp is fired, and closed immediately afterward. There were seven exposures for the mirror room—one for each of the six flashlamps and an extra one for a "special effect"—the torches on the mantel. These happened to be electric lights attached to a rheostat. With the room in total darkness, the rheostat was slowly turned up and down to make an effect in the picture of real torchlight flame.

With mirror pictures, be sure to scan every inch of the mirror thoroughly from the camera position to be sure that unwanted objects or people (including yourself and the camera!) are not accidentally reflected. And, of course, be sure that your lights are arranged so that they do not throw a glare on the mirror and blot out the reflection you are photographing.

Another way to use flashlamps is to direct them toward the ceiling and let the reflected light illuminate the subject. This is known as "bounce light" and gives a very soft lighting effect without any hard shadows. Exposure for bounce light depends on the height of the ceiling, and a few trial exposures are generally necessary. Other light sources besides flashlamps can also be used for bounce lighting, but off-camera flash is the most common. In the mirror-room picture, one of the flashlamps was bounced off the ceiling to fill some hard shadows.

Strobe Lighting

Electronic flash (strobe light) has one useful advantage over ordinary flashlamps: you do not need a new lamp for every picture. A strobe tube is good for thousands of pictures, and the battery that supplies the power

33. (Left) SR Stroboflash II and extra "slave" unit, both battery-operated. Stereo Realist camera synchronizes strobe flash at all shutter speeds.

34. (Right) ASCOR Midget 200-2 battery-operated strobe synchronized to Realist and used off-camera. Camera is braced against the arm that supports the lamp unit.

also has a long life if kept properly charged. The duration of a strobe flash is very brief—1/500 or 1/1000 second for average commercial units —but the flash is very powerful. For both these reasons strobe light needs extra care in stereo. Strobe outfits vary greatly in light output and efficiency, and the best way to find out about a particular unit is to try it out on a roll of film.

Strobe light is balanced for daylight color film and should be used with daylight film both indoors and out. It can be synchronized with the Realist at any shutter speed. See Chapter 3 for more data.

Strobe light is noted for its action-stopping power, and when people first started using it for still photography they pointed with pride to strobe pictures that showed "frozen" action. In stereo, we usually prefer not to freeze the action, so strobe should be used most carefully in photographing people. Figures 15 and 32 are both effective strobe shots of people. In Figure 15 the little girl is deliberately making a silly face, so the frozen action is not a distortion. In Figure 32 the frozen action enhances the magician's trick.

Daylight Flash Outdoors

A good method of filling in shadows in exterior photography, and particularly in portraits back-lighted by sunlight, is to use a *blue* flash-lamp on or near the camera. It is necessary, of course to balance the daylight exposure with the flash illumination to get a natural, overall balance.

The synchronizer built into the Stereo Realist camera makes its contact at the instant the shutter blades are fully open. For this reason it may be used with the normal Class M Flashlamps only at speeds of 1/25 second or slower. Thus, a simple method of balancing flash-fill and daylight is used. The camera lens and shutter are set for the daylight exposure; then the flash-fill ratio is adjusted by varying the distance from lamp to subject.

For example, the exposure for the daylight part of a given subject is 1/25 second at f/9. The guide number for Daylight Kodachrome with a 5-B Lamp is 50. Then dividing the guide number by the lens aperture will give the distance for a full-flash exposure—in this case $50 \div 9 = 5\frac{1}{2}$, and if the flash were the only source of light it would have to be placed at 5½ feet from the subject.

However, since the flash is being *added* to the daylight this will not result in a 1:1 balance, as might appear at first glance. Actually, parts of the subject will be illuminated by daylight and parts by daylight plus flash. To allow for this additive effect, the distance should be increased about 20 per cent (or approximately 1 foot in this case) to attain a 1:1 balance.

Artistically, however, a 1:1 balance of fill light to daylight looks some-what unreal, and more natural-looking pictures will result if the ratio is 1½:1 or 2:1. A rapid rule of thumb for attaining such ratios is to increase the calculated distance from lamp to camera by 25 per cent for a 1½:1 ratio and by 50 per cent for a 2:1 ratio.

Thus, for example, assume a Sylvania 25-B Lamp having a guide number for Daylight Kodachrome of 65 and a daylight exposure of 1/25 second at f/9. The calculated distance would be about 7 feet. For a 1½:1 ratio of daylight-to-fill, the distance would be increased to 8¾ feet, and for a 2:1 ratio the distance would be 10½ feet.

Strobe lights can also be used for flash-fill with daylight-type color films. Since the flash duration is very short, strobe lights will synchronize with the Stereo Realist shutter at all speeds; hence somewhat more flexibility is possible in choosing subject distances.

For example, take a strobe having a daylight guide number of 55 for Kodachrome Film. If the subject is 10 feet away the correct aperture for the strobe light alone would be $55 \div 10 = 5.5$, say f/5.6. If the daylight exposure has been determined to be 1/25 second at f/8, then we can use 1/50 second at f/5.6 in this case.

As before, this will not give a proper 1:1 balance, and the same rule previously given may be used. However, a better way to apply it is directly to the guide number. Thus, for a 1½:1 balance, the increase is 25 per cent, so the guide number for our flash unit becomes (for this purpose only) $55 \times 1\frac{1}{4} = 69$ and for a 2:1 balance $55 \times 1\frac{1}{2} = 82$. Having decided on a guide number for a given light balance, it may be used directly for calculating flash-fill exposures and will always result in that approximate highlight-to-fill balance.

"Handkerchief" Flash Outdoors

For quick flash pictures outdoors, when you do not want to spend any time figuring the distance for a well-balanced flash picture in daylight, there is a simple trick you can do for most average pictures. All you need is a man's white handkerchief. You cover the flashlamp with one or two layers of white handkerchief, depending on the distance to the subject. The table below is a handy guide for using a handkerchief to control the light intensity of blue flashlamps for outdoor exposure on daylight color film.

Exposure 1/25 Second—Lens Set Halfway Between f/8 and f/11

Lamp-to-Subject Distance	Use of Handkerchief with 5B Lamp
3½ feet	2 thicknesses
4½ feet	1 thickness
6-8 feet	no handkerchief

Incandescent Light

Most professional lighting in studios is done with incandescent light, and the array of lighting units in a studio is fairly staggering. The fashion pictures reproduced on the color pages of this book were all made with incandescent studio lighting. Notice how carefully the lights were arranged for a smooth effect throughout.

Without studio facilities, you are almost always hampered in handling incandescent light. You need lots of floor space for lamp stands and a lot of room overhead with beams or clips for hanging top lights. Then too, you need lots of gadgets to control the light: diffusers to soften it; snoots to spot it down; barndoors to direct it, and dozens of other things, not the least of which is a crew to push things around. This sort of operation is definitely not for beginners.

Still, without a great deal of working space and without any great capital investment, you can assemble a small and useful lighting outfit for the home or office. The backbone of such an outfit is the sealed-beam reflector lamp. These, as you might guess, have their own built-in reflector; they come in various sizes (floods, medium-beam and spot) and can be used in any household socket. It is better, though, to use them in some adjustable or swivel-type socket; there are many. A very good one, intended especially for photography, is the Gator-Grip. Small barndoors can be attached to the Gator-Grip, and the barndoor frame will also hold diffusers. The Gator-Grip can be clipped to anything at any angle, or it can be mounted on a lamp stand. With six Gator-Grips, six lightweight folding aluminum lamp stands and an assortment of sealed-beam lamps, you can do some pretty fancy work. Balance the lights carefully with an exposure meter, as explained earlier, and you can make good pictures on a not too limited scale. Such a lighting setup is very satisfactory for pictures of small groups, and more than sufficient for portraiture, many interiors, small products, etc.

Light Placement

All amateurs want to know the "secret" of light placement, and the professional always shrugs and says he just puts the light where it looks right. Alas, the professional is right, that's where the light belongs! This doesn't help you much, but neither will the diagrams with angles, heights and all kinds of mysterious symbols commonly seen. They'll work only for the sample picture shown, and only with the equipment in question, and that's all.

How then, to place lights? If you've been shooting outdoors in bright sunlight, you should have learned how the lights and shadows look when a face is properly lit. Try to get the same pattern with your floodlamps. Go back over the previous pages on sunlight, hazy light, flat light, front light, side light and back light. Try to make a picture of each type

144

indoors with your lamps, to match an outdoor picture you made and liked previously. This takes some practice, but once you get the knack you'll never again need a lighting diagram to match the slickest, most complicated lighting in any picture you've ever seen.

Light has to be balanced in floodlighting just as it does outdoors; the total intensity will be less, and the exposure longer, but the ratio must be the same. That is, if an outdoor shot has a highlight reading of 200 (candles per square foot on a Weston meter, if anyone cares!) and the shadows about 50, the ratio is 4:1, and you'll have a snappy picture. You'll get the same effect indoors if your highlights read 25 and the shadows 6.5—the picture will be exactly the same in quality, but you'll need 8 times as much exposure. And that's all . . .

Assorted Light!

Besides the main lighting categories we have talked about, there are all sorts of other things that you might want to photograph: street lights, neon signs, floodlighted buildings, lighted shop windows. Try them all; they are all picture possibilities.

The black night sky is a wonderful background for many things that get lost in the shuffle in daylight. Look at the pink magnolias in Figure 11, Page 102. They were photographed from a low angle against a midnight sky, with one No. 5 flashlamp, 1/25 second at f/11. The black sky is a much more striking background for the pale flowers than the light blue

35. Display-window lighting should be measured with an exposure meter, and tungsten-type color films should be used. Stereo by Dorothy S. Gelatt.

sky of daylight. And the night flash had another advantage for this picture—the light didn't carry far enough to show other distracting bushes and buildings.

In almost any fair-sized city some section will be found with an array of varicolored neon signs, traffic lights, white street lights, theater marquees, etc. Innumerable patterns can be made with these colored lights, and the effect can be further enhanced by shooting in a light rain or in mist. Reflections from colored lights and signs in wet pavements sometimes take on new, exotic shapes, almost abstract and frequently more striking than the signs themselves.

It is difficult to give any directions for estimating exposures under such conditions. In general, tungsten-type color films should be used, both for more accurate rendition of color and because they are often faster than daylight-type films in artificial light. An exposure meter can be used to estimate exposures for a preliminary test; however, a number of additional exposures should be made, both above and below the metered exposure. Where lights are included in the scene a decision must be made as to whether they need be rendered in color; if they are white lights, they may be permitted to burn up while the dimmer neon tubes and colored bulbs are registering. Floodlighted buildings photographed from such angles that no light sources are visible may take exposures running from 1 to 5 seconds with a wide-open lens; often shots may be made of store windows and under theater marquees at about the same exposure.

Where the lighted signs themselves are the picture, and there is no objection to a completely black background, exposures may be considerably less. In Figure 36 the illuminated signs in Times Square were photographed at 1/25 second at f/3.5 on Kodachrome Film, Type A.

Brightly lighted store windows may often be photographed in color with a short-time exposure. However, the lamps used in store windows usually burn at a lower color temperature than the photographic lamps to which the film is balanced; hence the pictures may be somewhat warm in tone. If this is objectionable, a Kodak Light Balancing Filter such as the 82-C may be of assistance. Meter readings will be some help in estimating the exposure of a store window, but often it will be found that the light level is lower than it appears to the eye, and meter readings are so low as to be unreliable. In such a case, the only solution is to make a series of tests and keep accurate notes of the results. The exposure for the display window in Figure 35 was 1/10 second at f/3.5.

Those who are lucky enough to be admitted with a camera to movie sets or television studios will have little difficulty making some excellent stereos. There is no problem getting enough light on a movie set if a color film is being shot—the shot of Jean Carmen in Figure 14, Page 103 had been lit by the movie cameraman for an exposure of f/3.5 on his Mitchell professional movie camera, which has a shutter speed of 1/50 second.

The stereo camera was therefore used at 1/25 second at f/4.5 for better depth of field.

Sets for black-and-white films or for television plays are usually not lighted to so high a level, and it may not be possible to make snapshot exposures in such cases. Even then, it is better to use a tripod and take a time exposure, rather than a flashlamp, which will destroy the modeling already carefully built up in the set lighting.

A bit of etiquette here: on a movie set, never shoot during a "take," and always ask the cameraman's permission before walking onto the set or crossing in front of the camera. The best time to shoot stereos on a movie set is while the still photographer is taking his production stills between takes. Often the cameraman, or the still photographer who is always part of the crew, will tell you the exposure being used on the particular shot, and you can depend on its being right!

Amateur theatricals are a problem of a different type; lighting for such affairs is likely to be a bit dim, even when well done, and in any case the lamps used are not designed for color photography. However, since the effect is intended to be theatrical, exact color rendition is not essential.

No matter how many subjects we might mention here, you will think of lots we have left out. In the end, your pictures express your own interests, and the lighting serves only to strengthen your own expression.

1. Window at San Felipe, Baja California. The entire view is practically in one plane, and the stereoscopy serves to differentiate the shapes of the various objects in this strikingly simple shot.

The realism of stereo must not be permitted to obscure the fact that an imaginative approach to three-dimensional photography is not only possible but desirable. All of the striking—and in some cases, fantastic—stereos in this chapter were made by Dick McGraw; several more will be found in the Color Sections.

148

5. A Personal Approach to Technique and Composition

DICK McGRAW

Consider, for a moment, the paradoxical implications of a stereo picture. Here is a reflection of reality which looks as "real" as its original. But it is only two pieces of transparent flexible material bearing on the surface various two-dimensional areas of transparent color. Under suitable conditions these two bits of colored film are capable of creating in the brain of the person who examines them a close approximation to the visual sensations, and to some extent even the emotions he might have experienced had he been looking at the actual scene when the exposure was made. But the appearance of depth and roundness, of the sizes, shapes, colors and textures of the objects, is formed only in the subjective world of the viewer's brain, not in the external "objective" world. There the stereo picture continues to exist only as two pieces of film which, when viewed together, "translate" in the viewer's mind into a three-dimensional representation of a scene or of objects which existed at some instant in the irrecoverable past. The actual objects represented may have long since disappeared from the face of the earth; the weather, the circumambient light, the subjective emotional atmosphere of the time and place may never again be the same. Yet by a facile magic we can evoke them again at will and make others see what we saw. If we are skillful enough with our camera we can even make others feel what we felt, so strongly that they cry out, "It's realer than real!". Two pieces of colored film!

It is precisely the ease of attaining this appearance of reality that is apt to limit us in our use of the stereo camera. Though our pictures are in three dimensions, they remain nothing more than records of what was before the lens at the moment of exposure. They seldom embody that integration between subject and photographer that is one of the criteria indicative of creative effort. This is not to say that the "realism" of stereo is a thing to be feared or avoided by anyone who wishes to work

2. View from Empire State Building tower, New York, looking toward Times Square (bright area in center). Wind vibration caused slight unsharpness despite the fact that a tripod was used.

in a creative way—or that it is to be sneered at by the art fancier who has probably come around to accepting photography as a fine art but may have to revise some of his preconceptions before he can embrace stereoscopy as a creative medium. On the contrary, this very realism may be thought of as the basis of a new art form—for the inhibitions and limitations that restrict the accomplishment envisioned by the creative worker in planar graphic media need not apply here.

One factor which indirectly contributes to the super-realism of the stereo picture is the "window" through which it is viewed. When one is viewing a real subject or scene in nature it has no boundaries, and the attention can and frequently does wander outside and beyond the principal subject of interest. In real life one can return to the principal subject again and again from this visual wandering. But in the stereo picture the "window" limits the scene, and one can examine only that part of it which the photographer has chosen to isolate from its surroundings. Nevertheless, though every person who sees the picture has the identical array of visual ingredients before his eyes, it is astonishing how different things are noticed by different people. For instance, it frequently happens that someone will comment on something in one of my pictures which I myself had not noticed, and which other people had also overlooked. On the other hand, details which seem quite important to me may not be seen at all by someone else. In other words, each person sees what he has been "conditioned" to see, so that his mental, and perhaps his

150

emotional, reaction to the picture may be quite different from yours or mine.

For this reason, as has been pointed out by Herbert C. McKay, the color stereograph can be considered "impressionism" just as much as "realism." Apparently no one person ever grasps the *entire* visual content and the resulting implications of a stereo picture, any more than he does when confronted with a living subject or a scene in nature. Although you can make the same general statement about a flat photograph, its entire visual content is generally much easier to digest. Because it is usually small and subtends a small angle when viewed, its whole area can usually be encompassed, if not always comprehended, in a single glance. But in a properly coordinated stereo-viewing system the scene is spread out over the same angle before your eyes that it occupied before the camera lenses, and therefore it appears to be not a *picture* but a life-size model of that segment of the world contained within the window. Here, as in nature, the eyes can move about—in fact, they *must* move about if the whole picture is to be examined—and settle on objects at different distances in space and at varying angles from the straight-ahead. Because of this constant shifting of attention, and because of the fact that some objects will have special meaning to a particular spectator, he may easily overlook other things that are actually right in front of his nose.

There are "quick discharge" and "slow discharge" pictures. By the former we refer to those whose main content is grasped almost completely

3. Floating "Shantytown" in Hong Kong. People live their whole lives on these boats. Crowded scenes like this are "slow discharge" pictures.

151

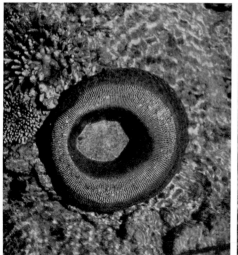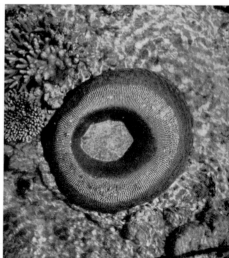

4. A "Brain Coral" photographed on the Great
Barrier Reef, Australia. A simple composition like
this is a "quick discharge" picture; the simple
shape has the quality of an art abstraction.

Compositions in depth have volume, location in space and a real feeling of "life-
sizedness" in addition to the line, shape,
tone, color and texture of flat pictures. This
"Brain Coral" looks like a small doughnut
in the flat picture; the stereo view shows it
to be quite large and at a good distance
from you.

in a single glance and whose importance therefore rests in what is conveyed at this first glance. Although we can continue studying the lesser details of such a picture, they are usually of considerably less importance than the quick impact that the principal objects make on our consciousness. In a "slow discharge" picture, on the other hand, there may not be any immediately apparent subject matter; or, if there is, it may be so surrounded or buried in a quantity of subordinate objects, colors or space relationships, all contributing to the total meaning, that it is not discovered at first glance. The viewer must give this picture more prolonged study if he is to get full value from what it has to say. In fact, in many pictures of this type there is frequently no subject matter except by implication—perhaps only a pleasing arrangement of shapes, lines, colors, volumes, textures, etc., isolated in such a way that the emotion they arouse in the beholder is the one that is called the esthetic emotion. The principal purpose of this kind of picture, whether planar or stereoscopic, is to stimulate visual pleasure — what I like to call "eye-delight" — by the way in which the eyes can travel around within the enclosed space and visually touch or caress and mentally "arrange" the component parts.

Composition in Depth

One of the most difficult ideas to get across to a beginner in picture making is that "composition" is not a thing which can be mastered by following rules. The so-called rules of composition are nothing but deductions made from the study of great masterpieces of painting. "Rules" are seldom if ever in the consciousness of an artist when he is working on a picture. Every earnest worker in a graphic medium has to find his own way to utilize the elements of construction — line, shape, tone, texture, color, balance, etc. — in the way which will most effectively convey the visual and emotional aspects of the subject or idea he is attempting to represent. There has never been a rule which has not been broken with vigorous success by later artists — those who came after the rules were deduced and reduced to formulas. Such deductive rules can be helpful in the study of existing masterpieces, and they may also have a limited use to a timid beginner. Nevertheless, if he does not develop an intuitive feeling for composition — a feeling not based on rules — he will not get very far in the creation of vital or original work.

Many writers have pointed out that in photography composition is not necessarily the same thing as in painting. The ability of the camera to reproduce minute detail and realistic textural values, and to capture in an instant a fleeting and intricately constructed subject, makes it almost inescapably necessary to avoid the "rules" of painting. Fortunately no one has yet attempted to write a book of rules for stereo, so that the way is open without restriction or limitation for serious workers to discover for themselves how best to make use of its possibili-

153

ties. It is not my intention here to lead the way, but only to point out that *there are ways to be discovered.* That is what makes it so exciting!

I know of no way to acquire this feeling for "composition" other than to consider the world about you, decide what interests you most, and then *look* at it — not just with your eyes, but with your mind and emotions as well. Having chosen a subject to be photographed, move around it. Watch what happens to it and its surroundings from different angles — how the parts change their size-and-space relationship and what shadows do to it, or absence of shadows. Observe it from very close by and from a little farther off, from low viewpoints and from high. Do not be afraid to shoot different pictures of it, for the study of these at leisure later on will perhaps be even more helpful than your preliminary observation before exposing. You can choose the one in which the arrangement of relationships most nearly conveys the emotional state in which you found yourself when the subject first began to arouse your interest and finally to excite it to the point where you had to photograph it. Pictures in series made from time to time as your capacity for "seeing" grows will teach you more about how to look at the world and photograph it than a whole shelf full of "rule" books.

You will learn by working that composition in depth is a very different thing from composition on a flat surface. In three dimensions, the components of which the picture is constructed — line, shape, tone, color, texture — are augmented by the concepts which might conveniently be

5. Hot food soon ready! Cooks at work in a Singapore market place. Taken on Daylight Koda-chrome with No. 5 flashlamp and blue shield over reflector for color balance.

154

called *volume, location in space,* and *"life-sizedness"* (this being an attribute which is seldom encountered in photography except in stereo). These new factors do not, however, necessarily add to the complexity of creating a satisfactory picture in three dimensions. In fact, they probably make it easier, because you can get away with many things that would be definitely unpleasant in a planar picture. The classic example of bad arrangement — the telephone pole apparently sprouting from your best girl's chapeau — causes no confusion in stereo because the position of the pole *in space* is immediately comprehended by the viewer. Tones or edges which merge in a flat picture — even in color — also do not exist in three dimensions, for the areas of like tonality and merging edge are separated by their volume and their varying distances from the eye.

On the other hand, it is well to remember some of the *don'ts* of flat composition, for they apply equally well to composition in space. For example, when the principal subject is somewhere near the center it is better not to have a large, bright object without subject-significance near the edge of the picture, for it will distract or annoy. Common sense in matters such as this is everywhere applicable.

Large-Scale Pictures

Much advice on stereo for the beginner is unfortunately based upon a superficial approach to the nature and requirements of three-dimensional

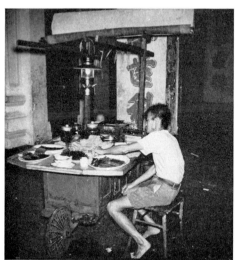

6. Singapore food vendor with pushcart at night. Notice modern gasoline lantern, and head of child ducking out of sight in the background. Day and night, you can find any kind of food!

7. Do you like pig's head? Market in Singapore; pig's head being covered with brilliant magenta-colored sauce. Taken on Daylight Kodachrome with No. 5 flashlamp and blue shield over reflector.

composition. You may read, for instance, that you should *always* have something in the foreground to establish the distance of objects farther away or to far-off landscapes. A moment's reflection, or the examination of pictures in which this "rule" has been rigorously followed, will demonstrate its invalidity. If the subject is a vast and distant landscape of mountains or desert, all of it at stereo infinity, it actually looks flat in nature; but because of its size (i.e., the angle of view it subtends) and the atmosphere between it and you, it does not look *small*. A stereo picture of it will not look small either, and it will retain the feeling of space and atmosphere if it has been properly mounted with respect to the "window," which then becomes the point of reference for the third dimension even when all the objects in the picture are at such a great distance that they look flat. Planting something in the foreground — your best girl again! — merely distracts attention from the distant scene and does nothing to mitigate its flatness. Of course if the purpose of your picture is not to show the scenery but merely to record the fact that you and your friend were there, I cannot reasonably object to your including her in the foreground! In this case you have the same thing as if you had used an ordinary camera—a snapshot which will not hold the interest of people for very long who are not acquainted with the person shown.

But here let me insert a further thought about landscapes. For many years before the Stereo Realist came my way I was primarily a land-

156

scape photographer, using a view camera with lenses of various focal lengths—mostly long—to picture large expanses of scenery in the western half of the United States, particularly the desert areas of the southwest. This kind of landscape is difficult to do in flat photography, even in color. The scene has a most discouraging way of reducing itself to inconsequentiality on paper. Its grandeur is elusive; its high emotional content is removed, along with the residual silver salts, by the fixing bath. Nevertheless it *is* possible to retain some of these qualities even in a black-and-white 8x10-inch print. It is also possible to retain them in a stereo picture. But of all kinds of subject matter, I have found that vast landscapes are the least suitable material for stereo. There is no stereo depth evident in distant scenes, and they suffer by comparison with the effectiveness of objects that are closer to the camera. In general, the nearer the subject the more effective it will be in the three-dimensioned picture. Because of this, the stereo camera taught me another kind of visual approach to the world about me. Since the big landscapes which I photographed in planar pictures were in general not very exciting in stereo, I began to look about me for more suitable subjects, and almost immediately found them right under my feet, so to say. I became aware of small things I had scarcely noticed before; and those who look at my pictures almost all agree that the most interesting are close-ups, for in them are revealed sources of beauty which many people, like myself, had never been aware of before.

8. Dramatic moment in Chinese opera, Singapore. A No. 5 flashlamp was used with Type A Kodachrome and no compensating filter, yet color balance was very good in the original film.

157

9. A soft coral photographed on Heron Island, Great Barrier Reef, Australia. This is primarily a record picture to show the coral formation, but it has considerable "eye-delight" as a semi-abstract.

Isolating bits of nature in a stereo view often gives a touch of fantasy to the most commonplace subjects. Of course everyone does not have the Great Barrier Reef at his back door, but there is a wealth of surprising backyard beauty available to anyone who looks for it.

158

Small-Scale Pictures

Bits of nature isolated and viewed close-up may be not only surprisingly beautiful but may even assume some of the elements of fantasy, for most of us are not accustomed to looking at nature in so concentrated a fashion. Some of my best pictures are therefore intimate glimpses of quite commonplace plants, rocks, water surfaces and other things to which we are so accustomed that we take them for granted and no longer "see" them. Some of these subjects remain matter-of-fact but are nevertheless fascinating when isolated in stereo pictures. Others partake of the fantastic even though treated in a straightforward manner. Still others can be taken completely out of the world of reality by the simple technique of pseudoscopy (transposition of the left and right frames of the stereo pair). Here, the spatial relationships are inverted so that what was nearest becomes the most distant, so that what was "out" goes "in" and what was "in" comes "out." By this means the worker can produce effects that approach surrealism and—by their mixture of interacting planes—strongly suggest more dimensions than three. Thus they become completely free of any "objective" associations.

In this connection it is interesting to note that recent exhibitions of contemporary art have presented occasional compositions or constructions in three dimensions which, since they are framed and hung on the wall, are evidently meant to be considered as pictures rather than as sculpture. They show that some painters have begun to try to escape from the limitations of their two-dimensional surface. It would seem, however, that no matter how hard the painter-sculptor may work in such forms as these, he will never be able to create things as fascinating and fantastic as the stereo photographer can make just by pushing a button (and of necessity by mounting the pictures himself).

"Seeing" for Stereo

Some beginners forget, when examining the scene through the view finder with one eye, that the finder delimits not just a flat scene but a three-dimensional arrangement in depth. Consequently they fail to choose the best possible position for the camera. To overcome this limitation in seeing, you should examine the subject again with both eyes after composing it in the finder. Keep your eyes as close to the camera lenses as possible in order to determine the depth relationships that exist within the camera angle. Sighting right over the camera is helpful. It may also help to cut a cardboard frame to the same proportions as the view finder, but larger, and look at the scene through it with both eyes open so that stereo perception is maintained. Such a frame can be very useful in examining the subject from various positions in order to determine just where to place the camera. When held at a suitable distance before the eyes, the cardboard frame will approximate the effect of the "window"

159

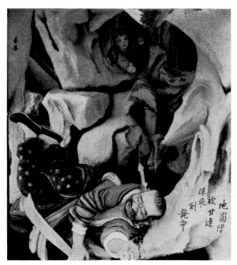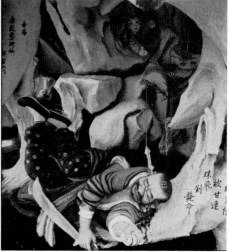

in the finished picture and enable you to see whether your composition is just as you really want it. By doing this every time you set up to make a picture, you will soon get the habit of automatically envisioning the finished picture in three dimensions.

Lighting Conditions and Filters

The light of a gray overcast sky is one of the most wonderfully revealing lights in nature. The all-enveloping illumination bathes everything softly and evenly, leaving to the forms and shapes the task of revealing themselves by their color and their placement in space rather than by the shadows they cast, and giving to the objects an almost self-luminous quality that is very lovely. This kind of light is especially suitable for close-ups of nature, such as small plants, rocks, etc.; and for successful pseudoscopic rendition of such subjects it is a *sine qua non*. Best of all, it is perfect for true color rendition, for it needs no filtering for splendid results on daylight color film. If the film is really in correct color balance for noon sunlight plus blue sky, then the gray sky illumination will render the colors of objects just about as they appear to the eye. However, if you prefer a considerably warmer rendering, the 81-C flash filters can be used.

As an outdoor color photographer for many years, I have made thousands of exposures on all kinds of color films in all types of cameras. I have made countless tests with all the suggested filters for the suppression

160

of excessive blueness due to haze or ultraviolet rays, and for the correction of variations in color rendition due to "incorrect" color temperature of daylight or sunlight at different hours of the day, to the kind and quantity of clouds in the sky, etc. My conclusion from all such test work is that there is only one condition of daylight that I wish to correct (and that one not always): the excessive blueness that comes from photographing natural subjects (including people) that are in the shade on a sunny cloudless day and so are illuminated by light that is predominantly blue. For this purpose I like to use the 81-C flash filter (which you probably already have in your kit for use with No. 5 flashbulbs on Type A Kodachrome). This is not the recommended filter for Daylight Kodachrome, but I prefer it. With this filter on daylight film under blue sky illumination you should increase the aperture about 1/3 to 1/2 stop for best results.

I do not care for haze filters and ultraviolet filters used with any kind of color film. I realize that this is contrary to everything you have ever read before on the subject of correction filters, and you will, of course, have to make your own decision. The color cast in color pictures is mainly a matter of personal preference: some people like a warmer cast, some like a colder tone. Filters, the prevailing light, small variations in film emulsion and processing all affect the final tone.

If the sunlight early or late in the day casts a warm or reddish glow on my subject, that only adds to its attractiveness. In fact, frequently it pulls the whole color composition together by relating all the colors within the picture to each other. Indeed, it is often the color of the light that incites me to take the picture in the first place, and I therefore would not dream of filtering it back to the color of noon-sunlight-plus-blue-sky. Of course in a portrait made in such light you may wish to make the flesh tones more "natural"—and in that case a correction filter should be used, if you want to bother with it. If you do not—well then, shoot the portrait at some other time of day, when the light is more like that for which the film is supposed to be balanced.

Polarizing filters are sometimes useful to reduce glare from highly reflecting subjects. However, they must be completely neutral in tone so as not to impart a color cast to the picture. Some polarizing filters tend to discolor with age and may cause an unpleasant greenish cast in the film. If you want to use polarizers, be sure that they are in good condition.

Concerning lighting and the color balance of film, I think it is often interesting to depart from the "recommended" procedure. It is not *always* necessary to use artificial-light film for artificial lighting conditions—or daylight film in daylight! For instance, if you are photographing city scenes at dusk when the lights are coming on, and even into the hours when daylight has gone completely from the sky, try daylight film; the pictures will look quite natural. Conversely, for odd color effects (which sometimes add to the impact of a picture which you want to look more

161

or less unreal or fantastic anyway), try indoor film out of doors; or use color-correction filters for deliberate distortion of color. You may get some fascinatingly beautiful things. But be sure to keep exact records of what you do when you depart from standard procedure, for otherwise you will not be able to control and repeat your results.

In short, don't be hidebound by "rules" in your approach to your creative efforts in stereo. Try anything—including the unorthodox or non-recommended procedures—in both your thinking and your technique. You have nothing to lose except, perhaps, a little film; you have everything to gain!

Long Exposures

In any condition of illumination where the exposures will have to be of considerable length because the light is dim and the subject is dark in tonality, you are going to run up against that distressing phenomenon known as "failure of the reciprocity law." Briefly this means that for exceptionally long exposures you will have an underexposed picture if you give what the meter indicates. The reciprocity law and its failure are described in any good text on photography, but usually there are no specific recommendations made for the amount of extra exposure that will overcome it when using color film. I have found, by testing, that the following rough guide will usually produce good exposures on Daylight Kodachrome.

EXPOSURE INCREASE FOR LONG EXPOSURES ON KODACHROME FILM, DAYLIGHT TYPE

If meter indicates	5 sec. or less	5-30 sec.	30-40 sec.	40-60 sec.	1-2 min.	Over 2 min.
Multiply exposure time by	1	1¼	1½	2	2½	3

You can make yourself similar tables for any type of color film by running a series of carefully timed exposures and keeping an accurate record.

Planning Stereo Pictures

After several years of work and thousands of shots of all kinds of subjects with the Stereo Realist, I find that my stereo pictures almost all fall into certain definite categories with respect to subject matter and approach. By listing these I do not mean to imply that there are no other kinds of subjects or no other ways to consider them. Rather these are the directions in which my own "seeing" tends, whether consciously or intuitively:

162

a) SUBJECTS
  1. Portraits (of people, of animals, of objects in general—such as ships).
  2. Genre (everyday life and activities of people in any part of the world).
  3. Landscapes—scenery.
  4. Close-ups of nature.
  5. "Record" pictures (made primarily to impart information).

b) APPROACH
  1. Planar confusion vs. stereo clarity.
  2. The design element: semi-abstraction; "eye-delight."
  3. Color schemes and harmony, including the approach to mono-chromatic or even achromatic pictures.
  4. Simplification of the depth effect: the approach to two-dimensional subjects rendered in three dimensions.
  5. The departure from realism and the approach to fantasy; pseudo-scopy.
  6. The "idea" behind the picture—the emotional aspects and the intellectual implications.

The classifications under each of these two headings are not mutually exclusive. The categories frequently overlap; a picture may fit into two or three of them at once: a travel picture showing people in the streets of an oriental city might be considered both as *genre* and as *information;*

11. Snow-covered trees in Illinois. Taken on a dull winter day, the original Kodachrome had no more color in it than this black-and-white reproduction.

163

12. Swamp scene on the Colorado River near Topock, Arizona. The tangled mass of foliage needs stereoscopy to be neatly unraveled.

A single stereo often has many different uses and many different appeals both to the emotions and to the mind. A nature study or record photograph will often have considerable design quality that stimulates "eye-delight" or creates an illusion of fantasy.

its treatment might fall under any or all of the first three headings under
(b) Approach; and if its content has in addition any sociological or politi-
cal implications it would also come under the heading of idea.

I do not necessarily think consciously of all this when I am getting
ready to make an exposure. Frequently there is no opportunity for reflection on such abstract ideas; sometimes there is scarcely enough time
to adjust focus, aperture and shutter! These things are felt rather than
thought about. The thinking comes afterwards, when I see the finished
picture. Then I may find things (and ideas) in it which I was not conscious of when I shot; yet I must somehow have been aware of
them, for they are what caused me to shoot in the first place. But when
there is time, I study the subject and its implications and try to arrange
it (by which I mean I arrange myself and the camera in space with
relation to the subject, for I don't like to tamper with nature by "arranging" it as if it were a still life in the studio) so that it will appear to the
best advantage and will most forcefully express what I have thought (or
felt) about it while preparing to photograph it.

With these considerations of technique and approach in mind, let us
examine some actual Stereo Realist pictures.

Making Stereo Pictures

The pictures of Singapore and Hong Kong are obviously and primarily
travel pictures and would come under the heading of genre in the above
classification. Figure 8, the Chinese opera, was photographed in an
amusement park theater in Singapore. The color of the production was
dazzling and the sound of the music beyond belief. The scene is a dramatic moment from a classical opera, and the head in the foreground
belongs to one of the players in the five-piece pit orchestra. Note the
microphone—a modern touch.

I found Singapore fascinating in many ways, particularly the street
life. Everything goes on right in the streets; all you have to do is wander
around and all sorts of wonderful picture material confronts you. Although the city was founded by the British its population contains more
Chinese than any other one race, and of course in Chinatown "Every
Day is Wash Day" (Fig. 6, Page 99), with the laundry poles projecting
from the upper stories of the dwellings and the teeming life in the
street below.

Food vendors are everywhere in the streets and marketplaces. Many
of them prepare and cook their wares right on the pavement where it
is easy to photograph them, and they always have a grin ready without
being asked. Figure 5 was shot in the daytime in a roofed open-
air market, the shade being so deep that flash was necessary.

The food vendor and his cart (Fig. 6) were photographed just outside the entrance to the amusement park at night. Behind the cart was

a shy youngster overcome by the conflicting emotions of curiosity and fright, who kept popping up to see what I was doing, but ducked every time I made a move to shoot. He was faster than I was, so that even with several attempts the best I managed to get was the blur of his disappearing head.

Another shy child trying to hide can be seen in the background with the woman and sleeping baby in Figure 8, Page 100, which shows an Indian food vendor in the street at night, pleased at being photographed.

The fabulous Tiger Balm Gardens in Singapore are one of that city's most fascinating sights. Here, spread out over several acres, is an astonishing conglomeration of narrative and comic sculpture and other attractions, created by the beneficence of Chinese multimillionaire Aw Boon Haw, who made his wealth from an ointment known as Tiger Balm that is in great demand throughout the Orient. The gardens provide endless camera material, of which Figure 10 is a typical example. Note that the path of the dagger is represented by a wire. Equally as interesting as the exhibits are the people who come to look at them. Mr. Haw has a similar establishment in Hong Kong, high on a hillside overlooking the beautiful harbor in one corner of which float hundreds of little boats on which thousands of Chinese spend their entire lives from birth to death eking out a skimpy livelihood. A picture such as this (Fig. 3) furnishes food for thought — the sociological implications under the subject of *Approach*, above.

The portrait of the great photographer Edward Weston autographing his book, "My Camera on Point Lobos" (Fig. 13, Page 103) was made in his home in Carmel, California. Facing him was a window through which came the daylight of a sunny day, and above and to the left was a diffused skylight let into the roof at an angle. The exposure was made without other light or reflector on Daylight Kodachrome, 1 second at f/8. The background is slightly out of focus, but it would have been unreasonable to require him to "hold it" longer so as to use a smaller stop and get greater depth. (And it would have been quite inappropriate to use flash or artificial light on a foremost exponent of natural-light photography!) As is often the case with Kodachrome film, the color contrast in the original slide is somewhat exaggerated, the flesh tones being ruddier, the blacks deeper, etc., than in the actual scene.

The night picture of New York City showing the Great White Way (Fig. 2), was made from the observation platform atop the Empire State Building on a bitter December evening, which was why I was able to use a tripod. In good weather the platform is so crowded with sightseers that tripods would constitute a hazard and are therefore not allowed; but on this occasion it was so cold that few people were about and permission for the tripod was readily granted. I remained there (frequently going inside to get warm) from before sunset until complete darkness, making a series of about twenty shots in various directions, of

13. Paint bucket and gasoline tank, Cuyama Valley, California. A composition of utter simplicity; the original colors were the yellow bucket and tank, blue sky, and blue trim on the tank.

which this picture is the climax. All were shot on Daylight Kodachrome without filter, and although the series progressed from warm sunlight through blue twilight and on to warm artificial light, all of them look quite reasonable and always impress everyone as being quite natural in color. It was so dark during the final shots that the Weston meter would not give a reading, so I had to guess. Although I kept no records, I believe this particular exposure was about 1 minute at f/8. One or two of the longer exposures in the series were spoiled by movement, although the camera was on the tripod. It was the building that moved! (The Empire State tower sways several feet in a breeze, it is said.) Note that in this picture everything is flat because the entire scene is at stereo infinity. Nevertheless there is an impression of great size and depth because of the "air" or space between the "window" and the subject.

The picture of the paint bucket hanging from a gasoline storage tank (Fig. 13) and the one of the window in San Felipe, Baja California (Fig. 1) both exemplify simplicity in subject matter, arrangement and color. The former, reproduced here in black and white, contains only two colors: the intense yellow of the bucket and the steel tank, and the blue of the sky and trim of the tank. The composition is so simple that a painter who looked at the slide exclaimed, "How pure can you get!" The window is practically a monochrome picture, consisting mostly of white with various shades of blue. In this it is primarily the design element that interested me, although the shot might also be considered as a record.

167

14. Cleft boulder with plant growth near Hemet, California. With dull light like this, the flat picture seems to have no modeling at all; in 3-D the separation of planes is very striking.

In close-up pictures where the stereo depth is very pronounced, there is often no need whatever for lighting contrast. Tones and shapes that would merge into oblivion in a flat picture will all be sharply separated in the stereo view.

168

The remaining pictures reproduced here come under the heading of "close-ups of nature," though they were not all approached in the same manner. The pictures of coral on the Great Barrier Reef of Australia are primarily "record" shots, made to show what various kinds of coral look like, as you can see in Figures 4 and 9. However, the color reproduction shown in Figure 2, Page 233, has some interest as a semi-abstract composition and a harmonious color scheme, and I believe it is quite capable of holding its own as a picture to stimulate "eye-delight" without regard to its subject matter.

In the picture of snow-covered trees (Fig. 11) we have an example of "planar confusion vs. stereo clarity." Seen flat, this is an inextricable jumble; viewed in three dimensions everything falls naturally into place even though there are no shadows and no color differentiations to separate one branch or twig from another. In fact, the original Kodachrome slide is as colorless as this black-and-white reproduction, there being no color in it whatever, only the black trunks and branches and the gray-white snow. It was shot on a dark overcast day with some snow falling.

Very little needs to be said about the picture of swampy plants at the edge of the Colorado River, near Topock, Arizona (Fig. 12), except that the lack of horizon puzzles me. I do not remember that it was invisible, but perhaps the camera was pointed down so far that the horizon was above the picture and what appears here to be sky is instead the reflection of the whitish overcast sky on the distant surface of the water. The color scheme is soft and pleasing, showing that a picture can be beautiful even though it has no garish qualities.

The intimate close-up of a boulder with colorful lichens and plants (Fig. 14) also needs little explanation. The light came from a blue sky, but no compensating filter was used—primarily because the subject did not look too blue to the eye, and neither does the color film. The camera was about as close as it can focus without supplementary lenses, and only hand-mounting keeps the scene beyond the window and without "ghost bands" at the sides.

The view of water plants on the surface of a creek (Fig. 17) is another near-monochromatic picture, being primarily a silvery green with touches of brown. At a casual glance the material on the surface of the water looked like scum, but close inspection revealed that it was a mass of tiny leaves. This was shot in the afternoon of a slightly hazy day, somewhat toward the light.

Pseudoscopy

We come now to the pseudoscopic pictures. They bear out my contention above that pseudoscopy is a procedure which can lend added interest and a touch of unreality and fantasy to the most prosaic subjects. But it will not work with everything! I suggest that when you do your own mounting you make trial mounts of such pictures as you think might

15. Wet spider web, Carissa Tittli, California. This picture is normally mounted and is viewed right side up for comparison with the pseudoscopic shot on the next page.

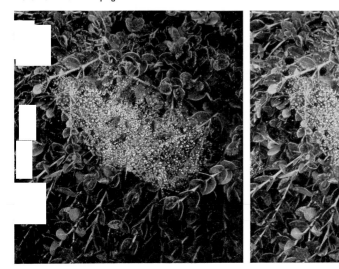

Rules were made to be broken, and the rule that the right eye must view the right picture, the left eye the left picture, can sometimes be broken for effects of sheer fantasy. Compare the picture above with the pseudoscopically mounted one on the facing page.

170

Not every subject can be photographed or mounted pseudoscopically, but one like this takes on a fairyland quality when so handled. Upside-down mounting enhances the effect still further, and the imaginative photographer is urged to experiment with subjects of his own choosing.

16. The same picture, with the two images transposed for pseudoscopic viewing. Such effects are often more interesting when mounted upside down as this picture has been.

171

17. Water plants and floating debris, Verde River, Arizona. This is another pseudoscopic view, also mounted upside down. Right side up, pseudoscopic mounting causes water to appear overhead.

Strong lighting contrast generally causes confusion in pseudoscopically mounted stereos. The lighting is successful in this picture mainly because of the unfamiliarity of the objects, and because of the near-monochromatic coloring.

172

be served well by this transposition technique. Merely mount the left-hand film on the right side of the mask, and vice versa; or leave them in their correct left and right locations but turn them individually upside down. If you use the Realist Metal Masks it takes no time at all to try a pair of films mounted in the normal fashion and then pseudoscopically to see which you like better for the subject at hand. When you have decided which way you prefer the picture, then you can place the films in the permanent mounts of the type you generally use.

Many pictures mounted as pseudograms look better upside down, especially when they have been photographed with the camera not parallel to the surface plane of the subject. Both Figure 17 (the water plants and scum) and Figure 16 (the wet spider web) are examples of upside-down mounting. If the former is viewed right side up, you seem to be under a ceiling (or under the surface of the water), which recedes in a plane *above* your eye-point. This will generally be true of any pseudoscopic subject which contains a horizontal surface at an angle to the camera. Although this does not hold quite true for the spider-web picture, there remains something disturbing about it if viewed right side up (compare it with the non-pseudoscopic version, (Fig. 15) which is right side up; the disturbance vanishes (for me, at any rate) when the picture is inverted.

Note in both these pictures the sensation of double exposure and the "impossible" intermingling of various planes and objects. That this effect of double exposure is due entirely to the pseudoscopic mounting is proved by looking at the pictures flat. These two shots also violate what is generally a valid rule for pseudoscopy: do not allow objects or lines to cross each other or partially hide one another. With most subjects crossed lines will cause visual disturbances that prevent successful fusion of the two halves into a three-dimensional whole, at any rate for many people. In these pictures I have been able to get away with it because of the "softness" of the outlines (in the web and leaves), and the unfamiliarity of the objects (partly due to their upside-downness) in the swampish picture.

The latter picture is also one of the few successful pseudoscopic pictures I have been able to make in direct sunlight. In general, the preferred light for a pseudoscopic subject is that diffuse and shadowless light that is at its best on an overcast day, such as that which lighted the leaf-and-rock shot (Fig. 18) where the leaves seem to be embedded in the rock. This would be far less effective if the leaves were casting sharp shadows on the surface of the rock, for the shadows would then be disturbing unexplainable dark areas in the pseudogram.

After you have made a few successful pseudoscopic pictures, you can usually tell in advance what subjects are going to work successfully for this technique. Frequently it is worthwhile in doubtful cases to make two identical shots and mount one of them in the ordinary way and the other as a pseudogram, for comparison. The picture of the

18. Autumn Leaves on Rock. Near Glendale, Utah. Pseudoscopic picture mounted right side up. Diffuse illumination from an overcast sky gives no shadows, and the leaves seem embedded in the rock.

wet spider web in the bush was done this way, and both versions are reproduced here. Note in this case, however, that the "normal" picture is not so normal after all, for it was made with two separate exposures with reduced separation of the lenses. (Lens separation, using Portra +1 supplementary lenses, was 1½ inches; camera-to-subject distance was about 20 inches). This was done in order to reduce the amount of unusable area at the outside edges which would either have to be hidden by the window frames (and thus make too narrow a picture for the subject) or would show up as "ghost bands" at the sides. The two-exposure technique is revealed here by the lack of perfect register of all the water drops, for it was drizzling when the exposures were made and drops were continually falling off and reforming. It was not necessary to use the two-exposure reduced-lens-separation technique for the pseudoscopic version because the interchange of frames made possible a picture of normal width without "ghost bands." Incidentally, this fairyland scene is a splendid example of the wonderful subject matter that exists everywhere for the taking. I found this beside my front steps one morning when I went out to get the daily paper.

How to Learn "Free Vision"

The ability to look at a stereo pair without any optical device comes in very handy at times, especially when mounting your own slides. "Free

174

vision" cannot be mastered by everyone, but it is worth a try, and is very likely to come with a little practice.

Here are some suggestions on learning to see a stereo pair in three dimensions with your unaided eyes. Stand before a window through which you can see clear sky. If there is a distant object, such as a building several blocks away, or a far horizon of any kind, focus your eyes upon it. In other words, your eyes should not be converged as they are when looking at near-by objects, but should be parallel, as they are when looking at objects at infinity, such as the stars at night. The relaxed condition known as "staring vacantly into space" is what you are after here.

Now, while your eyes are in this condition, hold up both hands at arm's length before you, with the forefingers pointed straight up and about 2½ inches apart. Continue to focus on the distant scene and move your two fingers a bit closer together or farther apart until you apparently see *three fingers*. When the two fingers are the right distance apart, the center finger of the *three* you see is opaque (because it is a double or superimposed image of both fingers), while the outer fingers are transparent (because each is a one-eye image, the distant view seen by the other eye occupying the same apparent location as the finger).

If you can see your fingers like this you can also see a stereo slide in three dimensions if you hold it up before you! The principle is identical, since the two frames of the slide are the same distance apart as your fingers were. But seeing the stereo clearly and sharply will probably take a little practice. So continue to maintain the relaxed stare, but direct your eyes upward towards the clear sky (that is, stop looking at the distant object), and then hold up one of your stereo slides at arm's length and interpose it in the beam of your vision. At first your eyes will want to converge upon the slide, but try to keep them from doing so. If they converge you will be looking at the slide merely as a flat object containing two pictures. But if your eyes remain unconverged you will see three pictures instead of two, the same as you saw three fingers when you held up two. The three pictures will be blurred at first because you are not focusing on the near distance. Remember that two different faculties are in operation here: *convergence*—the "toeing-in" (or lack of it) of the line of vision of each eye; and *focus*—the accommodation of the shape of the eyeball and its lens for objects at given distances. In natural vision, focus and convergence work together automatically; in viewing stereos (even in a stereoscope) they must work separately— which takes a little practice at first but soon becomes natural.

The center image of the three is what you must devote your attention to. Try to see it sharp instead of blurred. (If you wear glasses to look at objects at arm's length or closer, they should be worn when learning and using free vision.) The trick is to maintain your eyes unconverged, but to *focus* them on the plane of the slide held at arm's length. After a few attempts you will begin to see the details of the slide more sharply, even

19. Maple leaves in Utah. This picture looks like a wallpaper pattern when viewed flat, but takes on a definite, three-dimensional pattern when seen through the stereo viewer.

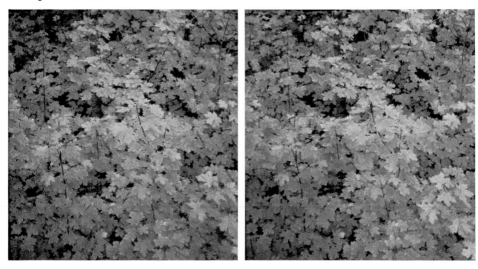

while maintaining zero convergence; and when this happens you will suddenly realize that you are seeing the center image in three dimensions. But if your eyes "slip" into convergence, all that happens is that you will be looking *at* the slide as a near-by object instead of (in effect) looking *through* it at a three-dimensional scene situated beyond it in space.

Note that the slide must be held horizontal and so must your eyes. If you tilt the slide a bit sidewise, you have to tilt your head too; otherwise you cannot fuse the images.

After a while you will learn to ignore the two outer images and concentrate on the center one. As soon as you can see the details *sharply* (which should happen after a few attempts), try moving the slide closer to your eyes while maintaining zero convergence. At first the picture will become blurred again as it gets nearer, but before long it will stay sharp until you can bring it almost as close as your normal reading distance. When you can do this, you've got it—that's all there is to it!

It is well not to practice too long at a time. Start with five minutes. Then wait an hour and try again for five minutes. After several such short sessions (some people can do it almost at once) you should master the trick, and from then on you will never have any trouble—the minute you hold up a slide your eyes will diverge automatically to zero convergence and you will see the center image in three dimensions. It is even possible to view a transparent slide this way against a variegated background. The eyes (and the mind) can learn to ignore lots of things!

176

You can also view the stereo prints in this book in this way. I believe, however, that your initial attempts at free vision should be with slides rather than with printed pairs. In the slide there is a considerable space between the two pictures which keeps the outer images separated from the three-dimensional image that pops into existence in the space between them; whereas the two pictures of a printed pair are so close together that the outer images tend to obtrude into the center one and may make it harder to accomplish fusion until you have mastered the trick. One way to look at these printed stereos is to stand a tall card on edge between the two halves and rest your nose on its upper edge (about 10 inches from the page) so that each eye can see only one picture. After you have learned to look at a transparent slide unaided it should not be long before you can dispense with the card when viewing the printed pairs. The page should be held flat, of course, and no shadow or glare should be on any part of either picture.

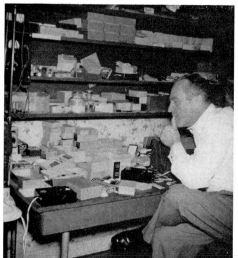

Harold Lloyd in his stereo workshop with the thousands of stereo pictures taken on his travels. Stereo by Willard D. Morgan.

6. Slide Mounting and Projection Equipment

JAMES H. CALDER

Stereo photography can be no better than the sum total of its many operations, one of the most important of which is the actual mounting of the slides for either hand viewing or projecting.

The introduction of the Stereo Realist camera using 35mm color film and the first *complete* system for taking, mounting, viewing and projecting stereo pictures made it easy even for beginners to enjoy their own stereo pictures from start to finish. Added boons were the factory mounting service and home mounting kit provided by Realist, Inc., for its camera customers.

To obtain factory mounting service, the photographer mails exposed rolls of film to a stereo slide service, along with the nominal fee and his name and address. The slide service has the film processed, mounts the film in metal masks in either cardboard folders with acetate protectors or glass, as specified, and then returns the mounted slides to the customer.

The Eastman Kodak Company has also engineered equipment for mounting slides on a mass production basis and has marketed special stereo rolls of film. The stereo rolls are mounted in a cardboard mount by Kodak and returned directly to the customer, the cost of mounting being included in the cost of the roll of color film. Use of the Eastman stereo roll is the most convenient system, but because the slides are in cardboard they are recommended for viewer use only. Those slides which the camera owner wishes to protect permanently or to use for projection should be mounted in either metal masks between glass or in plastic Permamounts.

Many stereo enthusiasts seem to be interested only in taking and viewing their pictures, preferring to leave the job of mounting slides to others. However, recent development of easy, accurate mounting systems produced greater interest in home mounting of slides, not only because it saves money, but also because it makes stereo more of a hobby.

1. The Stereo Realist Mounting Kit, including sorting tray, film cutter and tweezers.

Although slide mounting has been made easy for the public, the engineering problems which first had to be solved were many and extremely technical in nature. It was ultimately determined that the most reliable system of maintaining accurate alignment was to use the top and bottom edges of the film. The edges of the 35mm film are the ideal points with which to align film properly because they are true and accurate. When they are used, the cut edges (or sides of the image) become less important in slide alignment. Cut edges can be and are satisfactory only when an accurate film cutter, such as the Realist ST-24, is used.

Generally speaking, the vertical alignment of stereo pairs is of greater importance to successful stereo slides than the horizontal alignment. That is why all stereo slides employing a principle whereby the film pairs are inserted in a slot at the top of the slide are generally unacceptable for either viewing or projection. This also holds true for mounts which locate the horizontal spacing by using the film sprocket holes.

Certain plastic mounts using the top and bottom of film for vertical alignment are satisfactory for use in a hand viewer when they are new. However, plastic does scratch easily, becomes discolored, and generally tends to deteriorate after any length of time. Plastic slides are not acceptable for projection because the plastic depolarizes the light and causes "ghost" images.

The material from which masks are made is extremely important. Realist, Inc., learned that paper masks, for example, cannot hold extremely close tolerances because of humidity, temperature, warping, etc. Accordingly, a metal mask made of thin aluminum was developed, incorporating principles proved by experience. This mask uses only the top and bottom of the film for vertical alignment. The mask has horizontal guide marks, but variations are permitted in horizontal alignment so that the individual can adjust the picture in relation to the window of the mask. By varying the spacing of the film pairs ever so slightly, it is possible to place objects in the picture at a different plane. This adjustment is responsible for more comfortable hand viewing and projection.

Actually, any slide which is aligned properly for comfortable viewing when projected will be equally comfortable when viewed in a hand viewer.

During the years of experimentation and development of the Stereo Realist projectors, engineers learned that stereo projection could not be successful without a special mounting system. Projection limits the distance range that can be accommodated within a given slide. If the film were always placed in the same position in the mask, frequent major projector adjustments would be necessary. Audiences are subjected to considerable eyestrain during this adjusting process.

The Stereo Realist mounting system is based on three different spacings of the windows and three different openings. The center of each opening in the three different masks is on the same vertical and horizontal line. However, the size of the windows themselves varies with each type of mask, and the distance between windows also varies by approximately 1/16 inch. This slight difference is magnified many times when projected on the screen and is the major factor contributing to the success of the practical system of stereo slide mounting for projection.

The three types of Realist metal masks and Permamounts are: 1) a "distant" mask is used if the near object in the picture is at least 7 feet away from the camera, no matter where the most distant point falls. It is also used if the farthest point in the picture is 20 feet or more distant, no matter how close the closest point is in the picture; 2) the "medium" mask is used if the near point is from 4 to 7 feet away and the far point is no more than 20 feet away; 3) the "close-up" mask is used if the nearest point is from 2½ to 4 feet away and the far point in the picture is less than 5 feet away.

These three types were found to be a complete mounting system compatible to both hand viewing and projection. The actual differences in

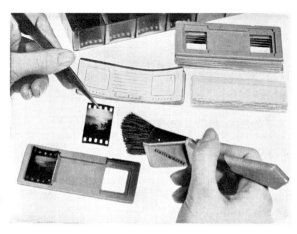

2. Each film is dusted with Staticmaster brush before putting it in the mount.

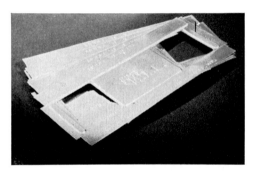

3. The new Stereo Realist metal masks for precise mounting of stereo pairs in glass.

the masks themselves are extremely slight, yet they make it possible to run through a complete projection show without making any projector adjustments when switching from a picture with a close-up object to a picture with a distant object.

They also do away, to a certain degree, with the need for an interocular adjustment on the hand viewer. Contrary to public misconception, this adjustment is actually not an eye-spacing adjustment but rather one to collimate the center of the viewer lenses with the center of the openings in the stereo pairs. Although the spacing of eyes does vary with individuals, the design of the lenses in the Realist viewer is such that anyone can see the stereo image whether his eyes are centered in the viewer lenses or to any side of the lenses. The human eye, when it scans a scene, changes focus with different objects. When you look into a viewer, however, the eyes merely converge or diverge with images at different distances in the picture. The majority of people will be able to set the interocular adjustment in one position and leave it there through a showing of slides using any of the three masks. The center of each slide remains the same no matter which of the three types is used.

Therefore, slide mounting for projection or hand viewing cannot and should not be separated. Because all slides mounted for projection are equally effective in a hand viewer, every slide can and should be mounted as if it were going to be projected.

As more and more projectors are sold for home use, you may some day wish to have some of your slides projected by a friend, or you may wish to enter slides in a salon competition or have them projected at a camera club meeting.

The Realist metal masks make this very simple to do because films can be mounted in them and placed in a cardboard folder. Then the outstanding ones can be removed from the cardboard folder and placed between sheets of glass and taped for permanence. Those slides left in the cardboard folders can be slipped into acetate sleeves for safe storage and hand viewing. This same procedure can be used with slides mounted by the slide mounting service of Realist, Inc.

182

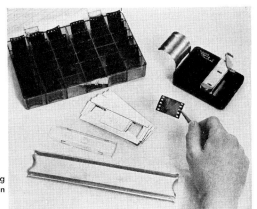

4. First step in mounting with sorting tray. Film is cut, and frames placed in proper compartments of box.

Mounting in Realist Metal Masks

METHOD A — USING SORTING TRAY — The easiest and simplest way to mount slides in the Realist metal mask is to use the ST-3 Realist mounting kit in conjunction with the ST-220 mounting jig and alignment gauge and loading tool. The mounting kit consists of film cutter, sorting tray and tweezers.

a) Place film in cutter by inserting through the guide at left and engage perforations on pegs, emulsion side facing you. Bring down film holder. Loosen lock nut on bottom of cutter. With the handle on the bottom, adjust perforation pegs so that the right film line of the first stereo pair is exactly on the cutting edge of the cutter. Hold the cutter up to a light to assure accuracy of alignment. If you have slight over-lap on stereo pairs, adjust to cut down center of overlap. Once the cutter is set it should not be necessary to reset for the length of the roll of film from this same camera, although it is always well to dou-ble-check because you may have variations due to failure to take up

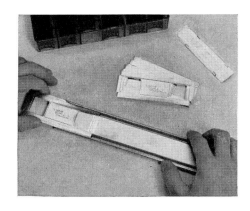

5. Second step. Place a Stereo Realist metal mask in mounting jig.

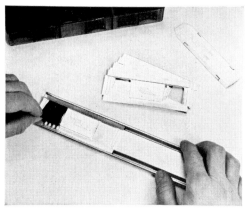

6. Third step. Place picture 1-L in left side of mask, emulsion side up.

all of the film with the winding knob on each shot. Start cutting at the beginning of the roll (the clear end with perforated number). As the stereo pairs are cut, place them in the sorting box in the rotation in which they are cut. Start at the upper left compartment and work from left to right. Cut all blank film and bad exposures. Do not discard but place them in the sorting box in proper order. Use the tweezers to handle film at all times. Move the film to the next film line with the tweezers. Fingerprints on film can ruin a good picture. A 20-exposure roll of film (15 stereo pairs) can be completely cut at one time. A 36-exposure (28 stereo pairs) should be cut in two operations. When cutting a 36-exposure roll, fill the sorting tray, stop cutting and go on to the next operation. After the box has been emptied, the balance of the roll can be cut, starting with the upper left compartment again.

b) Place a metal mask in the ST-220 jig with channels up (the trademark reads correctly from this side), remove transparency from sort-

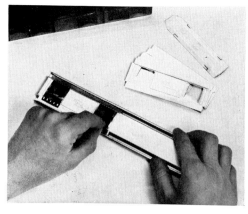

7. Fourth step. Place picture 1-R in right side of mask, emulsion side up.

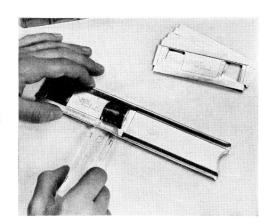

8. With loading tool, insert bottom edge of each film in channel of metal mask.

ing tray compartment marked 1-L. Place in the left window under top channel, emulsion side up, image upright.

c) Remove transparency from sorting tray compartment marked 1-R. Place in right window under top channel, emulsion side up, image upright.

d) Take loading tool. Place forked end in film sprocket holes. Push forward with tool and allow film to slip into the bottom channel. If film is properly cut, the edges of each side should fall right on the vertical guide mark of the mask.

e) Remove mask from jig. Check to be sure transparencies are in correct mask. (See instructions on page 189). Crimp channels down firmly on front side of mask at edges of channel with serrated end of loading tool. Place in cardboard or glass mount.

f) Continue mounting film in mask as above. Next, take 2-L, 2-R; then 3-L, 3-R, etc., until all film except blanks or rejects is mounted.

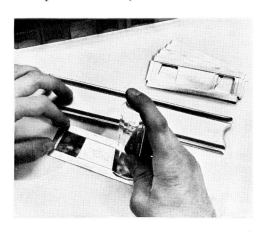

9. Crimp channels down on film with serrated end of loading tool.

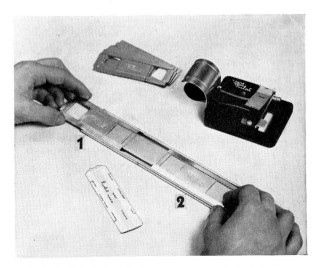

10. Mounting without sorting tray. First step: place a metal mask in each end of the loading jig, and put uncut roll of film in cutter.

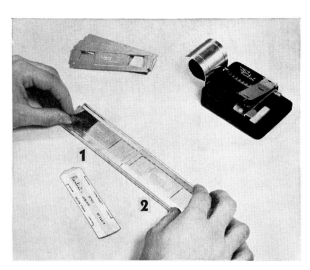

11. Step 2. Cut first picture and place in left channel of metal mask no. 1, emulsion side up. Then cut blank transparency and discard.

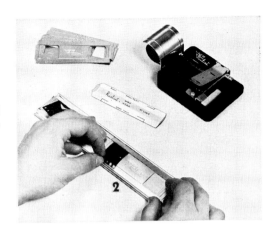

12. Step 3. Cut next picture and place in left channel of mask No. 2, emulsion side up.

METHOD B — WITHOUT SORTING TRAY

a) Place a metal mask in jig, as far as possible to the right, with channels up. Place a second metal mask to the left of the first mask.

b) Cut first transparency from roll with Realist Film Cutter. Place in left window of left mask under top channel, emulsion side up, image upright.

c) Cut blank transparency and put aside.

d) Cut second transparency from roll and place under top channel of left window in right-hand mask.

e) Cut third transparency from roll and place in right window of left-hand mask.

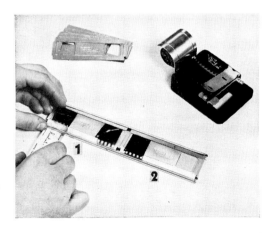

13. Step 4. Cut third picture from roll and place in right-hand channel of left-hand mask. Insert bottom edges with tool.

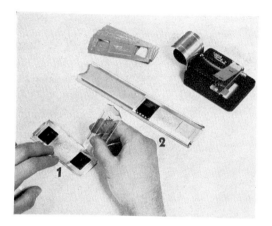

14. Step 5. Remove left-hand mask from jig and crimp film in place.

f) Take loading tool. Place forked end in film sprocket holes. Push forward with tool and allow film to slip into bottom channel. If film is properly cut the edges of each side should fall right on the vertical guide mark of the mask.

g) Remove left mask from jig. Check to be sure transparencies are in correct mask. Press channels down with serrated end of loading tool. Place in cardboard or glass mounts.

h) Shift remaining mask in jig to the left and place a third mask in its place, channels up, to the right.

i) Now a definite routine has been established. After each shift, and placing a new mask on the right-hand side, you work only with the two adjacent windows in the center of jig. First transparency goes into the window at the right, then the left. So it simply becomes right, left, shift; right, left, shift, for the balance of the roll.

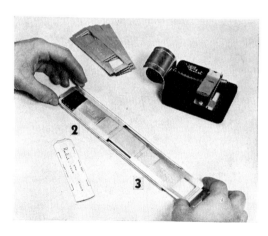

15. Step 6. Shift right-hand mask to left end of loading jig and insert new mask in right-hand end.

In case of confusion during this mounting procedure, it is possible to identify the left-hand picture of any pair if the film was taken with a recent model of the Stereo Realist camera. All current Realist cameras have a notch in the lower edge of the right-hand picture aperture, which exposes a nick in the margin of the picture. This identifies the picture which goes in the left-hand aperture of the mask, emulsion side up, and will be viewed by the right eye after mounting. A similar notch can be put in older cameras with a small round file. See Chapter 2 for further information.

Choosing the Correct Mask

Place plastic loading tool over the mask. Use the "far" guide mark on the tool and line up the same farthest points in each picture. Make sure these most important points fall on or inside the guide marks on the tool. If the "far" points fall outside of the guide marks and your film is properly aligned in the mask, change to the next more distant mask.

Now choose the closest point of each transparency, using the "near" guide mark on the tool. Make sure these "near" points fall on or outside the guide marks indicated by "near" on the tool.

a) If these "near" points fall right on the "near" marks, that object will be just at the stereo window.

b) If these "near" points fall beyond the "near" marks, that object will be behind the stereo window. This indicates the transparencies are in proper mask.

c) If these "near" points fall inside the "near" marks, that object will come through the stereo window. This indicates the transparencies are not properly aligned in the space provided, or they should be in a different mask, or there is too great a range of distance within the picture itself. Having an object come through the stereo window is sometimes used to create special effects.

The Realist mask is the only mask to offer opportunity for further adjustments. There are occasions when you may wish to change some plane of the picture in relation to the plane of the stereo window. For example, the closest object in the picture may fall in front of the stereo window and may not be pleasing. This can be easily seen in a hand viewer. To move this object back to the stereo window or slightly behind it, shift each transparency the same amount of distance slightly away from the center of the mask. Check again in a viewer, and if still not satisfactory, repeat. The amount of adjustment is limited by two things: the film must always slightly overlap the edge of the opening, and the farthest object in the picture must not be separated beyond the far marks on the loading tool. If you want to bring an object up to or through the window, move each transparency toward the center of the mask. The only limiting factor is the edge of the mask openings.

Mounting in Glass

When mounting in glass, cleanliness is absolutely essential. There are many ways of cleaning glass, from breathing on it and polishing with a lintless cloth to various types of commercial glass cleaners. One recommended method is to wash a considerable quantity of glass at one time, using a detergent and scrubbing the glass in this solution, rinsing in hot water and stacking in a rack to dry naturally without a cloth. One simple way of making a rack is to purchase an ordinary door spring at a hardware store and stretch it on a board to a point where it opens up sufficiently so that the glass will fit into the coils. One corner of the glass should rest on a towel, which will help draw off the water. After drying naturally in this way, there is usually little or no need for further cleaning. In localities with a high content of mineral substances in the water, a rinse with hot distilled water will prevent spotting.

Selection of the actual glass itself should be done judiciously for best results. Realist, Inc., holds extremely close tolerances on all of the glass which it ships, not only in width and length but also in thickness. This is important, particularly for projection, because the glass on the back of each slide should be of exactly the same thickness. Glass which is too thick will not fit conveniently in either the viewer or the projector.

Mounted slides can be taped evenly and quickly with a little practice. The key to this particular operation is to precut the binding tape to 11⅝ inches. Take a piece of tape in the right hand and sight over the slide so that the slide is in the center of the tape in the middle of one of the long edges. Sight down along the edges of the glass, and by turning the slide lay the tape all the way around without folding it down. After the final turn, you will find that the tape will overlap about ¼ inch. Take one of the long sides and fold the tape down in the center. Slip the fingers along both edges of the slide, snapping the fingers off the slide at the corners. Fold both long edges and then the two short edges. This will fold the corners under so there will be no protruding corners. A folded corner is desirable in that it provides a cushion between slides and helps protect the glass. This system automatically places the two pieces of glass firmly together and achieves a degree of neatness impossible in any other way.

Mounting in Permamounts

Prior to beginning mounting operation, film should be rolled in opposite direction from that in which it is received from the processing labs and allowed to set for several hours. This will remove the curl from the film. Windows from the Presto-Sealer can be used to hold the glass and film in place in Permamounts while the mount is checked in a viewer to make sure that the glass is clean and the film is in the correct position.

a) Cut and sort your film as described above for metal masks.

b) Select the correct type of Permamount for the particular stereo pair.

190

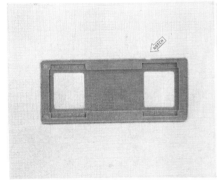

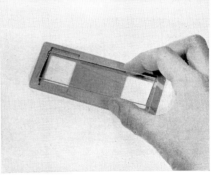

16. The plastic Permamounts. Notch should be up and to right during insertion of films in this mount.

17. First step in mounting. Insert a carefully cleaned piece of glass in the permanent plastic frame.

c) Place plastic frame with the recess area up, making sure the notch on the top of the frame is to the right.

d) Carefully clean glass.

e) Place one piece of glass in the plastic frame.

f) Using tweezers, take the film from sorting tray marked 1-L. Carefully dust film with Staticmaster brush or similar soft hair brush to remove lint and dust.

g) Place the film in the left opening of the plastic frame, emulsion side up and with the picture subject upright.

h) Remove the matching film from the compartment of the sorting tray marked 1-R. Dust film and place in the right opening of the plastic frame, emulsion side up and picture subject upright.

18. Now follow same procedure as with metal masks, inserting 1-L at left, 1-R at right, etc. Place cover glass over pictures.

191

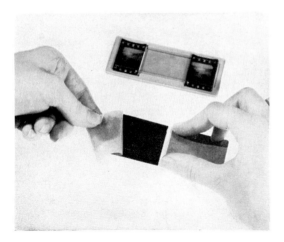

19. Carefully remove the cover-paper from the adhesive side of the mask, and push out apertures.

i) Place a second sheet of glass over the frame in its proper recess in the plastic frame.

j) Take a corner of the paper backing with the zip-strip on the Presto-Sealer. Pull it carefully across the sealer. Remove both sides of paper backing and make sure that window openings are removed.

k) Align the paper sealer to the plastic film by holding the glass down with the finger of one hand and the Presto-Sealer center with the other. Align the top edge, identified by the red strip against the top edge of the plastic frame. When it lines up properly, drop into place and press down firmly around all four sides and seal securely.

l) Permamount slides should be viewed with the plastic frame facing you — white label to the rear.

20. Holding glass in place with finger, place adhesive mask over cover glass and position it carefully.

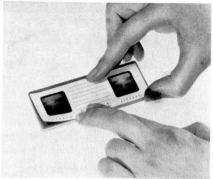

21. Rub down adhesive mask carefully to seal picture in mount all around. Identification can be written in spaces.

192

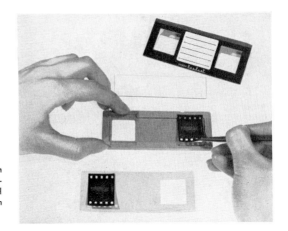

22. Transfering pictures from cardboard mount to Perma-mounts. Films must be cleaned carefully when removing from cardboards.

Remounting Cardboard Slides to Permamounts

Place open cardboard or glass slide below the plastic frame. Follow instructions c, d and e, above.

Follow same instructions f through k, but remove film from left side of the old mount and place emulsion side up in left side of plastic frame. Then remove film from right side of old mount and place emulsion side up in right side of plastic frame.

Stereo Projection

Practical stereo projection of color film became possible late in the nineteenth century when the principles of polarized light were applied. Basically, polarizers transmit light in definite "lines," or axes. Although both polarized filters in a pair are transparent, they become opaque when superimposed in a position where the "lines" are crossed.

In stereo projection, therefore, the two images are superimposed upon a screen by two different lenses. One image is projected through a polariz-ing filter with an axis at a 90° angle to that of the other image. Without wearing polarized glasses, the viewer sees two confused images on the screen. If the viewer looks at the screen, through a single polarizer, he will see a single image at four points as the polarizer is rotated 360° — the left image at two points and the right image at two points where the axes coincide.

Polarizing the light at the projector and viewing the images on the screen through polarized glasses permits the viewer to see the right image with the right eye and the left image with the left eye. This separation of images makes it possible to "see" stereo projection in 3 dimensions. The lenses in the glasses are so polarized that the axis of each exactly matches the axis of one projected image only and crosses the image of the other.

The spectator sees only the image intended for the right eye with that eye. (It is actually projected from the left lens.) He does not see the other image with the right eye. This same applies in reverse to the left eye.

However, if the images are to retain their polarization for viewing, they must be projected upon a screen with a metallic surface. When polarized light strikes a nonmetallic surface the polarization is lost, it becomes ordinary light again, and the Polaroid spectacles cannot separate the left and right-eye images. No other type of screen surface is acceptable for front stereo projection! Sheets, plaster walls, nonmetallic screens — none will retain polarized light in its polarized form and will result in complete failure of stereo projection.

Advantages of the Realist "Silvrscreen" include a wide angle of diffusion, giving better vision to those in the audience to the side of the screen, and "truer" color than on white mat or other screen surfaces. Also, the "Silvrscreen" has the least tendency to depolarize of any screen surface on the market.

Although there are several stereo projectors on the market, the Stereo Realist projector represents a major accomplishment in photo-optical engineering. It alone took into account that everything had to be coordinated — camera, mounting system, proved stereo principles, etc. — for maximum enjoyment of stereo projection.

23. Front and side view of Realist Projector. Numbered parts are described in text.

Two models of the Realist projector, Models 81 and 82, are available. Specifications are as follows:

Front View and Side of Realist Projector

All references to RIGHT and LEFT are from the operating position at the rear of the projector and facing the screen.

1) HORIZONTAL ALIGNMENT KNOB — Controls horizontal separation between images — rotates to either right or left.

2) LENSES —
    Model 81 — Lenses: coated; f/2.8; 3½-inch focal length.
    Model 82 — Lenses: coated; f/2.3; 3½-inch focal length.

3) LEFT LENS HOOD — Stationary — does not move for individual adjustment.

4) RIGHT LENS HOOD — Rotate this lens to make focus of both lenses identical. (Necessary only when setting up projector.)

5) FOCUSING KNOB — Moves lens housing back and forth — also used to remove lens housing for cleaning of lenses.

6) AIR INTAKE and FAN — Draws air from front and directs air to lamps and slide for cooling. So designed that it is impossible to cut off flow of air.

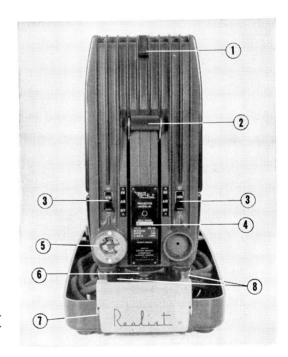

24. Rear view of Realist Projector. Numbered parts are described in text.

7) MOTOR or BLOWER —

Model 81 — AC-115 volts, 60-cycle, single-speed.

Model 82 — AC-DC, 115 volts, 60-cycle, 2-speed universal motor. Slow speed used on 500 watts and less. High speed with 750 and 1,000-watt lamps.

8) FRONT CASE HOLD-DOWN KNOB — To hold projector securely in position while carrying — must be loosened to elevate projector legs.

9) FRONT CASE SNAP LOCK.

10) FRONT LEG BASES.

Rear View of Projector

1) REAR DOOR LATCH.

2) SLIDE CHANGER LEVER — Rotates dual slide carrier when pushed down.

3) SWITCHES — Two 3-way switches, one for each projection lamp. When switch is at "air" position, only the blower is working. When switch is at "on" position, both the blower and lamp are in operation.

4) PROJECTOR SERIAL NUMBER — To be registered with Realist, Inc., for owner's protection.

5) TWIST LOCK SOCKET — Connection for power cord.

6) REAR CASE HOLD-DOWN KNOB — To hold projector securely in position. Need not be loosened unless projector is to be removed from base of case.

7) REAR CASE SNAP LOCKS.

8) REAR LEG BASES.

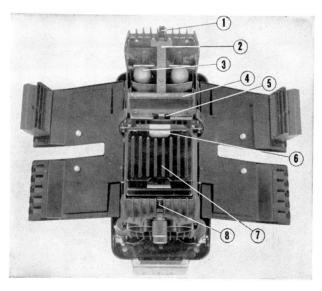

25. Top view of Realist Projector with doors open. Numbered parts are described in text.

Top View of Realist Projector

1) REAR DOOR HATCH — Locks projector doors.

2) DUAL SPEED BLOWER SWITCH (On Model 82 only) — Regulates speed of blower. When using 500-watt lamps or less, switch should be set at 500. When using 750 and 1,000-watt lamps, switch should be set at 1,000.

3) LAMPS — For greatest illumination, we suggest the following:
   Model 81

      500-watt — 120V, Medium Prefocused Base, T10P Bulb, C13D Filament, 500 T10P, average life 10 hrs.*

    Model 82

      500-watt — 120V, Medium Prefocused Base, T10P Bulb, C13D Filament, 500 T10P, average life 10 hrs.*

      750-watt — 120V, Medium Prefocused Base, 750T-12/24, C13D Filament, average life 10 hrs.*

      1,000-watt — 120V, Medium Prefocused Base, T12 Bulb, C13D Filament, 1MT-12P, average life 10 hrs.*

4) SHUTTER

5) DUAL SLIDE CARRIER — Rotary type, rotated by lever at back of projector. One slide is in projection position while other slide is being changed. Slides are positioned accurately by positive spring alignment.

6) SLIDE EJECTOR BUTTON — Pushes slide up from sequence slide file when button is pressed.

7) SEQUENCE SLIDE FILE — Holds slides with spring tension in projection order.

8) FRONT DOOR LATCH — Locks projector doors and sequence slide file in position.

Side View of Projector with Doors Open

1) CONDENSER DRAWER pulled partially out.

2) CONDENSER LENSES.

3) HEAT RESISTANT GLASS.

4) GLASS POLAROID FILTERS.

5) RIGHT LAMP CENTERING KNOB — Used to center lamps to obtain maximum illumination through the lenses. Left lamp centering knob found in same position on left side of projector.

6) DUAL SLIDE CARRIER.

7) RELEASE BUTTON FOR SLIDE CARRIER — To remove slide carrier push in black button. Until other types of slide carriers are available it

* Far longer life with Realist cooling system.

197

should not be necessary to remove carrier. Red button must be fully depressed when operating projector.

8) VERTICAL ALIGNMENT KNOB — Recessed to eliminate possibility of accidentally moving knob while projector is in operation. Tilts slide carrier to level images.

9) ELEVATION KNOB — Coupled to legs, permits raising and lowering front legs of projector for various screen positions. Front case hold-down knob must be loose to operate.

10) FINE ELEVATOR CONTROLS — Raises each leg separately for slight tilt corrections.

Model 81 provides ample illumination for a 6-foot screen at a distance of 25 feet. It has a comfortable audience capacity of 100-150 people.

Model 82 provides ample illumination for a 12-foot screen at a distance of 50 feet. With a 9-foot screen it has an audience capacity of 1,000 people, while a 12-foot screen will easily accommodate an audience twice that large.

Lenses of both models are highest quality projection anastigmats, coated for maximum screen brilliance and contrast. They were designed to fill the screen from corner to corner with a critically sharp image.

26. Side view of Realist Projector with doors open. Numbers refer to text on previous page and above.

27. Carrying case with six Realist Sequence slide files for use with Realist Projector.

The Realist projector was designed to accommodate a sequence slide file. This file holds up to 29 Permamounts or 35 glass-mounted slides. It has two slots at the top, one from which a slide is popped up when the button is pressed, and another for replacement of the slide in its proper sequence after it is projected. An adjustable tension spring keeps slides securely in place in the file at all times.

Use of sequence files for projection shows helps keep the show orderly and gives the projectionist complete control during his presentation. It is also somewhat of a safeguard against slides being mixed up by well-meaning friends. It is a simple matter to interchange sequence files when projecting a large number of slides. Realist also offers a versatile sequence file and viewer case which will hold six files, or a proportionate number of files and hand viewers.

How to Operate the Projector

a) Unlock cover of projector case by pulling up two snap locks and remove the cover.

b) Loosen front hold-down knob in base of case.

c) Connect cord into twist lock socket by pressing plug in and turning approximately ¼ turn. Plug into any AC outlet. (With Model 82, DC can also be used.)

d) Turn on left-hand switch, in rear of projector, to "air" until motor obtains full speed. This takes only a second. Then move switch to "on" position. Do not turn on right switch at this time!

e) Turn elevation knob until light is correctly positioned on your screen. (Also see directions on proper tilt of screen.) Legs can be raised about ¾ inch.

199

f) Pick out a clear, sharp, well-exposed slide from your collection to use as a setup slide. The slide should have a definite object in the near foreground — fences, poles, rocks, etc.; and a definite object in the distance — mountains, bridges, tall buildings, etc.

g) Place this slide in dual slide carrier as you would in a viewer, or with front of slide facing the operator. Hold slide at top center with thumb and forefinger, press slide down between slide spring and front of slide holder until slide locks under top ledge of carrier. To remove slide from carrier, grasp slide at top center and pull toward operator approximately 3/16 inch and upward.

h) Press slide changer lever all the way down. This rotates slide carrier and places picture behind the lenses. (*Warning:* Guide slide changer lever back into normal position — don't let it snap back.)

i) Rotate focusing knob until images become sharp. (Left-hand lens is stationary in lens housing.)

j) Center image on screen. If necessary, use the fine elevators on front of each projector leg to level picture.

k) Turn left switch to "air" position. This will shut off left lamp, yet allow blower to continue to operate.

l) Turn *right* switch to "on."

m) Focus (or sharpen) picture by rotating right lens hood. (*Note:* Do not use focusing knob.)

28. Streamlined carrying case for Realist Projector, designed and balanced for easy portability.

29. Polaroid spectacles for use with Realist projector, in regular frames for permanent use.

n) Turn *left* switch to "on."

You have now focused both lenses. Both images should now be sharp on your screen. Refocusing with the focusing knob is needed only when using different brands of mounting supplies. (See section on correct mounting for projection.)

o) Rotate vertical and horizontal alignment knobs until the outside edges of the two pictures are superimposed or blended as one, forming a definite frame around the picture.

Now it is necessary for you to check the vertical and horizontal alignment of the images in relationship to each other.

Note: Do not put on polaroid glasses. Proper alignment can only be accomplished with glasses off.

Aligning Picture Properly on Screen

a) Pick out the farthest well-defined object in the picture area to use as your two alignment points.

b) Rotate the vertical alignment knob until these two points are on the same level.

c) Turn the horizontal alignment knob until these two alignment points are approximately 2½ inches apart on screens up to 6 feet in size; 3 inches apart on a 6-foot screen; 4 inches apart on a 9-foot screen; up to 6 inches apart on a 12-foot screen. (On a 54x59-inch screen it is only necessary to superimpose the edges of the picture. Images will automatically fall into proper alignment when mounted in a Realist mount.)

d) Pictures should now be in perfect alignment.

You are now ready to start projecting. No other projector adjustment should be necessary if your slides are mounted in proper Realist mounts. (See correct mounting for projection.) Now put on your glasses and enjoy the marvels of 3-dimensional projection.

There are numerous stereo screens on the market. When making a choice, several important factors should be kept in mind, in addition to the fact that a stereo screen *must* have a metallic surface. One is that the screen should present an absolutely flat surface for best results. Bulges, wrinkles, etc., will show up under polarized light as shadows and detract from the picture. Another is that it should have some form of "tilt" control to assure maximum reflection from the screen surface. By properly adjusting the angle at which the screen is placed, reflected light will be directed back to the audience instead of being dispersed above or below proper eye level.

The Realist "Silvrscreen"

A stereo projection screen known by the trade name of "Silvrscreen" is offered by Realist, Inc. When assembled, the screen stretches perfectly flat because an elastic surface is used as a base for the powdered aluminum coating. The stand has a built-in tilt control to adjust the frame. Sizes range from 40x40″ to 144x144″.

RECOMMENDED DISTANCE FROM PROJECTOR TO
SCREEN FOR 3½-INCH FOCAL LENGTH LENSES

Screen Size	Distance to Fill Screen with Picture
40x 40″	13½ feet
54x 59″	18 ′
72x 72″	23½ ′
108x108″	35 ′
144x144″	47 ′

Proper tilt of the screen is reached by projecting a beam of light against the screen, then tilting it forward or backward. When the most intense portion of the reflected light is concentrated at audience eye level, set the tilt control. In the case of large audiences, concentrate the reflected light approximately at the middle of the hall. The important thing to remember is that the screen should be as nearly perpendicular to the projector lenses as possible. The tilt does away with the need for having the projector exactly level with the screen. This adjustment also eliminates "keystoning" (having the top of the projected image wider than the bottom) and keeps the image sharp over its entirety.

Glasses

The last important element in stereo projection is the polarized spectacles. V-type polarization is used with the Realist projector. Realist, Inc.,

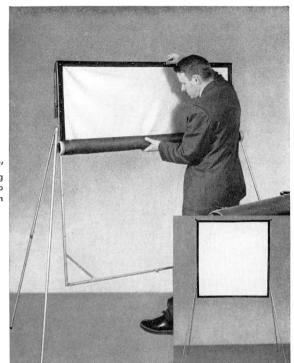

30. The Realist "Silvrscreen" for stereo projection, showing how screen is stretched into frame. Small insert shows screen erected on legs.

has found the polarizing material made by the Polaroid Corporation to be the most satisfactory. Polaroid spectacles provide the greatest amount of light transmission and, at the same time, the greatest "cut-off" of light. For comfort, economy and convenience, permanent-type glass Polaroid glasses are best in the long run for stereo projection.

* * * * *

Editor's Note: The instructions given in this chapter for the mounting of Stereo Realist transparencies, with and without the sorting box, will result in correctly mounted slides, with the right and left-eye images correctly oriented.

However, for those who like to know "how it works," as well as for some who already know and who may think they have noted a discrepancy in these instructions, the following explanation may be of interest.

In mounting stereo pairs it is, of course, essential that the picture taken with the left lens of the camera be viewed with the left eye, and the one taken with the right lens with the right eye.

Since the films are placed in the mask with the emulsion side up, but the finished slide is viewed from the opposite or base side, it will appear that the *left* picture, having been placed in the *left* aperture, will finally be viewed by the *right* eye when the slide is turned over for viewing. This is actually the case.

However, study of the camera will indicate that the first picture of the roll is the *right-hand* one and that in cutting and sorting, this was placed in the first compartment of the sorting box, which is marked 1-L. This picture, in turn, is placed in the left-hand aperture of the mask, emulsion side up, and when the mask is turned over it becomes again the right-eye picture, which is, of course, correct.

In short, the compartments of the viewing box have been marked, not with the actual positions of the pictures as taken and to be viewed, but with the positions which they will occupy during emulsion-side-up mounting. The result is a correctly mounted slide, without need for any explanation or possibility of confusion which might result if the user were told to mount the *right* picture in the *left* aperture, emulsion side up. Actually, that is what he is doing, but without verbal or mental gymnastics.

7. Viewing and Projection

ROBERT L. McINTYRE

Seeing stereo is an exciting visual experience. The Realist camera, with its two lenses, captures all the detail of a scene in an instant. In three-dimensional realism it remains imprisoned in the film for you to enjoy again and again.

Each slide contains two views, one left and one right. They show what each eye would see if it were back in the original setting in the position of the camera. When these views are properly presented to the eyes, you forget you are looking at pictures. The scene seems recreated before you, with all the realism inherent in this modern, two-eyed photographic view of things. To see it at its best you should use viewing equipment as good as the camera that takes the pictures.

The Hand Viewer

Old-timers will tell you that there is only one way to look at stereo pictures — with a hand stereoscope. That isn't entirely true. Stereo projection has taken great strides in recent years. Most people think, though, that the hand viewer is still superior to the projected image. It may be antisocial, but it does have some advantages unequalled by the best projection systems yet devised.

The technical requirements for a good viewer are simple. It should hold the slide flat, in a plane at right angles to the line of vision. The slide should be evenly illuminated from behind, with light of proper color and intensity. It should be viewed through a pair of matched lenses. Since the separation of users' eyes may vary quite a bit, these lenses should be capable of adjustment or should be big enough to allow for considerable variation in eye spacing. There should be some provision for focusing to accommodate variations in sight. All these requirements are fulfilled by the Stereo Realist viewers, which are designed to fit into the Realist stereo system.

1. Viewing stereo pictures with the modern Stereo Realist viewer is a far cry from the parlor stereoscope of Grandpa's day.

2. Looking at stereoscopic pictures with the old-fashioned parlor stereoscope may have been fun for Grandpa and Grandma.

The ideal conditions for viewing exist when camera and viewer are matched. This is called "ortho" stereo. To achieve it, viewer lenses should be of approximately the same focal length as the camera lenses. When they are, the stereoscopic reproduction of the scene is identical with the original view. It shows exactly what a person would see if his eyes were in the position occupied by the camera lenses at the time the shutter was tripped.

The Realist viewers are designed to produce a stereo image that is almost ortho. Their lenses are of 44mm focal length, which is slightly greater than the 35mm focal length of the Realist camera lenses. This difference results in a slight exaggeration of the stereo depth effect.

Whether the exaggeration is good or not is a matter of personal preference. It helps to make different planes more readily discernible at medium and far distances from the camera, which is all to the good. This makes it easier to achieve an effect of depth in most outdoor views. On the other side of the ledger, however, is its effect in extreme close-ups. Here the exaggerated depth is more noticeable, so that a subject's chin may seem to jut out from the neck unnaturally in a portrait. The amount of exaggeration due to this effect really is of much more technical interest than practical importance. Few untrained observers are likely to comment on it.

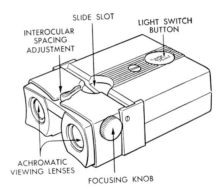

SLIDE SLOT

INTEROCULAR
SPACING
ADJUSTMENT

LIGHT SWITCH
BUTTON

ACHROMATIC
VIEWING LENSES

FOCUSING KNOB

3. The parts of the Stereo Realist Viewer, Model ST-61, showing the placement of all adjustment controls.

The Viewer Adjustments

The Stereo Realist viewer (ST-61) is a de luxe piece of equipment. It provides two adjustments, one to control the spacing between the lenses and the other to focus them on the slide. Together they make it possible for anyone with two reasonably good eyes to enjoy the full depth effect obtained in stereo pictures.

The focusing knob is located on the right side of the viewer. It is the first adjustment to make after the slide has been placed in the viewer and the lamp has been turned on by pressing the large red button near the back of the top of its case. Turn the knob until you find the position at which the picture appears sharpest. Then you are ready to adjust the lens spacing.

Lens spacing is controlled by a lever at top center of the viewer, right between the eye lenses. Moving the lever to the left draws the lenses

4. The Stereo Realist Viewer Model ST-61 is a de luxe piece of equipment, made entirely of black plastic except for the lenses.

207

5. One of the handy
carrying cases for the
Realist Viewer and a
group of slides.

closer together. Moving it to the right pushes them farther apart. The setting to use is that which makes the muscles of your eyes feel most relaxed as you look at a slide. It will vary somewhat for different individuals, and also when viewing slides that have been placed in various types of mounts that provide different spacing between the transparencies.

Viewer Adjustment Theory

The controls of the viewer need not be adjusted with extreme precision for generally satisfactory results. Our eyes are surprisingly flexible in their ability to compensate for different viewing conditions. Nevertheless, there are certain settings that will add to the realism of seeing stereo for each one of us. It isn't practical to find them by physical measurement, but you can increase your viewing pleasure by experimenting with the adjustments and finding the setting that is best for you. A little theory will help guide you on your way.

Seeing stereo is a very personal experience. Cameras, transparencies, mounts and viewers lend themselves to accurate measurement. We can compute all sorts of information concerning the image the eyes receive when an individual looks at a real scene or its stereoscopic counterpart. From this point on, though, we know less about what happens.

We know that an image is formed on the retina of each eye and that somehow these two images of the scene are fused together to give the brain a mental image that has three-dimensional depth. We also know that certain changes in the way these physical images are presented will affect the way they are interpreted by the brain.

208

This is where the finer points of slide viewing technique come in. They probably won't interest the casual viewer, or even be apparent to him, but they are important to the connoisseur of stereoscopic photography. They are the tricks by which he can squeeze out every last bit of realism as he looks at stereo pictures. Both viewer controls are involved — the focusing knob and the lever that controls lens spacing.

When you look into the viewer and focus it, you aren't focusing the viewer alone. You are also focusing your eyes. Since the eyes are capable of changing focus to accommodate for a wide range of distances, it isn't surprising that the slide in the viewer appears sharp at more than a single point in the focusing adjustment. The eyes are focused at *infinity* when the viewer lenses are at the closest distance to the slide at which the slide can still be seen sharply. It is as though you were looking off into a scene at a great distance. The eyes are focused at their *shortest viewing distance* (perhaps 8 to 12 inches, depending on your age and whether you have graduated to bifocals) when the viewer lenses are at the farthest point from the slide at which it can still be seen sharply.

It's slicing it mighty thin, admittedly, but distant scenes in which nothing of importance is close to the camera gain added realism when the eyes make their normal accommodation for distance in viewing. Thus it follows that you will get more satisfaction in viewing outdoor scenes if you position the viewer lenses at the point nearest the slide at which the picture appears sharp. Extreme close-ups work the opposite way. They will seem more real if the eyes must accommodate for near-by objects. Hence the viewer lenses should be as far from the slide as possible.

Thus far we have been discussing *accommodations* for distance without considering *convergence*. In vision, of course, the two go hand in hand.

6. The smaller case is handy for salesmen who may need only a few slides at any one time.

7. The largest carrying case holds still more slides when necessary—space for viewer is also provided.

In stereoscopy these two functions are separated, and the eyes remain focused on a single plane to view all parts of a slide, although convergence changes as we shift our gaze to look at near and far objects within it. Convergence is by far the stronger of these two factors. Accommodation was taken up first only because focusing should be done before the lens spacing is adjusted in using the hand viewer.

Convergence Control in Viewing

You can't go far wrong if you adjust lens spacing by "feel" after the viewer is focused. Here again, however, you can gain an additional effect of realism if you know some of the theory behind the use of this adjustment.

When we look at far-away objects the lines of sight of our two eyes are parallel. There is no convergence. The same thing holds true when we look at pictures of distant objects with a properly adjusted stereo viewer. The eyes are parallel when we look into faraway parts of the picture, and converge only when we inspect things in the foreground.

Our eyes converge very readily. They are accustomed to making this adjustment in daily life. They are not willing to do the opposite. When the viewer is misadjusted to necessitate divergence instead of convergence, we have difficulty in making the two images fuse. If we force them to come together, a headache is likely to result. This is the sort of thing that has given some people the false impression that stereo pictures are hard to look at. With a properly adjusted viewer, it's easy — it may even prove restful and relaxing to the eyes after a day of close work requiring prolonged convergence.

The best setting to use is the one that enables you to look at infinity objects in a slide with eyes parallel, just as they would be in looking at the scene itself. To find it, first select a slide that has well-defined objects at a great distance from the camera. Insert it in the viewer and look at the distant objects as you move the convergence control lever to its extreme adjustments, first at the left and then at the right.

This little experiment will not be easy on the eyes, but you only have to do it once. What you see will depend on your own personal eye separation and on how far apart the two stereo transparencies are held in the slide mount. With the adjustment lever at the left you will probably feel some discomfort. You may find it impossible to fuse the two images of the slide. Don't keep trying if this is the case. What you are doing is trying to force your eyes to turn outward, the left one to the left and the right one to the right. They just don't want to work that way, and prolonged use of the viewer with the adjustment off in this direction leaves a headache as its only reward.

Keep looking into the viewer as you shift the adjustment lever to the right. You probably will experience a feeling of relief as the lever moves toward the center of its adjustment range. As you move it to the extreme right you may get a feeling that the slide and the objects within it are becoming smaller.

This is a natural reaction. We are accustomed to viewing small things at close distances and big things at large distances. When we create an artificial situation in which the eyes converge excessively while looking at a distant scene, we are likely to interpret it as a setting in miniature, close to the camera.

The best adjustment of the convergence lever to make the most of this depth effect is the point at which viewing first becomes relaxed and easy as you shift the lever from left to right. It avoids painful divergence and the headache likely to follow it, and it also avoids excessive convergence and its attendant feeling of miniaturization. Individual eye spacing determines the convergence setting in many cases. Eye spacing varies considerably from person to person.

8. A small file-type case for both carrying and library storage of slides.

9. A larger file-type case for permanent library storage of slides.

Personal taste also enters into the use of this adjustment. Some people habitually use more than normal convergence. It is easier for a beginner to see stereo for the first time this way, perhaps because he is conscious that he really is looking at a little slide in a viewing box and automatically feels he should have to converge his eyes to see it.

If there is any error in using this adjustment, it should always be on the convergence side. The slightest divergence will make itself felt, while excessive convergence merely detracts a bit from the realism of the stereoscopic effect.

The Handi-Viewer

The original Realist viewer (ST-61) is a fine instrument. Its adjustable interocular unavoidably adds to its cost, however, and isn't strictly necessary for a large majority of individuals whose eyes are set anywhere near the average distance apart. Furthermore, the presence of this adjustment can even become a handicap when the viewer is placed in the hands of beginners who don't know how to use it. This line of thinking led to the design of the Handi-Viewer, a compact unit that performs the same functions as the ST-61 but is more convenient to use and less costly to manufacture. Its lenses and illumination system are similar to those of the ST-61. Focusing is accomplished by a centrally located wheel, and the light is turned on merely by depressing a slide in its channel. These features make it possible to operate the viewer with one hand.

The main functional difference between the two units is that the convergence control has been omitted from the Handi-Viewer. Its only viewing control is the focusing wheel. This adjustment has some influence on convergence, however, when the individual's eye spacing is more or less than the distance between the centers of the lenses. Focusing should be used to obtain the adjustment that feels best to the eyes. The related convergence influence will take care of itself.

10. For continuous use of the Stereo Realist viewer, a transformer is available to operate lamp from the 115-volt AC line.

11. The inexpensive Handi-Viewer has all the features of the Model ST-61 except that interocular adjustment is not provided.

Care of the Viewer

The viewer requires very little attention to keep it in tiptop shape. If your favorite slides begin to look a little bit dark, the batteries probably are weak and should be replaced. This effect first becomes visible after the viewer has been in use for some time. During a period of inactivity, weak batteries will build up enough strength to provide adequate illumination for viewing a few slides, but then the light will grow dim. With normal use replace the batteries every three months or so to guard against weakness.

A Realist transformer is available to provide a steady, dependable power source when the viewer is used a great deal. It is wired into a line cord near the end that is plugged into the wall, and the end of the cord that attaches to the viewer is equipped with a pair of clips. The batteries are removed when the transformer is used, reducing the weight of the viewer considerably.

The transformer is designed for use with the regular viewer bulb, a No. 14 G-E or Westinghouse lamp rated at 2.5 volts and 0.3 amperes. The bulb will require replacement when it burns out or darkens with age, and a spare can be stored conveniently in a corner of the battery compartment if it is wrapped in tissue or stuck in place with mounting tape so it won't rattle about.

If the lamp flickers as the viewer is handled, or fails to provide good illumination when batteries are fresh, poor contact somewhere in the circuit is indicated. Remove the batteries and wipe them vigorously to eliminate any trace of corrosion at either end. Clean the contact points that press against them, too. If the batteries aren't held tightly enough, increase the tension by bending the clips slightly so you have to force them apart to insert the batteries again. Make sure the lamp is tight in its socket.

The white reflecting surfaces must be kept clean to get good illumination. They can be cleaned with the moistened corner of a handkerchief, exercising care to avoid scratching them. Dust should be removed from them and from the entire viewer case each time the batteries are changed. More frequent cleaning may be indicated if the viewer is used a great deal, especially when cardboard mounts are employed.

The viewer lenses should be cleaned with all the care used in handling camera lenses. Lens tissue or a soft, much-laundered handkerchief will do the job safely. First remove surface dust by brushing lightly. Then breathe on the lens and polish it without applying pressure. Outside surfaces will require more frequent cleaning. Those inside seldom need attention except for brushing off surface dust. Never disassemble the viewer lenses. They are mounted carefully so that their focus is matched, and disturbing this relationship will make viewing difficult. If dirt between the lens elements calls for taking them apart, the job should be done at the factory.

A good hand viewer is capable of providing the ultimate in stereoscopic enjoyment. If you learn to get the most out of it by mastering its controls, and keep it in good operating condition, it will help you enjoy the thrills of stereo for many years to come.

Projection: "The Magic Window"

The stereo screen has been likened to a "magic window" through which you can enjoy glimpses of an ever-changing world outside. When well-mounted slides are shown with a good projector under proper conditions, you can come amazingly close to fulfilling this fanciful description.

Each step toward putting on a successful projection showing is a simple one, from mounting the slides to returning them in order to their cases after they are shown. There are enough different steps in the process, though, to make it worthwhile to learn something about them before you start.

12. Inexpensive Polaroid glasses, for viewing projected stereo images, have cardboard frames and plastic earpieces.

214

13. The Stereo Realist projector, with carrying case and Polaroid glasses for viewing the projected images. Glasses are available separately in different types for permanent and temporary use.

The development of modern polarizing materials made today's stereo projection system possible. The basic problem is to show the two images of a stereo pair on a screen in such a manner that the left-eye image is visible only to the viewer's left eye and the right-eye image is seen only by his right.

Polaroid filters within the projector orient the light beam for each picture at right angles to the other. Similarly oriented polarized eyeglasses worn by viewers will allow the light of the proper image to reach each eye and will cut off the image intended for the other one.

The screen surface must be covered with a metallic material which reflects light without affecting its polarization, and viewers' heads must be held upright so their eyeglasses remain in correct relationship to the images on the screen. These requirements are met when the Stereo Realist projector is used according to the manufacturer's recommendations.

Hand Viewing vs. Projection

Can projected stereo ever equal the results that you get with the hand viewer? There is no clear-cut answer. Both systems have their advantages. The hand viewer is the traditional instrument for enjoying stereoscopic pictures. Only in recent years has it been seriously challenged by the projector. The choice depends a great deal on individual requirements and preferences.

Most obvious and important is the fact that projected stereo can be enjoyed by a group, while using the hand viewer is a solitary pastime. Of course a group of people, each holding a viewer and passing the transparencies along, can enjoy slides, too, but the experience lacks the feeling of group participation that is generated when everyone is looking at the same pictures at the same time.

The hand viewer has two major advantages that you should bear in mind when planning projection showings. First, it automatically places the individual in the correct position for viewing slides — you have to hold it up to your eyes to use it. Second, it blocks off your view of everything but the slide, making it easier to imagine that you are looking at a real scene. These things are important, but by setting up proper audience seating in relation to screen size you can create the same "ortho" stereo effect that you get with a properly adjusted viewer. By darkening the room you can subdue distractions that might destroy the illusion of reality.

There is one hand viewing trick you can never duplicate in projection, and it is interesting to note. Slides taken by shooting down from high places are enhanced when you look at them with head bent forward so the viewer is pointed toward your knees. Those taken with the camera aimed upward seem more real in viewing when you tilt your head back so the viewer is held at about the angle the camera was.

These experiences suggest that there is more to seeing stereo than merely presenting images to the eyes — and so there is. The impressions we get from a set of slides may vary considerably from one individual to another and from one showing to another. The enjoyment of stereo pictures is a mental thing, subject to many influences. To put on the best possible show, use all the factors you can control to make the grand illusion seem like the real thing.

The Projector

In principle, the Stereo Realist projector is like two projectors with twin lamps and lenses, but is designed so that they work together as a unit. The model recommended for home use has 500-watt lamps and uses about 10 amps of current. To get maximum efficiency it should be plugged into an electrical outlet on a line which does not serve appliances like deepfreezers or ironers, which consume considerable electricity.

Each transparency of the stereo pair is shown on the screen by a separate optical system. In front of the lamp are condenser lenses which gather the light rays and make them parallel. Then come the polarizing filters, which serve to hold back heat as well as to polarize the light for viewing. The polarized light passes through the transparencies, and then through the projection lenses which form the images on the screen. A blower sys-

216

14. Control switches of the Realist Projector operate fan motor and lamp for each image individually. Lamp cannot be lighted without first starting fans.

tem keeps cool air flowing into the projector, over the slide and around the lamps, to eliminate danger of overheating.

Projector Controls

The Realist projector provides several adjustments and controls to help you show your stereo slides at their best and to aid you in presenting a well-run program. They are listed here, for quick identification, and their use will be discussed in detail later on:

FAN SWITCHES are located at the bottom rear of the projector; they should be turned on and allowed to gain speed before the lamps are turned on.

LAMP SWITCHES are just above the fan switches; they should be turned on last and turned off first. At the end of a show the fans should be allowed to run for a few minutes after the lamps are turned off to cool the projector before returning it to its case.

THE SLIDE CHANGER is a lever at the center of the rear of the projector. Pulling it down automatically performs a series of operations to darken the screen, change slides, and then illuminate the screen again to show the succeeding picture. There's a little knack — easily acquired — to depressing it firmly and yet not too fast, so that slides change smoothly.

VERTICAL ALIGNMENT is controlled by a knob on the right side of the projector, opposite the slide carrier. It is the adjustment most often required and is the easiest to reach. When one picture appears higher than the other on the screen, turning this knob will bring them into alignment.

15. Lens controls of Stereo Realist projector. Upper knob controls spacing between lenses, and convergence of images on the screen. Lower knob focuses the two lenses as a unit.

HORIZONTAL ALIGNMENT or convergence is accomplished by turning a knob located at the center of the front of the projector. Turning it one way brings the images on the screen closer together. Turning it the other moves them farther apart.

FOCUSING is controlled by a knob at front center of the projector, just below the horizontal alignment control. Turning it moves the two projector lenses in and out in unison. When slides are properly mounted the adjustments should be made only once — at the start of the show. Minor deviations from normal image placement on the screen are not nearly so distressing to an audience as moving the images while the slide is being viewed.

The Stereo Screen

An efficient screen for showing projected stereo pictures must be perfectly flat and covered with metallic material that reflects light without affecting its polarization. The Silvrscreen makes use of a lightweight, four-sided frame with detachable legs. This frame supports the screen itself, which is cast as one piece of live rubber. Powdered aluminum is bonded to the surface to give proper reflectance. The screen is stretched slightly as it is placed on the frame with the aid of snap fasteners. This stretching serves to flatten it perfectly.

The screen supports are designed to permit tilting the screen forward slightly for maximum efficiency. To make this adjustment, set up the screen facing the audience and turn on the projector with no slide in it. Take a position at one side of the screen, loosen the tilting knobs, and tilt it forward from vertical while watching the beam of light it reflects back toward the projector. Adjust the tilt until the brightest part of this beam of reflected light falls in the center of the seating area.

218

Stereo Spectacles

For effective stereo viewing, each eye must see the picture intended for it, and only that picture. Polarizing filters within the projector differentiate the left and right-eye pictures by polarizing them at right angles to one another. To maintain the effect, viewers must wear stereo spectacles of polarizing material, which orient each eye for the projected polarized picture.

This is accomplished with inexpensive polarizing spectacles. There is only one important point to be observed in using them. The head should be held straight, not tilted to left or right. When this is done, each eye sees the correct picture with maximum brightness, and the other picture is cut off as completely as possible. Tilting the head makes a "ghost" image of the second picture visible to each eye.

Screen Adjustments

There was a time when mounting was likely to vary greatly from slide to slide; it was standard procedure to throw the pictures on the screen and then adjust the image placement to align them vertically and obtain the proper horizontal spacing. An occasional focusing adjustment was required, too, and it was all this manipulation that caused quick audience fatigue.

The ideal for which every projectionist strove was to get perfect vertical alignment, so that a horizontal line passing through a given point in one picture would pass through the same point in the other. He also

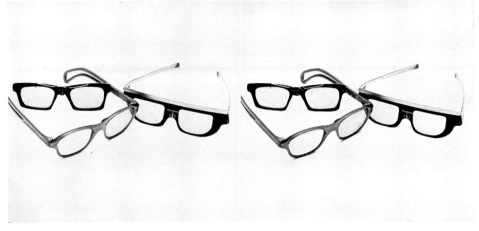

16. Several different types of Polaroid glasses. Above left: clip-on type to go over ordinary eyeglasses. Lower left: permanent plastic frame type. Right: less expensive type.

219

17. A typical outdoor picture which should be mounted in the *distant* mount, since no object is closer than 7 feet from the camera. Stereo courtesy Realist, Inc.

attempted to get normal horizontal spacing, which meant separating the two pictures sufficiently so that images of points representing objects at infinity would be 2½ inches apart. Such adjustments could be made for every slide, but it took a little time — and it was hard on viewers' eyes to watch the images while their placement was being changed. The solution was to provide a mounting system that would place the transparencies in the projector in the same position every time. Then the adjustments could be made for the first slide, and subsequent ones would fall into position automatically.

It's an axiom that the viewer's eyes will converge with ease, but won't turn out. Because of this, mounting systems are planned to avoid placing infinity points more than 2½ inches apart on the screen. Another limitation, less obvious, governs the placement of subject matter close to the camera.

When we look at properly adjusted infinity points on the screen, they are 2½ inches apart — the same as the distance between our eyes — and our eyes look straight ahead and parallel. This is as it should be. Our eyes do exactly the same thing when we look at a distant object in real life.

When we look at a near-by object, our eyes converge on it. They turn in, and the amount of turning in required gives us some measure of its distance away. When the two stereoscopic images of a given object coincide on the screen and our eyes converge on them, we get the impression that the object is located in the same plane as the screen. In most cases

220

it is desirable to keep the planes of the picture located *behind* the screen, which gives us a range of displacement from 0 to 2½ inches with which to work. When a picture is properly adjusted to cover this range on a screen 54 inches wide, objects that were 7 feet from the camera will coincide on the screen. The images of things farther away than 7 feet will be separated, farther and farther, until objects at infinity appear 2½ inches apart.

Sometimes, however, it is desirable to include in the picture things that are closer than 7 feet. If this were done and the transparencies were mounted in regular masks, the objects closer than 7 feet from the camera would appear to be *in front* of the screen. The images would not overlap. The right one would appear on the left, and the left one on the right. The eyes would converge at a point closer than the screen in order to fuse the two images together. Except in special circumstances, where an object extends *through* the screen without touching the edges of the picture, this condition is not desirable. It can be avoided by limiting the subject matter to avoid taking extremes of depth beyond the range of projected stereo. When this has been accomplished, it is then possible to move the two transparencies farther apart, within the mount, so that the most distant points take over the positions that normally would be occupied by infinity points and the near points move back to the screen or behind it. This is what is done, automatically, when you use special mounts with projection masking.

Projection Mounting

Three types of mounts are provided in the Realist mounting system. They cover any picture-taking situation likely to be encountered while using the Stereo Realist camera. They require limiting the depth of scenes — a limitation which is inherent in taking pictures with an amateur stereo camera for projection.

DISTANT MOUNTS will handle most stereo pictures the average photographer takes. They cover subject matter at any distance from 7 feet to infinity. The only precaution necessary in shooting pictures for these mounts is to avoid including anything closer than 7 feet from the camera.

Thus far we have discussed placement of objects within the pictures of a stereo pair without considering their "frames." Any mount masks off the two picture areas with apertures. The apertures appear on the screen along with the pictures, and their placement governs the distance at which they seem to be. They create the stereo "window" through which the picture is viewed. The apertures of distant mounts are so separated that they create a stereoscopic window at 7 feet when the pictures are projected on a 54-inch screen and the projector is adjusted so the openings overlap. Anything farther than 7 feet from the camera appears beyond the window.

MEDIUM MOUNTS cover subject matter at distances of from 4 to 20 feet. Indoor flash shots often fall in this range and should be placed in medium

18. A typical medium shot, with objects in the range of 4 to 20 feet from the camera. Such a picture should be in a *medium* mount. Stereo by Dorothy S. Gelatt.

mounts when they include anything nearer than 7 feet from the camera.

The transparencies are moved farther apart in medium mounts so that objects 20 feet away will be separated by 2½ inches on the screen. Immediately after showing a picture in a distant mount, without projector adjustments, the view in the medium mount will fall into proper position. This is what makes the system so valuable — mounts of different types can be intermixed and shown in any order without need for adjustments.

Close-up mounts are needed only for real close-ups where the subject matter is from 2½ to 6 feet from the camera. Here the images of objects at 6 feet are moved apart so they appear the same on the screen as infinity points would in a distant mount. You don't have to think about moving them, though. All you have to do is select the right mount, and it does the rest.

*   *   *

Selecting mounts for transparencies is not a difficult chore. Outdoor scenes that contain distant objects must automatically go into distant mounts. Their near limit is 7 feet. If subject matter closer than 7 feet is included, the far distance should be limited at the time the picture is taken. If it is no more than 20 feet, a medium mask is in order, and it will permit showing near objects as close as 4 feet. The best way to work is to think in terms of these mounts when you are working with the camera.

222

That way you can limit the depth of your scenes as may be required. When a picture exceeds the range of any of these mounts, the problem is one of compromise. Usually the more distant mount is the best to use. It will take care of the distant points in the scene, keeping them from displaying excessive separation on the screen — which calls for painful divergence on the part of the audience. It is better to let the picture come through the stereo window and appear to extend out into the room from the screen than to force the viewer's eyes to diverge to see more distant objects in it.

Putting on the Show

Presenting a stereo slide program involves little more preparation than putting on a home movie show or displaying ordinary color slides. The show will go more smoothly if you have the projector, screen and chairs in place before the audience arrives and the slides organized in proper sequence.

It saves valuable seating space to have a high projector stand that will permit shooting over the heads of the audience. That way, the best area — that immediately in front of the screen — can be used for seating. A substantial wooden box, placed atop a solid table, will serve nicely. You can build one to serve double duty as a place to store slides as well.

With the 54-inch screen recommended for home projection, the best viewing position is directly in front of the screen and 7 feet from it. Audi-

19. A typical close-up, which should go in the close-up type of mount, designed for objects from 2½ to 6 feet from the camera. Stereo by P. E. Springer.

ences naturally seem to gravitate away from the screen, so it is necessary to keep reminding them that the choicest seats are forward. A person 7 feet from the screen is in the "ortho" stereo position. He sees essentially what the camera saw, in true perspective and stereoscopic depth. From there back to the projector is the best seating area. Brightness diminishes rapidly at the sides of the room. From seats that are too far back, the perspective of pictures appears exaggerated. Hence it is best to confine the audience to seats that are as close to the screen as possible and as near as possible to the line from projector to screen.

Screens 6 and 9 feet wide can be used under special circumstances where it is necessary to present a program before a large audience. There is one important point to remember in projecting on a large screen. You can no longer use the mask windows of the mount as a guide in adjusting the projector. As each picture of the stereo pair is enlarged on the bigger screen, the difference between the left and right-eye views also is magnified. The masks are designed to be overlapped when the image is 54 inches wide. When it is bigger, you have to go by the actual separation of infinity points on the screen. This must be kept at 2½ inches. If you went ahead and blindly superimposed the windows while projecting on a 9-foot screen, the infinity points would be almost 6 inches apart and your audience would soon complain because of difficulty in fusing them.

If you are forced to set up the projector after the audience is seated, ask them to keep their viewing glasses off while you make the adjustments on the screen. If the group is small you can explain what you are doing as you go along to hold their interest. Without the glasses, the overlapping images won't make much sense, but at least they won't cause discomfort. It takes only a minute to align the first slide on the screen. From there

20. Side view of Realist projector showing condenser mount partly removed. Also note horizontal alignment control, just under slide carrier.

on, if the slides are mounted properly, there should be no need for adjustments.

The slides go into the Realist projector's carrier right side up, just as they go into the hand viewer. This simple system is different from other projectors and is made possible by a rotating carrier.

Even with perfectly mounted slides it is possible to have the images fall on the screen out of alignment once in a great while. The projector repeats its movements faithfully time after time, but the human factor plays a part in two operations that are important: 1) inserting the slide in the carrier and 2) depressing the slide-changing lever.

The slide should be inserted in the carrier right side up, with sufficient downward pressure to bring its top edge below the top of the slide retainer. At the same time slight forward pressure should be applied to bring the front glass surface into contact with the locating pads of the carrier. Then, with forward pressure continued, the downward pressure should be released to let the retaining springs raise the slide into position against the stops which hold it in place. Failure to seat the slide properly in the carrier can cause the images on the screen to appear out of focus. Usually the error is caused by tilting the slide, so it cannot be corrected by the focusing adjustment. At best, only part of the slide can be made sharp. In this case it is usually best to show the slide briefly, or skip it entirely if it is unimportant. But if it makes a key point in your stereo story, you can first pass on to the next slide, and while it is on the screen remove the one that caused the trouble. Replace it in the carrier, making certain it is seated properly. Then show it again. As you become more and more accustomed to placing slides in the carrier, you will find yourself seating them accurately every time.

There's a knack to depressing the slide-advancing lever smoothly and firmly, with just the right pressure to bring each succeeding slide into position for showing. It isn't hard to learn. If you bring the lever down too fast, the carrier may come to rest with the two images slightly out of horizontal alignment on the screen. This condition is painful to the viewer who tries to fuse the images, for one eye is forced to turn up while the other turns down—an adjustment we are ill equipped to make. Hence it should be corrected the instant it is seen.

The adjustment for this important correction is located where it can be made most quickly and conveniently, on the right side of the projector housing. Rotating the knurled knob there turns the slide carrier to bring the images into alignment.

Showing Mixed Slides

Occasionally the projector owner is called upon to present a program of mixed slides, mounted in different ways. It may be at a camera club competition, or it may be a set of slides belonging to a friend whose pictures are mounted for hand viewing. It may even be a group of your

21. Lens mount removed from projector for cleaning. Convergence control on top, focusing knob at bottom.

own slides—pictures you want to show so rarely that it doesn't seem worth the effort to get them into new mounts for a really smooth show.

Such a presentation should never be made before a large audience. If a show is worth putting on at all, it is worth doing well, with proper mounting. Camera club competitions in particular, however, offer the projectionist little choice. As long as varied mounting systems are employed, there seems little to do but make the best of it.

One solution in such a situation is to adjust the projector as each slide is thrown on the screen, first correcting vertical alignment and then horizontal separation. Instead of attempting to achieve a 2½-inch separation of far points in each slide, some projectionists overlap the images of near points on the screen. This has the effect of placing everything in the picture at the screen or behind it. Far points may not seem as distant, stereoscopically, as if the 2½-inch separation were adhered to. Nevertheless, it is a quick solution that will speed up showings considerably. In clubs, the projection adjustments are sometimes handled by one man while another takes care of the slide changing. A two-man operation of this sort is never necessary, or desirable, when a set of properly mounted slides is to be shown. It does help, though, when it is necessary to project an assortment of slides in different mounts. Whenever it is practical to separate the slides into groups that have similar mounting, much work can be saved.

Projector Maintenance

The Stereo Realist projector is designed to give years of dependable service. With just a little care you can keep it in tiptop shape to show your pictures at their best. The first requirement is cleanliness. Slides will always appear clear, bright and sharp on the screen if the projector optics are kept clean and free from dust.

226

Open the projector by pushing the front and rear locking levers outward. This will release the two sides of the case, which are hinged to open outward revealing the lamp housing and condenser assemblies.

Remove the condenser assemblies by sliding them out of their seats and lift out the lenses and heat-absorbing filters. Using lens tissue or soft cloth, wipe them lightly to remove surface dust. Then polish lightly. Dust the polarizing filters lightly, making certain they are not rotated out of position in their cells. A white dot on the filter ring should align with the index mark on its seat. If a filter is rotated out of position, "ghost" images will be visible on the screen. When the optical elements have been cleaned, replace them in the condenser assembly and put it back into the projector housing. Do not use force at any step along the way. The elements will fit only in their proper positions and will be damaged if an attempt is made to force them in any other way.

The front surfaces of the projector lenses can be dusted without removing them. Turn the focusing knob to the left as far as it will go. This will move the whole lens assembly forward until finally the adjusting screw disengages and the entire assembly can be withdrawn. Normal cleaning can be accomplished without removing the individual lenses.

The lenses are held in snap-in mounts. When it is necessary to remove them the assembly should be taken out of the projector. Then each lens can be removed by grasping it by its outer rim and pulling straight out with a twisting motion. They are replaced by inserting them and then pressing straight in firmly until they snap into place.

Changing Lamps

Projector lamps are expendable. The 500-watt T-10 Medium Prefocus base lamps used in the Realist projector have an average life of 25 hours.

22. Condensers removed from projector for cleaning. Note position of index marks for correct orientation of polarizing filters on each mount.

It's amazing how uniform their life is when they are used side by side in a stereo projector—when one burns out you can be sure that the other will go in a very short time. For this reason, and to keep the brightness of the two pictures matched, it pays to replace both lamps when one burns out.

When a lamp burns out, turn out both lamps but leave the switches in the "fan on" position. This will force a stream of air through the projector, cooling the lamps and the metal parts you may touch in removing them. In a minute or two they will be cool enough to handle.

Grasp the top of the lamp and press it down firmly while turning to the left. Once it starts to turn you can release the downward pressure. Less than a half turn is required. When it reaches the right point, you can lift the lamp out. You will notice that there are two flanges on the base of the lamp, one wide and one narrow, and that there are corresponding wide and narrow openings in the socket. Remove the new lamp from its wrappings and turn it until its wide and narrow flanges are aligned with those of the socket. Then lower it into place until the flanges seat in the openings. Press downward firmly and turn to the right until the lamp is seated. If it is in place it will stand straight up in the housing.

The Stereo Realist projector provides an adjustment for centering the lamps behind the condensers to obtain even light distribution. This is accomplished by turning wheels at the bottom of the lamphouse, one on each side of the machine. For best possible illumination, turn on one lamp with no slide in the projector and check the light distribution on the screen. If it is even, as it probably will be, the adjustment is right for the particular lamp you are using. If there are dark corners at one side of the screen, turn the adjusting wheel for the lamp you are checking until the light pattern is centered on the screen. Then turn off that lamp and make the same adjustment for the other one.

Projector lamps come in 110, 115 and 120-volt ratings. Most efficient operation usually is obtained with 115-volt lamps in locations where a normal current supply is maintained. If lamps burn out more often than they should, chances are that the voltage is higher than normal and that higher voltage lamps should be employed to obtain normal life. It is not desirable to use 120-volt lamps universally. When operated at lower voltages than that for which they are intended, lamps will burn longer but they will not give illumination as brilliant as they should and their light will have a slightly yellowish cast.

The Rotary Slide Carrier

The only maintenance the Realist slide carrier requires is a drop of oil once a year or so on the center bearing upon which it rotates. Two buttons will be found on opposite sides of the carrier. To remove the carrier from the projector, simply press the two buttons together and lift it straight up. To replace it, seat the carrier with the buttons pressed together and then release them.

An auxiliary carrier for standard 2x2 slides (not stereo) is also available for the Realist and need only be slipped into place to convert the projector for showing them.

Slide Files

Keeping slides in order during a showing is always a problem, but it has been simplified by a special pop-up filing unit designed for use with the Realist projector. It fits into a depression in the top of the projector housing, immediately in front of the slide carrier. The slides pop up in order as a lever is pushed, making it easy to lift them from the file unit and insert them in the carrier.

The pop-up slide holder is designed as a part of a filing system, and cases are made to take sets of holders. Since the slides are replaced at the back of the holder as new ones are withdrawn from the front, they remain in order automatically. To assemble a show, all that is necessary is to line up the holders containing the slides you want. After showing they can be returned to their cases again.

The Projector Case

An unusual case has been designed for the Realist projector. In addition to housing the projector and protecting it when not in use, it will also serve as a firm projection stand. Sockets are built into its base to receive three collapsible, telescoping legs that will hold the projector up high enough to throw its beam over the heads of the audience.

The carrying case for the legs serves a dual purpose. It can be fastened beneath the projector, where it extends at both sides to provide table space for the projectionist.

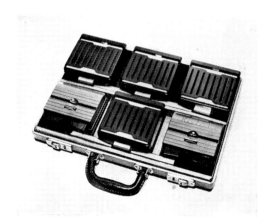

23. Combination carrying case for two Handi-Viewers and four Sequence files used in the projector.

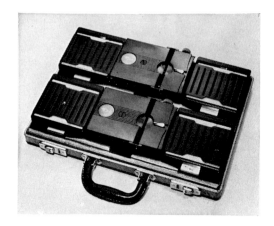

24. Another combination case for two Realist Viewers ST-61, and four Sequence files.

Stereo Showmanship

Proper handling of the mechanics—like audience seating, slide mounting and projector adjustments—is only a part of what it takes to put on a top-notch stereo program. Modern stereo packs a tremendous punch all by itself, but by injecting a little showmanship into the presentation you can give it still more impact. First thing to remember is to pick a show to fit the audience.

For a family group there's nothing better than family pictures. Holidays, birthdays, vacations and other outings can be recorded in slides that make it fun to recall those happy days. Family album pictures are a valuable part of every fan's slide collection, but their popularity is likely to be limited to the family and close friends. When you are putting on a show for a more general audience, try to stick to slides that have a broad appeal.

Any group except a camera club will be far more interested in what the pictures show than in how they were taken. A brief explanation of stereo is helpful at the start of the program, particularly when few members of the audience have seen three-dimensional pictures on the screen before, but from there on it's best to skip the technicalities. Let your commentary describe the subject matter instead, telling interesting things about the scenes that can't be seen by looking at them. You don't have to keep talking all the time, by any means. Give the audience a chance to explore the pictures. Don't try to show too many or to put them through the projector too fast.

The experience of viewing projected stereo is a far richer one than looking at flat pictures. The viewer participates to a much greater extent, for his eyes must adjust for different planes of depth as they explore the scene. All this takes time. The first few slides are particularly important in any show, and audience reaction to them usually sets a pattern that continues through the performance. Hence it pays to put your best foot forward at the beginning. You needn't be afraid to include pictures later on that are not too strong stereoscopically, if they are good color shots and fill an important place in the continuity of the story. Just remember to get the show off to a good start, save a few strong slides for the finale, and your program will be well received. The experienced stereo worker is likely to become too sophisticated in his choice of material. Every picture doesn't have to shout "stereo." Some scenes that are essential to a travelog, for example, may not happen to lend themselves to producing strong depth effects.

Even if everything in the scene is 200 feet or more from the camera—far enough away so that very little stereoscopic relief is observed—the slide is not necessarily a total loss. It may be an excellent two-dimensional picture. A certain amount of depth sensation is gained in any stereo picture, merely because of the stereo "window" created by its mask. Selecting pictures to make up a show is different from choosing slides to enter in a contest. In competitions you want to enter your very strongest pictures so they will stand out among the rest of the entries. In a show of your own you can afford to have some relatively quiet slides in between the impressive ones. They provide change of pace and give the outstanding depth effects even more impact by contrast.

Only half the fun of stereo is in the taking. Looking at slides in the hand viewer or on the screen is an enriching visual experience. It is doubly rewarding when you can share it with a group in a projected showing. The spontaneous response of an audience to good stereo slides will rekindle for you the enthusiasm you felt when you first realized the possibilities of the scenes you are showing.

Color Stereos 2

1. MINIATURE ORCHIDS. Photographed at Golden Gate Park, San Francisco. This beautiful flower study was made with the camera focused to 3½ feet, and no special accessories. *P. E. Springer.*

2. ALCYONARIAN CORAL. This record picture of coral on the Great Barrier Reef, Australia, has considerable design quality and can stand on its own for eye appeal. Essentially a one-color picture, shades of yellow to brown. *Dick McGraw.*

3. BLUE STRIPED GRUNT. An underwater stereo made with the equipment described in Chapter 11. Colorful corals and undersea plants add an aura of fantasy to this prosaically-named fish. Flash is generally used with color film underwater. *Harry Pederson.*

4. NILE VALLEY. In a single picture the lush green vegetation along an irrigation ditch and the dry brown of the parched ground tell the whole story of the miracle wrought by water brought to the desert. *Julien Bryan.*

5. RED PEPPERS. This close-up is fascinating because of the color contrast which would be lost at a greater distance. Taken near Antioch in Turkey, it was made at a distance of 3½ feet without special attachments. *Julien Bryan.*

6. BALANCED ROCK. One of the many overwhelming rock formations in the Garden of the Gods, Colorado Springs. Here again, it takes only two basic colors for contrast through the entire stereo. *Willard D. Morgan.*

7. BODILESS COWBOY. This is one of many illusions which can be produced with the aid of the Image Dividers described in Chapter 10. Such tricks are effective in flat pictures, but have more shock value in stereo. *Tommy Thomas.*

8. MULTIPLE EXPOSURE. The differently colored images here were made by covering the flash reflector with cellophane of the three primary colors, the remaining exposure being made by the light of a clear flashlamp. *Tommy Thomas.*

9. SEATED NUDE. A plain background is usually best for figure studies. In this case the color of the background was of light beige, not very different from flesh tone, and with flat lighting the modeling in this picture is due entirely to the stereo effect. *John Meredith.*

10. INFORMAL FASHION. The strong color of the costume is emphasized here by the use of relatively neutral colors throughout the remainder of the picture. The man in the background provides another plane for stereo interest. *Courtesy of Vogue.*

11. SILVER BIRD. The cold metallic bird contrasts with the warm flesh tones, the deep beige hosiery and the red drape. Simplicity is maintained by the use of a completely plain pastel background. The pose is sufficiently detached to be used in advertising. *John Meredith.*

12. FORMAL FASHION. A striking use of color film for costumes which are entirely black and white. The temptation to the amateur might be to use a brightly colored background. Here the neutral background and soft flesh tones provide all the color contrast needed. *Courtesy of Vogue.*

13. BRIDAL PORTRAIT. Outdoor fashion pictures are often enhanced by being photographed in the shade with sunlight filtering through foliage to add interest to what would otherwise be a large expanse of plain white. *John Meredith.*

232

1. MINIATURE ORCHIDS   P. E. Springer

2. ALCYONARIAN CORAL   Dick McGraw

3. BLUE STRIPED GRUNT   Harry Pederson

4. NILE VALLEY   Julien Bryan

5. RED PEPPERS   Julien Bryan

6. BALANCED ROCK   Willard D. Morgan

STEREOLUSIONS

7. BODILESS COWBOY   Tommy Thomas

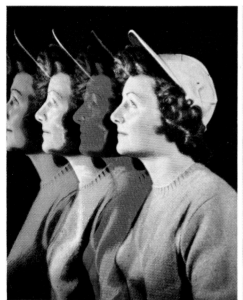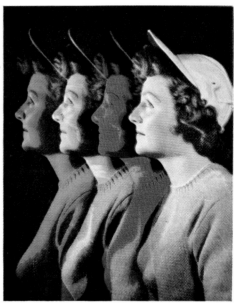

8. MULTIPLE EXPOSURE   Tommy Thomas

STEREOLUSIONS

237

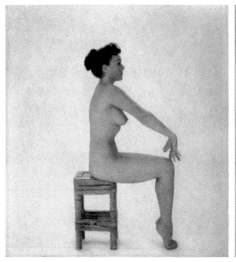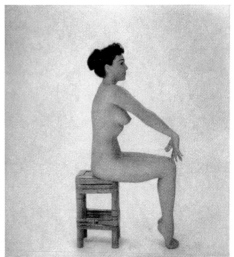

9. SEATED NUDE   John Meredith

10. INFORMAL FASHION   Courtesy of Vogue

11. SILVER BIRD   John Meredith

12. FORMAL FASHION   Courtesy of Vogue

13. BRIDAL PORTRAIT   John Meredith

8. Portrait and Fashion

JOHN MEREDITH

Three-dimensional photography has, in truth, added a new dimension to portraiture and to fashion photography as well. Whatever has been lacking in representation of face and figure on a flat plane has been fulfilled by the realism of the stereo photograph. But this must not be taken to mean that realism is the ultimate aim of stereo photography. Having the third dimension in our pictures should serve, rather, to unshackle our imaginations, to liberate us from the restrictions of flat photography. There are rules, of course, to stereo photography, but these rules should be used like all other rules — as a starting point for personal experiment and interpretation.

If realism is desired in three-dimensional pictures, it will be found that liberal use may be made of natural or "existing" light. Outdoors or indoors, light exists; with time exposures, and sometimes by judicious boosting with flash or floodlighting, such light can be made to show things quite as they are. But realism is not everything, and when fiction, flattery or fantasy are desired, the gamut of light effects may be added to the striking separation of planes possible with the stereo camera to produce effects unknown to photographers previously.

In between these extremes lies the work of the commercial portraitist and fashion photographer. If the stereo camera is being added to the regular studio complement of equipment, of course, nothing much beyond the camera itself is required. If, on the other hand, one is starting from scratch and plans to do much work on location, the compactness of the camera itself should be matched by simplicity in the accessory equipment.

Accessory Equipment

The two basic accessories on which it does not pay to skimp are the tripod and exposure meter. The best type of tripod is one which is slightly heavier than the lightest amateur models, and preferably one having a center-pole extension. It should be possible to lower it to within 24 inches of the floor; maximum height should be 6 feet at least, and 7 feet is better. Such tripods as the Quick-Set Elevator Hi-Boy and the Linhof channel aluminum model meet these specifications admirably, though similar units are available from other manufacturers.

Some of these "pole" tripods attain their lowest level by inverting the center column and hanging the camera upside down from the head. If this is done with the Stereo Realist, it may make for some confusion in later mounting of the pictures, since the picture which would normally be identified as the "right-eye" picture of a pair will now be the "left-eye" picture and vice versa. Unless a foolproof system and identification is worked out, it is better to avoid such setups.

Whatever tripod is used, it should have a good rigid pan-and-tilt head and a spirit level to assure exact sideways leveling of the camera. On the other hand, fore-and-aft tilting as well as slight changes in height and direction of the camera should be possible without having to adjust each tripod leg individually.

Any good professional exposure meter, such as the G.E., Weston, DeJur and Norwood, will be satisfactory for stereo. Incident-light attachments for these are available and will be particularly valuable when working in interiors by natural light, since with their aid it is possible to read much lower light levels than with reflected-light meters. Meters which are calibrated to show the highlight-to-shadow range of color films directly on the calculator dial are particularly valuable for this type of work.

1. A simple pose for the stereo fashion sample case. Stereo by John Meredith.

Lighting equipment for location work should be kept as light and portable as possible. Clamp-on light brackets are the best, used with or without some of the newer ultralightweight folding stands which are made of aluminum and reach heights of 9 or 10 feet. The heavy-duty Gator-Grip type of light clamp will be found more rugged than the bent-wire type, and only a little heavier in weight.

A fine all-around lamp for location work is the General Electric Photo Medium Beam PH375/34R4. It puts nearly twice as much light in the picture area as the well-known Reflector Photoflood and draws only three-quarters the current. Each lamp takes 3.3 amperes; 4 of these may be operated on a 15-ampere fuse, and a maximum of 8 may be used in a dwelling with a 30-ampere meter.

When a more powerful lamp is needed to "cut through" the basic illumination, the Reflector Photospot RSP-2 is used, but allowance must be made for its greater current drain, 4.4 amperes.

Always carry a supply of spare fuses, "just in case." And if you expect to use the maximum of 8 lamps possible in the average home, it is well to have two 50-foot extension cords, made of a wire no finer than No. 14, and having a 4-way outlet box on the end of each. By careful checking of the house circuits, it will be possible to connect each cable to a different branch so no one branch will have more than 15 amps. When full load is being drawn, it is well to shut off all other lights in the house and temporarily disconnect the refrigerator, whose motor may otherwise start at an inconvenient time and blow the meter fuse.

3. PORTRAIT. Stereo by John Meredith.

Often, a pose which would not be satisfactory in a flat picture will actually be the
best in stereo. Here, for example, the hands
are too close to the camera for ordinary
photography, and would simply look big. In
stereo, however, it is obvious that they are
nearer the camera, and added stereo relief is gained.

244

Where the background is neutral, the only stereo relief that appears is within the subject itself. Turning the model at an angle to the camera helps add some depth and avoid a "cardboard cut-out" effect. But it would be better either to have the hands in the foreground as in Figure 3, or a more definite background plane.

4. PORTRAIT. Stereo by John Meredith.

5. Application of the principle shown on the preceding two pages. Having the hand in the foreground increases the stereo illusion by adding another plane. Stereo photograph by John Meredith.

Proper balance of key and fill light is the secret of good portrait lighting. The main light is placed well above the subject, at a 45° angle; the fill light is placed near the camera. The main (or key) light is closer to the subject than the fill light.

General Lighting for Portraits

You might imagine that since roundness and modeling are inherent in the stereo process, all that would be needed for lighting a stereo would be sufficient light from a single source. It is not that simple; the basic principles of lighting should be followed with stereo just as with any other type of photograph. A single light will inevitably produce black shadows unless it is directly on the camera axis, and axis lighting, in turn, is a technique suitable only in special cases. At any rate, there is no reason to make the stereo illusion carry the entire burden of modeling; judicious use of light will add still greater depth to your pictures and make your results that much more striking.

Thus the basic light for a portrait is still the old reliable 45° main light plus axis fill light. The foundation of this method is the use of two lights of equal intensity, one placed closer to the subject than the other.

The nearer of the two lights is called the "key" light; it is placed to one side of the subject at approximately a 45° angle. The main error most beginnners make in the placement of the key light is to have it too low; for a seated figure it should be 6 to 7 feet high, and for a standing portrait, 8 to 9 feet. That is, the light should make a 45° angle with the subject vertically as well as horizontally. The key to the placement of this light is the shadow of the nose; it should fall at a 45° angle and just touch the corner of the *upper* lip. If it falls short of the upper lip, the lamp is too low; if it reaches the lower lip, the lamp is too high. If it falls on the cheek rather than on the lip, the lamp is too far to the side, while if it falls vertically below the nose, the lamp is too far forward. When this lamp is correctly placed, take a meter reading of the face, then shut off the light.

Now the second, or "fill" light is placed, near the camera and slightly above eye level of the subject. It should be just high enough to produce one small round catch light in each eye, just under the upper lid. If no catch light is seen (from the camera position!) the light is too high; if the catch light appears in the center of the eyes, the lamp is too low. Now take a meter reading; the light level in candles, or whatever your particular meter reads, should be from 1/3 to 1/2 that key light reading. If too bright, move the lamp away from the subject; if not bright enough, move it closer.

Now, turn your key light on again, and proceed with your effect lighting. This is the "frosting on the cake," and here you're on your own; any effect you may care for is built up with the extra lights — just make sure they land anywhere except on the front planes of the face. A light on the far side of the subject, facing the camera but not shining in the lens, can be used to put some highlights in the hair, or to throw a small kick across the shoulders and *side* of the face. Two "kickers" may be used

6. Cross-lighted outdoor stereos often need a flash to avoid black shadows. Flash was subdued here by using a handkerchief over the reflector, so that shadows are lightened but not washed out. Stereo by John Meredith.

in this manner, one on each side, to narrow a wide face; this works just as well in a stereo picture as in flat photography. Another light should be used in any case to illuminate the background; if this lamp is the only one available, the best trick may be to use a bare No. 2 Photoflood lamp, without reflector of any kind, and conceal it behind the subject's body. In this position it will not only illuminate the background, but will also throw a rim or halo of light around the subject's shoulders and hair. The effect is particularly striking with long-haired blonde women!

The difference between high-key and low-key lighting lies mainly in the amount of light placed on the background and the relationship between key and fill lights. If the 2:1 or 3:1 ratio given above is followed and the background lighted to the average of the two, a medium-key picture results. If the lighting ratio on the face is raised to nearly 1:1 and the background is equally bright, a high-key picture can be made by overexposing no more than 1/2 stop. Changing the key-fill ratio to about 4:1 and keeping the background down to fill-light intensity will produce a striking low-key effect, especially if underexposed about 1/2 stop.

Flash Lighting

Except for press photography it is poor practice to try to make a flash picture with just a single lamp on the camera. Basically, the same arrangement of light should be used with flash as with floodlighting; the flash-lamps should be placed in the same positions as the floods in the preceding setup. High, low and medium key pictures are made with flashlamps in the same manner as with floodlight.

When a number of flashlamps are used to make a single picture, they may be connected to a central battery such as the Heiland "Booster-Box" and fired at once, along with the lamp (if any) on the camera. Another method which does away with stringing wires about the room is to use the photoelectric "slave" units, in which each lamp is an independent unit with its own battery, and have a photoelectric cell which fires the lamp when tripped by the light of the main flash on the camera. Such units as the Heiland Fotoeye and some others work on this principle and are extremely convenient.

In general, whether using flash or floodlighting, the principle by which maximum depth is attained in stereo is to light as many planes as possible. Each plane will then stand out in the picture, not only by virtue of its distance from the camera, but also as a result of lighting contrast.

Posing the Subject

Maximum depth in stereo is attained by lighting several planes, so it is always well in planning a shot to arrange the subject and related objects in different planes to facilitate lighting each.

7. Clothes and the model should always figure more prominently than the props in a fashion picture. While this is an interesting stereo shot, it would not be used for fashion because props overpower clothes. Stereo by Nina Bourne.

8. For maximum modeling, a stereo picture should be lighted for roundness, just like a flat picture of the same subject. Here props are subordinate to clothes. Stereo courtesy of *Vogue*.

In a bridal portrait, the bouquet and train of the gown form the first plane. The bride herself forms the middle plane, and the background or background objects form one or more additional planes. A very effective bridal pose, for example, may be set up in front of a grand piano. The farthest plane, of course, is the wall behind the piano. The piano itself and objects on it form a second, nearer background plane. The bride is seated on the piano bench, at the forward corner, three-quarters to the camera (the bench having been turned at right angles to the piano). This, of course, is the major plane of the picture and the one on which the camera is focused. For a seated bridal picture, the hoop of the gown, if there is one, has been removed; the train is simply lifted and allowed to fall in a semicircle in front of her, and with the bouquet on her lap forms the nearest plane.

The face is lighted as already described. A single lamp, low and to one side, is used for the train, bouquet and as much of the floor as is visible; one or two lamps on separate stands are used to illuminate the piano; and, finally, a bare photoflood lamp concealed behind the piano lights the back wall and backlights all objects within its range. Another bare lamp, directly behind the subject, will illuminate her hair and rim-light veil and headdress. This lamp is kept from shining into the camera lens, by careful placement behind the subject's shoulders.

250

The same technique can be carried out with an equal number of flash-lamps, either wired to a Booster-Box or each in an individual Foto eye, a photoelectrically controlled slave unit. The same applies as well to strobe lights, which may likewise be a number of extensions from a single large power pack, or photoelectrically tripped slave strobes like the S/R Mono-strob to be used in connection with a single main flash at the camera.

Portraits in Daylight

For the utmost naturalness, portraits may be made outdoors. Usually direct sunlight should be avoided; if the sun filters through trees or foliage, however, it may be softened sufficiently to be satisfactory. In either case, the subject should face away from the sun so that the strong direct light will be used only for back light or rim lighting. It will often be found that white dresses will pick up and reflect enough light to the face so that artificial light will not be necessary. (See the bridal picture in Figure 13, Page 240.) Sometimes the picture may be taken on the shady side of the house or under a tree and reflections from near-by sunlit walls depended on for fill light. However, it is well to remember that when a subject is photographed in open shade, the main source of illumination is blue sky, and the picture will have a blue cast overall. The use of a haze or skylight filter will usually help somewhat to warm up such a picture, though the heavier Wratten 2B may sometimes be necessary.

9. A distant background makes stereo fashion shots even more impressive, especially when the subjects are in several planes. Stereo photograph by John Meredith.

10. Lingerie advertisement by John Meredith.

Compared to the picture on page 245, this one has a definite background to add another plane to the picture. In addition, the background objects themselves are in a receding plane. Therefore, the pose is arranged to come forward, adding another element of depth in the foreground. The cacti add a touch of fantasy.

It is necessary again to remember to have objects in both foreground and background for the most interesting depth effects. In ordinary circumstances it is not good to have any part of a stereo picture out of focus; however, an exception may sometimes be made here. You will find it is not very easy to get an out-of-focus background outdoors due to the very short focal length and great depth of field of the Stereo Realist lenses. However, by using the lens wide open, with a fast shutter speed to avoid overexposure, and focusing somewhat in front of the subject so as to place the subject at the far limit of the depth of field, it is possible to soften the background when it contains objects which might be disturbing.

Daylight portraits can be taken indoors as well, near windows or in greenhouses and conservatories. Again, however, the light tends to be bluish and the shadows extremely heavy; a single flash with a blue lamp on the camera may be used to open up the shadows in such cases. The skylight filter should be used to tone down excessive blueness in all such shots.

If a large number of both indoor and outdoor pictures is to be taken on a single assignment, it is well to carry with you both daylight and tungsten-type films and use each in the type of light for which it is intended. This will produce optimum color quality in all pictures. The ideal way to handle such assignments is to own *two* Stereo Realist cameras and to have one loaded with each type of film. It is not easy to unload a camera in the middle of the roll and later reload it in such a way as not to spoil a few pictures by overlapping. If one camera is all that is available when pictures are desired both indoors and outdoors in rapid succession, it is best to use tungsten-type film only and to employ the conversion filter when the film is used in daylight.

Fashion Photography

The type of fashion photography most often done with the stereo camera is what we might call the "photographic sample case." It offers the salesman the opportunity to carry his complete line in a little case of stereo slides, with a viewer, rather than bulky trunks full of samples. In addition, the clothing is shown on professional, big-city models, carefully posed, and lighted to bring out the best in color and design.

The majority of my clients prefer original photographs, and we find it necessary to shoot a large number of original slides of each model, having the model hold a single pose while the required number of shots is taken. We have averaged as many as 500 shots an hour, giving the model a chance to relax while the camera is being loaded. Using two cameras and reloading one while the other is in use will expedite matters still further.

Naturally, each costume is photographed from various angles. A full-length is always taken first, followed by close-ups of details such as belt, buttons, embroidery, appliqués, etc. It must be remembered that close-up

11. ACCESSORIES. Stereo courtesy of *Vogue*.

Close-up pictures of small objects usually have even greater stereo depth than more distant subjects, and only a small separation of planes is needed for striking results. Pictures of accessories such as these form a very large part of the fashion photographer's work and there is room for considerable imaginativeness in making them.

Where costume and accessories are the essence of the picture, the composition should be kept simple. In this case, a plain background was used, and the lighting was very soft and diffused. By so doing, all attention is focused on the costume and accessories with minimum distraction.

12. DRESS AND PUPPY. Stereo courtesy of *Vogue*.

slides should be mounted in the special close-up masks for easier viewing and projection.

Such slides are used not only by salesmen, but also in the main offices of the fashion houses, some of whom have installed projectors in their waiting rooms so that customers may inspect the line at their leisure.

The fashion world has also found stereo an outstanding way of presenting new clothes both for openings of collections and for important fashion shows. In the autumn of 1953, *Vogue* magazine presented a complete collection in stereo to a large fashion audience gathered in the auditorium of the Museum of Modern Art in New York. Photographs of the models were projected on a large screen and the guests were able to see minute details of the clothes not ordinarily visible in regular fashion shows. A few photographs from the *Vogue* collection appear in this book. These pictures, reproduced by courtesy of *Vogue*, represent the first major use of stereo pictures for fashion presentation.

The designer or manufacturer who presents his clothes in stereo can always be sure that important details of style, line, color and texture will not be overlooked. He needn't worry that a model may turn too quickly, that wrinkles may appear from nowhere, that makeup may run. All of that is avoided by careful posing in the studio or on location. And the pictures can be planned in advance to highlight a neckline, a flowing skirt, a smart jacket or perhaps just magnificent tailoring. And most important, each costume can be presented in a setting that complements it the best!

The regular fashion photographer who turns to stereo will find things a bit different at first. Since there is so much more to look at in stereo than in a flat picture, the stereo picture can generally be a good deal more simple and direct. Too many props, or surroundings too elaborate, will distract the eye from the clothes and the model. On the other hand, a plain white background, often used for simple, direct, flat pictures, may contribute nothing to the stereo fashion shot. Of course for figure photography, a plain white background is often the most suitable; but figure photography is quite a different thing from fashion work.

In planning stereo fashion pictures you must always remember that they have an inherent reality found in no other pictorial recreation. The setting, then, must contribute to that reality. Remember, too, that the sole purpose of the picture is to make someone want to wear the costume herself. In short, fashion pictures are intended to sell clothes! The stereo fashion picture makes clothes more desirable because they "look so real," and a woman can picture herself in them much more readily than she can from looking at a flat picture.

Finding the right models is of paramount importance in fashion work. See to it that the girl complements the clothes: there is no sense, for instance, in weighing down a fragile, petite, pale blonde in heavy, horse-blanket tweeds. See to it also that the clothes are perfectly fitted to the model. If it is impossible to alter the clothes for the model, you can fit them yourself in a jiffy with spring-clip clothespins. Be sure that the clothespins are well out of sight.

It is always well to point out to the client in advance that the color of the costume may look a little bit different in the color stereo transparency. Films do not react exactly the same as the eye to many artificial dyes and pigments, and it is important to let the client expect this from the beginning so that there are no misunderstandings later on. Most people are perfectly satisfied with modern color film renderings, but there are occasional dyes that will not reproduce on film as the eye sees them. Sometimes a test will indicate that a change in lighting or filtering can correct this; most often there is little you can do about it.

Studio Pictures

The busy photographer will have to do a great deal of work in the studio, since going on location takes a lot of extra time and is limited by weather conditions. Props and studio backgrounds should be clean and without blemishes: furniture scratches and dirty walls will leave their telltale mark on the finished picture. Large sheets of movable wall board that can be repainted and pushed around at various angles are a basic studio requirement. Drapes, furniture, rugs, trapezes, animals — anything that space, finances and imagination dictate — can be used for props. If your props are frankly fake, use them effectively. Fashion photography has never been known for reticence! Color is also extremely important and should be chosen to complement the clothes. Usually, the fewer colors the better. If there is any splashy contrast, let it be in the clothes themselves.

Lighting in the studio is much the same for stereo as it is for flat pictures. Color film has a limited range, and the shadows should always be brought up to the general level of illumination — unless, of course, you specifically want to make heavy shadows a part of the composition. Lighting cables and lamp stands must not be allowed to obtrude on the picture area; it is less trouble to keep them out than to mask them from the finished picture.

Location Pictures

Fashion assignments often specify a location: a town house, a night club, a yacht basin, a mountain top or an airport. Even without an assignment, you may feel that some clothes cry out for a natural setting. Weather is your first problem, and permissions your second. In many public places you need permission to set up a tripod and camera equipment; always be sure that you are allowed to take pictures before you arrive with all your traps and models. I can make no better weather recommendation than to suggest that you locate someplace with a low annual rainfall! I find California very cooperative in this respect.

Wherever you are, always keep your eye out for likely location backgrounds — good-looking buildings or houses, a pleasant country lane, a good beach — any place that's pictorially interesting. Train yourself to look for locations wherever you go. You never know when they might come in handy. And most people don't know what they have in their own neighborhoods unless they have a strong curiosity and good habits of observation. It is a good idea to keep your camera with you wherever you go, to make stereo records of interesting locations. A stereo file of good locations can be a lifesaver when a client is looking for new and different backgrounds for special lines of clothes.

In fashion photography outdoors, it is generally best to pose the model near some detail of the background. A whole house or a whole vista in the picture will overwhelm the model unless she is very close to the camera. Simplicity is just as important in outdoor stereo fashion as it is in studio work.

Direct sunlight is very hard for even the most experienced models to work in, so try to use side light or back light whenever you can. You can fill in the shadows with flash or with large reflectors. Large sheets of newspaper will serve for makeshift reflectors if you don't want to carry a lot of equipment around.

A thought to bear in mind is that regardless of where you live or work you have a great variety of natural lighting effects. Notice the lighting at different times of the day and different seasons of the year. Study it and remember it. There will be times when you want a special lighting

258

effect, and it is good to know where and when you can find it. Morning light, midday light, late afternoon sunlight all have different effects and different moods, any of which might be just right for a special picture. Or perhaps you will need to know when the sun will hit a certain part of a building or a certain side of a street that you have picked out for a background. Always be on the lookout for lighting effects that will be useful.

Stereo Fashion Markets

Stereo is growing constantly in the fashion business, and an enterprising photographer will find lots to keep him busy. This sort of work need not be limited to the big fashion centers, either. Department stores and specialty shops all over the country are interested in stimulating promotions, and they should not be overlooked by photographers outside of the fashion centers. Very often a stereo photographer in a small or medium-sized city can combine fashion with other commercial work — or fashion, portraiture, wedding and other general photography. Make up your own sample case of Stereo Realist pictures and let it be your own salesman.

1. The part is often greater than the whole, and a few columns produce a better picture than the entire temple. Stereo taken near Luxor, Egypt, by Julien Bryan.

9. Traveling With a Stereo Camera

JULIEN BRYAN

We have all seen travel pictures made by beginners, with some towering structure like the Acropolis or the Eiffel Tower far in the distance "to get it all in." Such pictures are always disappointing, but particularly so in stereo, where the resulting lack of depth is puzzling to those who believe that shooting with twin lenses should automatically produce full, round pictures no matter what the subject. Skilled photographers have long since learned the trick of simulating depth in an ordinary photograph by including some object in the foreground of the picture; this establishes an auxiliary plane of reference by which the distance of farther objects may be visually estimated. Beginners in stereo have a tendency to forget this simple expedient, in the belief that the 3-D photography will supply the missing depth element.

Actually, with our eyes set about 63mm apart, we see little depth in objects more than about 30 feet away. For distant objects we get our impression of depth by visual comparison with closer objects. When these closer objects are omitted in a photograph, the result is disastrous; the stereo effect is reduced to nothing.

In travel photography, where many subjects are comprised of large and historic structures, it is essential to include some foreground object if the entire structure is also to be shown. When this is not possible, it is wise to consider the parts of a building as more important than the whole. Take, for example, the Egyptian Temple, near Luxor (Fig. 1). The temptation to the beginner would be to get back about 100 feet and take the entire building in one shot. The result would be just about as flat as if it were taken with an ordinary camera. Look at Figure 1 again. The first column is only 5 feet from the camera; the great depth of field of the short-focus Stereo Realist lenses makes it sharp and clear. The next column is 10 feet away, the next 15, the next 20, etc. The man in the dark Egyptian gown is about 30 feet away. The result in stereo is a

2. Another view of the same temple, showing more detail. The entire structure is of uniform color, and depth is obtained entirely by stereoscopy without assistance from cross lighting or color contrast. Stereo by Julien Bryan.

sharp separation of planes, and the picture is a perfect example of good stereo.

But, you say, you want to get a picture of the entire temple, not just a few columns. You can do it, of course, and the method is simple. Just be sure to have some object in the foreground to establish at least one more plane. Take Figure 2, for example—a longer shot of the same temple, this time framed in an arch in the foreground to strengthen the feeling of depth and space.

The same thing applies not only to distant objects but to close-ups having little depth within the subject itself—for example, the close-ups of Egyptian hieroglyphs, etched deeply into the hard stone. With the camera distance of 6 feet needed to include the entire drawing the engravings will be noticeable but not very striking. What to do? In this case, I simply included fragments of temple columns in the close foreground and in the background to establish a plane of reference, with a touch of blue sky for the infinity plane. This way the picture is much more striking in depth. Figure 8 shows the results.

Foreground objects can often be people. In fact, they usually are, even in beginner's pictures. The crucial question is—who are the people? The answer makes the difference between the beginner and the experienced travel photographer. Including your wife in every shot (or the pretty girl you met on the boat), while understandable, adds nothing to the picture.

262

The danger is that your people will take up 90 per cent of the picture area, and the country you came thousands of miles to see will be completely obscured. Even if this is not the case, the picture will be much better if the people in the picture *belong* there. It is wiser to photograph Egyptians in Egypt, Greeks in Greece, and Turks in Turkey. Don't, though, simply ask people to pose for you—look for people going about their daily lives as usual.

Keep your people natural and photograph them at work or play or worship (though you have to be careful of local religious restrictions in the latter case). If they are farmers, picture them at the plow. They'll probably mug at the camera when you first start taking pictures, but they're like people everywhere—their work is important and they'll return to it after a short while. That's the time to take your pictures. And the farmer at his plow, the water-drawer with his oxen, the carpenter sawing, hammering or planing. . . . these are the real pictures, the ones that will keep the true flavor of the places you have visited.

Take the picture of two farmers hoeing (Fig. 3). Here the men really are hoeing, not posing for a picture. Again we have the foreground and background principle; in the middle distance loom the two great Colossi of Memnon, and in the background the great tan cliffs and the bluest of blue skies. You have them all in one picture, the stereo clearly setting one apart from the other. And with this separation of objects and

3. Farmers hoeing, with Colossi of Memnon in the background. People, at home or abroad, make the best pictures when photographed pursuing their normal activities, not simply posing for a picture. Stereo by Julien Bryan.

planes we are able to concentrate more on details—the hard tough skin of the feet of the youth on the left, the unlaced shoes of the man on the right.

Color adds the finishing touch to such a picture; one man in white, another with a black coat, the green texture of sprouting grain leading into the pinkish tan cliffs in the background. For the same reason, Figure 4, Page 234, is one of my favorite Egyptian shots, because in a single picture of date palms and an irrigation ditch we have the lush greenness of the Nile valley and the dryness of the lifeless desert—the starkly visual contrast between life and death.

Don't be afraid of movement and action. Even though it is a little blurred, the camel shown in Figure 4 is better with the whip not fully stopped in the air than if the picture had been taken at 1/1000 second. It denotes action and movement and avoids the danger, occasionally encountered in stereo, of having people appear like wax dummies.

Always carry a tripod or some kind of clamp-on camera support. A time exposure will often solve the problem of shooting interiors when no other source of light is available or permitted. I made several beautiful interiors in an ancient Egyptian temple with exposures of 1 or 2 seconds. You can do the same—for example, in churches with stained glass windows and worshippers in the foreground.

Simplicity of color makes more effective pictures. At Luxor, two colors were especially good: the pinkish tan limestone and the blue sky. Three

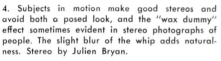

4. Subjects in motion make good stereos and avoid both a posed look, and the "wax dummy" effect sometimes evident in stereo photographs of people. The slight blur of the whip adds naturalness. Stereo by Julien Bryan.

5. Greek temple columns. The eroded details are nearly invisible in a flat picture, but stand out in this stereo. A slight underexposure was necessary for contrast in the original color film. Stereo by Julien Bryan.

colors are not too many if they harmonize—the pinkish tan stone, the green of growing things and the blue sky. When your people are dressed in black or white, as they usually are in Egypt, they will stand out nicely against such a background. Yet, on the other hand, color contrast is not always essential in stereo—see Figure 2, which has no color contrast at all, just a succession of pinkish tan limestone archways ending in the limestone cliff as a background. Such a scene provides an excellent background for natives in colorful dress, yet in stereo it can stand entirely alone, with no other colors present.

A row of trees disappearing into the background on a long straight road is always good in stereo, but such pictures can still be strengthened with a foreground object. I made such a picture in Iran—just such a road with a row of acacia trees on each side. Close to the camera was a small boy leading a herd of goats, actually unposed and moving down the road. A few additional men and animals appear in the background, more than 50 feet away. See Figure 7 for the final result.

The foreground frame, so popular in salon photography, has a place in 3-D travel pictures too. Figure 6 shows one of the most famous religious edifices in the world, the Mosque of St. Sophia in Istanbul. This would be a good flat picture, although two-dimensional without any foreground; but it is a lot better in stereo, with the dark, overhanging frame of close-up branches at the top of the picture. This is a particularly good example of stereo composition: notice the graceful progression from

the foreground frame of the tree branches to the silhouetted figures in the middle foreground, thence to a few small trees in the middle distance, and finally to the mosque itself, photographed so that the minarets appear of different heights for variety in outline.

Pictures in Series

The picture of the mosque suggests an important fact, one which is even more important in travel stories. It is seldom that a single picture can tell all about any place or any building, no matter how good the picture. This mosque is a story in itself, and it always pays to take many pictures of such a subject. To the Turks this mosque is their religion and their life. It is a vital and stirring thing to them, and you should attempt to get this feeling into your pictures. Above all, you must have *people* in your picture. Find out from your guide or host if picture taking is permitted in or around the mosque. Then work very quietly, quickly and unobtrusively.

Let's say, for example, that you are in the Blue Mosque and it is Friday, the Holy Day. Take several shots of the great building first; next a medium shot of crowds entering the courtyard; then several close-ups of Moslems washing themselves at the fountain in the courtyard; a medium shot again when the worshippers take off their shoes (and keep on their hats) as they enter the mosque; then a final shot, a time exposure, of worship-

266

pers in the mosque itself. This may not always be possible in all Moslem countries, but we were able to do it in Turkey.

So you have taken ten or a dozen shots on this very simple story of the mosque and the Moslem worshippers. You may feel at the time that you are wasting film, that one or two shots would be all you could possibly want on this subject. You will find that you feel differently when you get home; you will be proud to have a connected story of the mosque and the Turkish religion, whereas if you simply make one shot, you will find yourself wishing you had made more. It would be a good story in two dimensions; in three, it will be priceless.

Just a word in passing to those who may wish to sell their pictures: it is always easier to sell a series on one subject than a number of disconnected shots.

Close-ups Are Always Good in Stereo

Figure 5, Page 235, was taken near Antioch, in Turkey. It is simply an extreme close-up of red peppers, at about 3½ or 4 feet. This is about the closest limit of view of the Stereo Realist without special attachments, but many equally striking close-ups can be made at this distance. This one is particularly fascinating because of the color contrast, which would be lost at a greater distance. We stopped the car and stayed half an hour to get three or four pepper shots, simply because the color was so brilliant.

8. Close-ups of carvings need the stereo camera for best rendition of small details. At the 6-foot distance of this picture, much detail would be lost in a flat picture, but the combined effect of stereoscopy and cross lighting preserves the carvings. Stereo by Julien Bryan.

The Stereo camera is rapidly becoming an important tool in archaeological research, as well as in other scientific fields. The picture above is not only interesting pictorially, but as a document of the place and the civilization it represents.

No expedition, no vacation jaunt is complete if the pictures only show buildings, streets and scenery. The essence of travel is the introduction to new people, and their pictures are a vital part of the record of the trip.

9. Native and child in Ispahan, Iran. While this is a posed picture, it is not stiff, and shows not only the faces and dress of the native people, but some small details of the peasant home as well. Stereo by Julien Bryan.

10. Never be satisfied with just a long shot showing a building as a whole. Details are equally important. Compare this close-up of the Mosque of St. Sophia with the long shot (Fig. 6). Both are needed if we want a complete picture. Stereo by Julien Bryan.

Figure 9 comes from a small village near Ispahan in Iran. It is an excellent close-up of the baby, about 5 feet from the camera, and of the grandfather, about 6 feet away. In the background can be seen a lesser but equally important detail—the cracks in the mud walls of the home.

Even underexposed shots look better in stereo—see for example the foreground columns of the Greek temple in Figure 5; in a flat picture they would have no modeling at all, but in stereo they stand out strikingly in the sunlight, and with the bas-relief carving in the shadows they bring back the 2,500-year-old glory that was Greece.

Travel Photography in General

There are some rules which apply to travel photography no matter what kind of camera you use.

RULE No. 1:   Don't go on a trip with brand-new, untried equipment. Get your Stereo Realist weeks or months before you are ready to go abroad, and practice with it at home. Make your mistakes on unimportant subjects at home; on your trip, every shot counts.

RULE No. 2:   Have an intelligent plan for the trip and for the pictures you intend to take. Whether you are going to Mexico, Europe or the Far East, if you haven't been there before, become familiar with the places before you go. Read about them, visit museums, rent 16mm movies. Then set up a plan for your travels, allow plenty of time for picture taking at

270

the places which interest you most, but leave gaps for the unexpected. Too tight a schedule spoils the fun.

You cannot, of course, photograph everything you see on a trip unless you have unlimited means, time and film. So the thing to do is to establish a story line. What interests you in Greece, for example? Do you wish to emphasize history, archaeology, agriculture, theater, city life, folk dances, music, education? All are interesting, but make one of them your main theme; other shots can be related to it. Write down a simple story outline before you arrive—follow it as carefully as you can when you get there.

For example, on a recent trip to Turkey I made one short series on American aid in road building. It was very simple, but 20 shots on a single theme are more interesting than 100 disconnected snapshots of Turkish countryside. We began with a map of Turkey showing the paucity of roads, went on to a close-up of the map showing the new 400-mile link between Istanbul and Ankara, and followed with a series of 18 simple pictures, starting with the old bad road, close-ups of young Turkish engineers at work and in conference with American advisers, more shots of the Turkish engineers using a transit, long shots of American bulldozers at work, medium shots of the sheepsfoot tamper and roller, close-ups of a Turkish mechanic repairing a bulldozer.

With such a plan or outline, we give meaning to what would otherwise be disconnected shots, we make sure in advance that no important part

11. Turkish natives sifting wheat. This was an incidental shot taken during the making of a series on another subject. Often such sidelights fit into another story and while traveling it is always well to grasp such opportunities for extra shots. Stereo by Julien Bryan.

12. Dutch Canal. It is in just such shots as this that the charm of Old World architecture is most evident. Again, the rail in the foreground helps separate planes. Stereo by Willem L. Berssenbrugge.

of the story will be omitted, and we budget our film allotment; in this case, for instance, one 20-exposure roll covered the entire story.

RULE NO. 3: Exposure is important, but be sure your exposure meter is working right for you. If your meter gives you a reading outdoors in bright sunlight of 1/50 second at f/6.3 for color film, it is probably right, but if you get overexposed pictures with it, then it is not working in conjunction with your particular camera. It is best to run a series of tests, shooting at the meter setting, then ½ stop above and below. If the meter setting is the one that gives you the best picture, fine; if it is one of the others, then you can make it a rule to give ½ stop more (or less, as the case may be) whenever you are using *that* meter with *that* particular camera. Repeat this check every few months; even the best meters and the best cameras will vary somewhat in their calibration with use, particularly if roughly handled.

At high altitudes or in the tropics, you will often get exposure readings as high as 1/100 second at f/11 for color film. The manufacturer of the film warns that such readings should be viewed with suspicion, and will often lead to underexposure; on the other hand, some of my best shots in Egypt and Jordan were made at such exposures. When in doubt under such circumstances, you may use your judgment, but always make one shot at the meter setting too; it will be instructive later to compare your judgment with that of a good exposure meter!

RULE NO. 4: Ask questions before you shoot. Many countries have restricted areas in which photography is not permitted, even casual snap-shooting. You will avoid many embarrassing incidents—and possibly a night in the local lock-up—if you make it a point to inquire of the authorities when you arrive as to regulations concerning picture making. Very often you will find that such circumspection will bring you permission to photograph places ordinarily forbidden, even to natives.

In this connection, it also pays to inquire about customs regulations. Some countries do not permit mailing undeveloped films out of the country; they must be developed locally and censored. In such a case, make sure there is a Kodak processing station before shooting Kodachrome. Otherwise, the censors will develop your Kodachrome in a black-and-white developer and ruin it utterly.

When there is no Kodachrome processing station locally, and undeveloped film cannot be taken from the country, your cue is to locate some local brand of color film which can be processed where you are. Some of the European color films produce excellent pictures, others mediocre, but anything is better than having your Kodachrome ruined and no pictures to show at all.

There are few places now, however, where Kodachrome processing stations do not exist; consult the list packed with the films.

14. Another receding road picture, this one without a foreground object for reference. Compare this shot with the one having a foreground object (Fig. 7). Tamiami Trail, Florida. Stereo by Henry M. Lester.

15. Reflections in water make fascinating stereo subjects, emphasizing the fact that a reflection lies as far behind the mirror as the subject is in front of it. Mirror Lake, Yosemite. Stereo by P. E. Springer.

274

RULE No. 5: Check customs regulations. Before you leave home, find out how many cameras and how much film you are permitted to take to every country you plan to visit. Ignorance of the law is no defense at home *or* abroad, although many tourists try to plead otherwise.

RULE No. 6: Protect your equipment. It is always a good idea to insure your camera equipment. In any case, keep a record of all serial numbers and special identification, in case of loss.

Pack your equipment in suitable carrying cases or gadget bags sturdy enough to withstand the hazards of travel. Take along a camel's-hair brush and a good supply of lens tissue to keep camera and lenses clean. If you are traveling in hot, humid climates, you can put a small cloth bag of silica gel or some other desiccant in your carrying case to keep the equipment from getting moist and mildewed. A good carrying case for the tropics can be made out of a fiberglass-insulated plastic bag used to keep food cold on picnics. These bags zip tightly closed and are also very good for protecting film from the rigors of high temperature and dampness. If, on the other hand, you are traveling in cold climates, the only important thing is to have your camera conditioned in advance for cold weather.

In any case, be sure that you have everything you need in good working order before you leave on any trip. If you take good care of your equipment while you are traveling, you'll be entirely free for the fun and fascination of making pictures. The journey you bring home in stereo will be worth every bit of the effort you put into it.

1. Little Poker Player. Not a trick shot at all,
but depends on incongruity for interest.

10. Stereolusions

TOMMY THOMAS

Creative or trick effects with a Realist camera are almost limitless, depending upon your imagination and the accessory apparatus you work with. By beginning with the simpler "illusions in stereo" and gradually working up to the more complicated effects, it is easy to build up a working knowledge of the basic principles of this branch of 3-D photography — principles that you can apply continuously thereafter to derive more pleasure from your stereo camera. Since this is a relatively new and uncharted field, it will be necessary for you to build a certain amount of your own apparatus to be used in conjunction with your Realist. But then, that's part of the enjoyment of making your own "Stereolusions."

It's possible to take some of these photographs with a minimum of accessory equipment. In fact, that's the way to get started. Take the photograph of the Little Poker Player (Fig. 1), for instance. It's certainly not a trick shot — yet the incongruity of seeing a little mongrel dog playing cards (with five aces!) makes for a wonderful photo. The theme to use when photographing animals is to think of a human situation and then coax the animal to fit into it. And dress him up to fit the part. It takes a certain amount of preparation and a great deal of time, but the end result will be worth it.

Remember to "dress up" your photos; it's important. A proper regard for showmanship will often transform a simple idea into something quite arresting. A good example of this is the Head of Barbara Salad stereo (Fig. 17). It was set up by having the young lady sit under an old card table and stick her head up through a hole cut in the top, just large enough for her head. The tablecloth background also had a hole in it, as did the wooden salad plate. This latter hole, by the way, was made just large enough to accommodate the young lady's neck, the plate being

---

The title "Stereolusions" is a registered trademark. Stereo Realist slides such as illustrated in this chapter may be obtained from Dimensional Enterprises, Prudential Building, 4063 Radford Avenue, Studio City, California.

further cut directly in half to permit appropriate assembly. The colorful salad serves double duty in hiding the deception of the plate and adding that extra touch that makes for a good "Stereolusion."

Using a Black Background

One of the most continually useful items in special-effect photography is the black background. When you photograph something black you're not really photographing anything at all. Remember this, it's very important: *dead black will not register on your film; therefore you can re-expose that portion of film to succeeding images.*

There are various types of black backgrounds available. The professional photographer will very likely have a standard black velvet drop that is just about perfect for this purpose. The amateur can approach this ideal fairly closely by taking an old wool blanket of sufficient proportions and having it dyed black at the neighborhood cleaner's (a G. I. blanket works fine). Of course, just to get started, there's a way you can get around needing anything special at all: take your photos outdoors at night. Flashbulb lighting fades out quickly into blackness as the distance behind the subject increases, so just pick out a spot where there is nothing in the background for the first 50 feet or so and use *that* as your black background.

An easy *idea* to start with is making one person into "twins" (Fig. 2). With the aid of one of the black backgrounds, taking the stereo is sim-

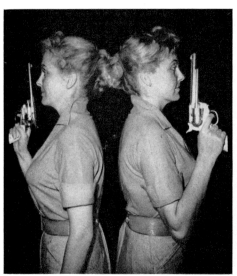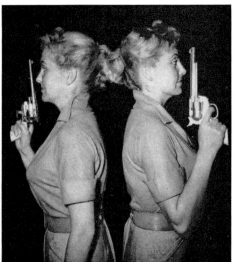

2. "Duel" Personality. A simple double exposure against a black background.

278

3. White string fastened with two small bits of tape divides view finder in halves for double-exposure shooting.

plicity itself. The procedure goes something like this: Line up your subject so that she takes up room on only one-half of your area as seen through the camera view finder. This is easy if a white string is taped vertically directly across the front of the Realist finder (Fig. 3). Be sure that the black background is in the *entire* scene, of course. Take the photo in your regular manner. *After taking this first photo, recock your shutter, but do not advance the film.* Now take the second portion of the photo by having your model pose on the other side of the vertical string, as seen in the view finder — still with your black background in place. Take this photo. Now you can advance the film. That's all there is to it. Don't forget to experiment with having your model at different distances away from the camera (Fig. 4). And try "overlapping" that center line as you gain in practice — that's where the *Image-Locator* (to be described further on) will come in handy.

4. More "Twins"—Jean Jack of Shipstad's and Johnson's Ice Follies.

279

5. FAIRYLAND EXPRESS—Illustrating the "floating power" of a black background.

Another use for your black background is in the taking of subjects that "float." The Fairyland Express stereo (Fig. 5) is a good illustration of this. A black background was hung on the wall of the little girl's nursery, a brightly decorated sofa cushion was supported by a box covered with black cloth. Four hydrogen-filled balloons were added to explain the floating power of the cushion, and then the little girl was properly posed and photographed on her Magic Pillow for the result you see here.

Cᴇʟʟᴏᴘʜᴀɴᴇ Exᴘᴏsᴜʀᴇ-Fᴀᴄᴛᴏʀ Cʜᴀʀᴛ

Color Cellophane	No. of Sheets Over Flashlamp	Open Up Your Camera Lenses
Yellow	3	1 full stop
Red	2	2 full stops
Blue	2	3 full stops

Another effective way of using a black background is in connection with colored lighting. Through multiple exposure, using colored cellophane in front of some of your flashbulbs (Fig. 6) you can obtain intriguing effects not otherwise possible (Fig. 8, Page 237). This combination of normal and colored images is an easy variation of the technique described earlier for taking multiple images — "twins." The only difference is in the judicious use of colored cellophane in front of your flashlamps for some

6. The Image-Locator Device fastened over the lenses of the Stereo Realist camera. Outlines of subject to be located have been marked on the plastic in white for better visibility in this photo, but a red or black crayon will usually be used.

of the exposures. The use of cellophane in front of a flashlamp naturally cuts down on the light output, so you must open up your lenses a corresponding amount to make up the difference. The Cellophane Exposure-Factor Chart on the previous page suggests how to do this.

Image-Locator Device

Much special-effect work is based upon multiple exposures on the same film, as you have noticed. Therefore, it is distinctly to your advantage to have a method of temporarily registering these various exposures *in front of the view finder*. The piece of apparatus known as the *Image-Locator* will do just that. It is a piece of clear plastic attached in front of the view finder and serves as a surface for outlining the images being photographed. This is accomplished by mounting the camera on a tripod with the plastic *Image-Locator* in place, aiming at your subject, and then using a red grease pencil to outline the subject on the plastic as you view it through the view finder (Fig. 6). From then on — until it is rubbed off — this outline, plus a record of carefully measured camera-to-subject distances, will permit you to line up any succeeding exposures (on that same film, of course) with almost mathematical exactness.

To get personal a moment, I'd like to mention that this *Image-Locator* of mine has been my greatest single "secret weapon" in making "Stereo-lusions." It also explains why the Realist camera, with its dead-center, non-parallax view finder, is my choice for the stereo camera that makes trick photography in stereo not only possible, but practical as well.

Making the *Image-Locator* is relatively simple. You'll need a set of Realist sunshades, a piece of clear plastic (⅜ inches thick, 2¼ inches wide,

7. The two separate exposures which combined to make the picture on the next page. (Top) the "portrait" against a black background. (Bottom) the girl and picture frame with inside of frame blacked out.

6 inches long), some machine screws, washers, and wing nuts, plus some simple shop tools necessary to work the plastic. Start off by mounting the sunshades on your Realist — then put the camera face down on the piece of plastic so that you can trace around the sunshade rims to mark the exact size and location of the necessary holes. Careful consultation of the photo (Fig. 6) and the diagram-sketch (Fig. 8) should enable you to finish the apparatus as illustrated.

It's easy to see how useful the *Image-Locator* would be in making the previously described black-background, multiple-image stereos. Now you're prepared to go on with more elaborate ideas.

The photograph of Snoka with a stereo portrait of herself (Fig. 9) makes a good representation of a basic idea that can be used in many ways. Here's how it was accomplished:

1. The first exposure was taken in a normal manner, the only thing special being the black velveteen cloth in the picture frame. The camera was on a tripod, and the *Image-Locator* was on the camera. After the exposure, the outline of the black cloth inside the picture frame was drawn upon the plastic surface of the *Image-Locator* (while looking at it through the view finder). The exact distance from the camera to the center of the picture frame was measured. The camera shutter was recocked, but the film was not advanced (Fig. 7 top).

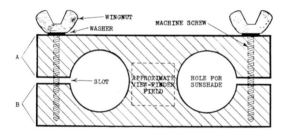

8. Sketch of the Image-Locator Device. It is made of thick transparent plastic, such as Lucite or Plexiglass.

2. The second exposure was taken outdoors at night, the darkness serving as a large black backdrop. Snoka was posed with black velvet covering all except her face. The camera — still on the tripod but in a new location now — was aimed and focused so that the face was exactly centered in the previously drawn red outline on the *Image-Locator* as seen through the view finder. The distance was measured to be sure that the camera-to-face distance was exactly the same as the previously measured camera-to-frame distance (Fig. 7 bottom).

3. These two exposures, one "over" the other, made up the completed stereo (Fig. 9).

The Variable-Interocular Apparatus

To continue still further into the realm of stereo magic it is necessary to have some more apparatus. An entirely new field is opened up when you are able to take "dual" exposures in stereo. A "dual" exposure occurs when the stereo camera is used in conjunction with a sliding-bar device, thus enabling you to control the stereo interocular (distance between the lenses) by taking the left and right pictures separately — moving the camera in between exposures. There are various commercial versions of these sliding-bar devices on the market, but it's easy to construct your own. The *Variable-Interocular* apparatus that I use is a bit more elaborate than you'll need, so it is suggested that you build one conveniently smaller. Three views of the construction of the Variable-Interocular Device and sliding base are shown in Figure 11 for your guidance.

The length of the apparatus determines the range of your interocular possibilities — from absolutely zero interocular to as far apart as you wish (12 inches is suggested as sufficient). You'll need a set of Realist sunshades and a single lens cap (to fit over one of the sunshades at a time) to complete your equipment. Basically, this is how a "dual" exposure works. Determine the interocular that you are going to use (this is explained in a special chart (Page 285). Slide your camera to the "0" point on the apparatus (Fig. 11 lower left) and look through the view finder to line up your subject. Slide the camera over so that the left marker (A) is where you want it. Cap the right lens with the lens cap and take the first part of the stereo "dual" photograph. Recock the camera shutter, but don't advance the film. Then slide the camera over so that the right marker (B) is where you want it. Cap the left lens and take the second part of the photograph. Now advance the film. *There must not be any movement of your subject during the time the two exposures are made — this is very important.*

Now you're prepared for some serious stereography. This apparatus is perfect for taking hypo-stereo (narrow-interocular) photos of small subjects close up. With the aid of the proper auxiliary lenses (see a standard photo data book or ask your dealer), you can apply the information given in the chart (Page 285) to make any number of distortionless close-up stereos. The Just Landed stereo (Fig. 10) of the butterfly resting on the flower is a good example of what can be accomplished. Despite the realistic appearance of the finished result (especially effective in the original full-color Realist stereo with a sky-blue background), this is an

10. JUST LANDED. Close-up stereo taken with the Variable Interocular apparatus, 1-inch interocular separation between right and left-eye views.

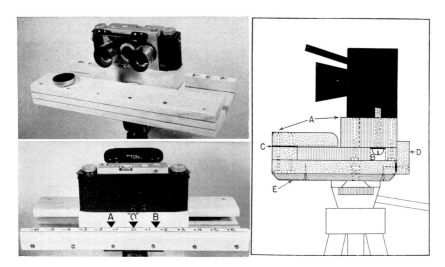

11. Three views of the sliding base, Variable-Interocular Device.

(Above left): Front view of sliding base with camera mounted.

(Lower left): Rear view of device showing calibration scale and pointers.

(Right): Cross-sectional diagram showing construction of the unit. Camera is fastened to block by means of long screw "B." The scale is fastened at "D," and plate "E" on bottom of the entire gadget has a ¼"-20 threaded hole to fasten it to a tripod head.

indoor photo made with a dead butterfly. This was essential, of course, because there couldn't be any movement between the two "dual" exposures.

INTEROCULAR SEPARATION FOR CLOSE-UP PHOTOGRAPHY

Lens-to-Subject Distance	Total Lens Separation	Scale Position For Pointer "A"	Scale Position For Pointer "B"	*Diopter Lens
30"	2.0"	− 1.0"	+ 1.0"	1
27"	1.8"	− 0.9"	+ 0.9"	1
24"	1.6"	− 0.8"	+ 0.8"	1
21"	1.4"	− 0.7"	+ 0.7"	1
18"	1.2"	− 0.6"	+ 0.6"	2
15"	1.0"	− 0.5"	+ 0.5"	2
12"	0.8"	− 0.4"	+ 0.4"	3
9"	0.6"	− 0.3"	+ 0.3"	4
6"	0.4"	− 0.2"	+ 0.2"	6

*Use Series V Portra Lenses: +1, +2 or+3 (Eastman Kodak Company), singly or in combination to get the total power desired. Full information regarding the proper distance settings of your camera is supplied with the auxiliary lenses.

12. Three-Dimensional Painting. The Variable-Interocular Device was used to move the girl forward into the plane of the painting.

Since you have the apparatus, you can experiment with hyper-stereo (wide interocular) too, for those stereos of distant subjects (such as many scenics) which are too far away to give satisfactory depth. Follow the previously described routine exactly, but without Portra Lenses. Compare a "regular" stereo photo with the same scene taken with 6-, 9- or 12-inch interoculars. *Take special care that the Variable-Interocular device is absolutely level before shooting. Don't photograph moving objects.*

To get back to our special effects, we have the Primary Colors stereo (Page 237), a combination result that involves many of the techniques which have already been described. Stated briefly, the photo was taken by mounting the camera on the *Variable-Interocular* apparatus and taking a quadruple exposure against a black background, starting with the blue image at the left and ending up with the full-color image at the right. (The camera was pushed an appropriate distance to the right between successive exposures.) DATA: The *Image-Locator* device was used on the camera to determine initially how far to move the camera between exposures for the desired effect. A single flashbulb off to the left (directly in front of the model) was used for the colored images, with appropriately colored cellophane used in front of the flashbulb each time. Two flashbulbs were used on the last full-color exposure; the second lamp was added high and off to the right to balance the shadows of the first lamp. The girl remained absolutely motionless during the entire two minutes consumed while the four separate exposures were made – this, perhaps, being the greatest trick of all!

286

Well, if that isn't enough for you, let's get really complicated this time with the Three-Dimensional Painting stereo (Fig. 12). Repeating the photo yourself and solving the problems involved is well worth serious effort, not only because you will find the finished stereo photo a worthy addition to your collection, but also because of the practice in control that it will give. The entire finished stereo represents a double-exposure idea, where the second exposure is also a "dual" exposure. It was made in this manner: First the scene of the man at the easel was taken. It's a straight photo with the easel board painted a dull black as shown, even where the girl is to be located in the finished stereo. This black area was outlined on the *Image-Locator* device before the camera (mounted on a tripod, of course) was moved to a new location, where the girl was posed in front of a large black background. In order to reduce her size enough so that she would fit on the easel, she was located 13 feet away from the camera. It was necessary to photograph the girl with a wide interocular (equivalent, in this instance, to a stereo camera having lenses 6¼ inches apart) in order to bring her forward — through stereo control — onto the plane of the easel 5 feet away. This was accomplished with the Realist camera mounted on the *Variable-Interocular* apparatus and used as described previously — a "dual" exposure. Naturally, the girl was perfectly motionless during the entire set of two (left and right) exposures. Determining where to locate the girl was easy; the outline sketch of the easel drawn on the *Image-Locator* made centering her on the easel a simple matter. Determining the correct interocular so as to "move" her toward the camera and onto the easel was a bit more difficult. Experimentation, using black-and-white film (see text further on), was the answer here. Trial and error, rather than complicated mathematics, was chosen as the most expedient method of solving this portion of the problem.

The Image-Divider Gadgets

Now that the use of the black background has been pursued through somewhat complicated setups, let's change our trend of thought completely and return to more easily produced illusions.

Some really amusing results may be obtained by using the simply-made *Image-Dividers*. Their purpose is to block off one-half of the camera lenses — either vertically or horizontally or any other way — so that you expose only one-half of the film at a time. The photos of Alan Young as "Twins" (Fig. 15) and the Bodiless Cowboy (Fig. 7, Page 236) illustrate the type of results that may be obtained. The variations are endless.

The *Image-Dividers* consist of nothing more complicated than a pair of cardboard pillboxes, 1½ inches in diameter, from the neighborhood druggist. The boxes have been shortened in length, the bottom trimmed as shown in the accompanying photograph (Fig. 13), and then the final result dyed a dead black with India ink. Putting them to use is quite

13. Steps in making the Image Divider Caps. Starting with a pill box of the right diameter, the caps are cut open for ½ their width, and then painted black with India ink.

easy: just attach a set of Realist sunshades to your camera and then slip the *Image-Dividers* over the ends of the shades. You can turn them any way you wish, depending upon the result that you wish to obtain (Fig. 14).

Let's use the stereo of Alan Young as "Twins" (Fig. 15) to demonstrate their actual use. The camera, mounted on a tripod, was aimed as shown by the photograph. Alan was seated in the chair on the right so that the *Image-Dividers* were turned to be exactly vertical and open on the right side (Fig. 16a). The first photo was taken, then the shutter was recocked, but the film was not advanced. (Sound familiar?) Alan next moved over to pose in the chair on the left. Meanwhile the *Image-Dividers* were rotated exactly opposite to where they had been before, leaving the left halves of the lenses open this time (Fig. 16b). The second photo was taken then, resulting in the completed stereo. Notice that the center of the scene was not used; this is the *fusion area* where the two images, left and right, merge into each other.

This fusion area is very important. It's necessary to have it wide enough so that there is a gradual, undetectable blending of the two exposures;

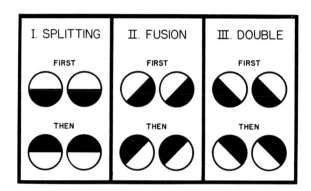

I. SPLITTING	II. FUSION	III. DOUBLE
FIRST	FIRST	FIRST
THEN	THEN	THEN

14. The Image Dividers may be positioned in various ways according to the effect desired.

288

15. Alan Young as Twins. This shot was made with the Image-Dividers, placed as shown in the picture below.

yet it can't be too wide or it will take up too much room in the picture. Only objects that remain unmoved during both of the exposures can remain within this area. You have full control over the width of this fusion area by your choice of lens opening (Fig. 19), so it's up to you to decide upon the proper diaphragm setting for your camera. Actually, like so much else in the illusion line of stereography, it comes down to being a matter of trial-and-error practicing. An opening of f/9, such as was used in this "Twins" stereo, makes a good starting point.

The stereo photo of the Bodiless Cowboy (Fig. 7, Page 236) is a different version of the same principle, only this time the *Image-Dividers* were horizontal, with the fusion area being directed along the top rail of the

16. Positioning the Image Dividers for the picture of Alan Young above. Top picture (a) shows dividers set for first exposure, bottom (b) for second.

289

17. Head of Barbara Salad. This is not a trick shot, the effect being obtained by specially built props.

18. THE NEGATIVE APPROACH

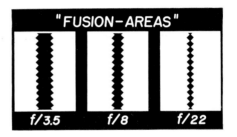

19. Fusion Areas. The amount of overlap, or double exposed area in the middle of the picture when using the Image Dividers varies with the lens aperture.

fence. The "cowboy" posed leaning against the top rail for the upper portion of the photo; then he moved out of the scene so that the second (lower) portion of the photo wouldn't have his body in it. A lens opening of f/22 was used here to produce a very narrow fusion area that would correspond with the narrow top fence railing.

In Conclusion

Here's a final suggestion. Use ordinary negative film when making any of the tests that you might find necessary. By using 35mm black-and-white film in your camera you can make tests at a fraction of the cost of color film. A negative stereo (Fig. 18, for example) is rather a strange thing to become familiar with, so try out a sample roll soon to discover its potentialities.

Well, I leave you here. You have the fundamentals: the basic "Stereolusion" principles; designs for the necessary apparatus; concrete examples. Now the rest is up to you. Have fun!

1. BANDED BUTTERFLY FISH AND ELKHORN
   CORAL

The vivid and exciting display of undersea life
is so real in stereo pictures that it makes an
experienced diver feel he is back on the bottom.

*Underwater Stereos by Harry and
Verne Pederson.*

11. Underwater Stereo Photography

HARRY PEDERSON

Stereo photography under water presents no problems that do not exist for the photographer taking pictures in two dimensions. There are the questions of shutter speed, of how far to go toward correcting with filters the imbalance at the blue end of the scale, the problem of whether to use flash and if so how much; and of course, the paramount problem of using a camera under water for many hours and bringing it up to the surface again dry as a bone.

On the other hand, the stereographer can look forward to an end result that is infinitely more satisfying than anything he could hope for in two dimensions. My brother Verne and I have made transparencies in cameras from 4x5 to 35mm. The 4x5 produces a beautiful positive, but with the long lens necessarily wide open, the depth of field is paper-thin, and out of 15 or 20 exposures perhaps two or three will be usable. The 2¼ square picture is much better, but still one is always fighting a combination that cannot be overcome if daylight is to play any part in the exposure—the necessity for great depth of field plus a fast shutter.

So we back on down to 35mm, which has depth of field at a large aperture and consequently can use a faster shutter. The Realist, being essentially two 35mm cameras in one, combines these advantages with the added realism of third dimension. And I feel that this matter of third dimension cannot be overemphasized. The realism of a stereo is so great that when the experienced diver looks at one he really feels that he is back on the bottom. The representation is so exact as to be uncanny. My belief is that when three-dimensional projectors are in greater use, most classroom visual instructions will be done with stereo. Nothing else can do the job so well.

The business of shooting stereo color undersea—and I assume here that anyone proposing to make the effort of equipping himself for the job will use color—resolves itself into two main categories: 1) an understanding

2. QUEEN ANGEL FISH IN ROCK GROTTO
The underwater photographer often whiles away
hours on the bottom waiting for an obliging fish
to mosey past the selected background—in this
case, rocks.

of the problems of color correction, lighting and exposure, and 2) the mechanical equipment that will enable the stereographer to make use of this knowledge when he has it.

Color Correction

One of the most important factors involved in satisfactory photography undersea is proper filtering. The terrestrial photographer analyzes his light source before making an exposure and uses a filter to balance the light to his emulsion. He can then proceed to shoot until the light value changes if he is shooting close-ups or landscapes. The submarine photographer has a new variable to work with—light travel. As he descends, the light reaching his subject becomes rapidly bluer and bluer. Or if he backs away from his subject the same thing happens. It is simply a matter of how far the light travels through sea water before striking the emulsion that determines the amount of filtering necessary. He can shoot at a distance of 6 feet from his subject in 7 feet of water and achieve practically the same results that he would if he were to shoot at a distance of 3 feet from his subject in 10 feet of water. But if he varies an established formula by more than a small amount he is in for trouble.

Of course the matter of filters can become such a mountain that no man can climb it. I know of a gentleman who has spent two summers and many thousands of dollars doing nothing but establishing filter tables

294

for different depths and distances. His charts and graphs will cover a large wall. Unfortunately the island on whose fringing reefs he made his studies has an infinite number of brackish streams emptying the mangrove swamps. Consequently the surrounding water is much yellower than it is anywhere else, and his innumerable filter calculations have no validity except for one Bahamian island—during the rainy season!

Sea water has a different color at high tide than at low; it changes after a rain, is different in a bay than out on a reef, and sometimes changes for no discernible reason. It is simply not humanly possible to anticipate all of the color variations that will occur undersea and correct for them with a multiplicity of filters. The man who tries to do so will become so snarled up in filters that he will not make any photographs. We use a basic set of filters and stay with it unless some decided change in location or color content of the water demands that something be done. Then to lick the variable of light travel we establish our own light source at the camera. This will not change no matter how deep we go. The only variation will be in the color of the background areas illuminated by sunlight.

Kodak makes the CC-R filter series which is especially good for undersea work, and we find those filters to be quite satisfactory. Because gelatin filters are less expensive than those mounted in glass and offer less chance of flare, we ordinarily carry a good supply of gelatin squares to be cut up as needed. They can be mounted in front of the lens in a Series

3. BLUE SHARK
The short focal length of the Realist lenses gives ample depth of field for pictures like this where near, middle and far planes are important.

295

V adapter or mounted back of the shutter with a dab of rubber cement. The latter method is more trouble-free as far as scratches and dust are concerned, but the filters are more difficult to change. On the open reefs in blue water we use quite consistently the CC-50R plus CC-15Y. This combination gives almost perfect correction when the subject is not more than 4 to 6 feet from the camera and the correct fill-in flash is used. Naturally, at greater distances from the camera correction falls off. However, there is little that can be done about it. Covering the camera lens with a heavy red filter when nothing but blue light is hitting it is about the same as putting on the lens cover.

Naturally, if a person is working undersea for a considerable period of time he will make many exposures at distances greater than the ideal 4 to 6-foot range. Many photographs have to be made when the opportunity presents itself. And there will be some degree of correction on any shot. But the filter combination I referred to reduces the emulsion speed of Daylight Kodachrome to 1.5 Weston, and I suggest this to be about as far as it is possible to go and still take pictures.

In shoal areas or at low tide when the water goes greenish blue or even to the yellow side, the filter pack must be changed. Sometimes it will be necessary to drop the yellow entirely and lower the red to CC-40R or CC-30R, or even switch to magenta. Some workers use the Harrison meter and filters and work out their combinations as they go.

4. GORGONIAS, STINGING CORALS, PURPLE FAN
Marine life in shallow water is often well illuminated by sunlight, as in this picture which is actually back-lighted by the sun.

5. GREY ANGEL FISH
Another shallow-depth picture, illuminated with
sunlight coming from almost directly overhead.

Such a system is fine on land, but it rapidly becomes complicated when a man is working under water.

Much filter knowledge has to be picked up by experience, unfortunately. When we are shooting in a strange area we invariably run a series of filter tests, using previous results as a base to start from. If we are using Ektachrome we process it on the job. If our material is Kodachrome we will have made arrangements beforehand with the processing laboratory and will have the answer in our hands within a few days.

Lighting and Exposure

Now, suppose we consider the exposures themselves. The person who has had no experience undersea usually thinks of it as a place of soft, muted tones, almost lacking in contrast. That is definitely not the case. The brilliant white wave patterns racing over the bottom at depths to 20 feet will kick the needle of an exposure meter all over the dial. More than that, when excessive blue is taken out by a set of filters, shadows become very heavy. A Weston meter will read 400 on the sand and drop back to 25 for the shadows—a very tough proposition to handle with the present latitude of color emulsions. There is no appreciable light bounce undersea except over white sandy areas. Most of the light that does bounce has traveled far enough to be deep blue and therefore of no value to the color photographer. And unfortunately most of the subjects he swings his lens at—with the exception of rays and flounders— are standing on edge.

297

6. A tripod and large base holds the Realist and a movie camera for simultaneous shooting. Coveralls protect the cameraman from coral scratches, not fish-bite!

The answer, then, is to fill in with some sort of light. Reflectors are out of the question in the surge and push of moving water, so we turn to flash. And it takes more light than one would imagine for adequate fill-in. We have established a guide number of 15 for the Press 40, and 25 for the No. 2 with Daylight Kodachrome when these bulbs have been blue-dipped in Jen-Dip for 5 seconds. (You can buy blue flashlamps if you don't want to dip your own.) In other words, with the Stereo Realist and a blue Press 40, the exposure would be 1/50 at f/3.5 for adequate fill-in at a distance of about 4 feet. The effective range of the blue No. 2 is about 7 feet. Beyond 10 feet or so the single bulb has no value whatever.

At first blush it may seem queer to be adding blue to the light fill-in and at the same time slapping on heavy red filters to cut down on blue. However, if daylight is to play a part in exposing the background and the highlights, there is no alternative but to balance the fill-in to the main light source.

We have tried bare bulbs or faintly tinted ones, but the results have been most unsatisfactory. If the photographer is planning to do his shooting at depths where sunlight is not a factor, it seems reasonable to assume that he could use lights of a color temperature that would make filters unnecessary, with a consequent increase in emulsion speed.

In such a case his backgrounds would all go dead black, of course, and some of the stereo realism would be lost. In the stereo shooting we have done so far, our aim has been to make photographs that reproduce the scene exactly as it looked to the diver. This aim calls for stereos made only in full sun, with flash used simply to pull the shadows up into the exposure range.

The great headache in using color on the bottom, then, is an inability to shoot at high shutter speeds and maintain realism. I have tried anchoring a main light high over the area to be photographed, ignoring the sun, but I soon became as involved in clanking and clattering contraptions as the White Knight—and about as effective. On the bottom, the photographer is the only thing that moves like a zombie. Everything else zips about like mad. A fiftieth of a second is very slow, but it can be managed — and successfully — when the photographer has a quick eye and some experience with the action of marine life.

With some of the theory of undersea shooting out of the way, the next step is to consider the mechanical setup that will make the knowledge effective.

Underwater Equipment

Since submarine stereo photography is seriously indulged in by a modest number of people, almost all of the apparatus to be used will

7. Schools of small fish do not travel too fast to be caught at 1/50 second. The experienced undersea photographer will study the habits of the fish and learn to catch the action.

8. Our first Realist undersea case, built of cast aluminum by Verne Pederson. The screw-type flashlamp socket was not convenient, and is replaced with a push-in socket on a later case.

be devised by the man who is going to operate it. In essence, an undersea camera case is simply a watertight box that has the camera controls extended to the outside. It must be made of rigid material, have a glass or plastic lens port, and be so constructed that it can be opened with a minimum of time and effort. Some individuals go to fantastic lengths to keep the public from seeing their creations. This, of course, is nonsense. The packing glands, levers and knobs devised by one individual will look much like those dreamed up by anybody else. A system that will get the job done is all that is necessary.

A great many kinds of materials are used in constructing undersea cases. The Scripps Institute of Oceanography makes a Stereo Realist case completely of heavy Lucite, lens port and all. I know one individual who insists that all he needs is a heavy balloon with a watch crystal cemented somewhere in it as a lens port. He operates his camera by feel, he says. Some use cast brass, others use cast aluminum.

My belief is that while Lucite is most beautiful to look at, one may encounter a lot of trouble with leaky joints, and screws and bolts are apt to pull their threads. Also, Lucite is a relatively soft material, and for a lens port it is not so good. A lens port should be made of sturdy plate glass with a cover over it when it isn't being used, and it should be so arranged that it can easily be replaced. A scratch or two in the wrong spot on a lens port may cancel a year's effort.

The less said about the balloon-and-watch-crystal job the better. It belongs in the stall with the fellow who proposes to sail the seas on a clutch of barrels filled with ping-pong balls.

300

Our first Realist box was built by my brother Verne of ⅜-inch cast aluminum. Brass is also used for undersea boxes. But brass or cast aluminum both have their disadvantages. Brass is pretty heavy, but it does not corrode or change in any manner undersea. Aluminum is easy to cast and easy to work after it has been cast; its drawback is that it tends to be porous unless the casting is made by a skilled foundry man, and it must be painted regularly—about once a month—during periods when it is being used daily undersea.

Our original Realist box is 6½ inches high, 9½ inches long and 5 inches from front to back, including the lens port. The halves of the box are held together by four brass tie bolts and are sealed with a rubber O-ring gasket. The lens port is of ¼-inch plate glass sealed into the box. In the center at the rear is the view-finding lens, which looks directly over the top of the camera so that parallax is at a minimum. The controls are all simple brass shafts running through packing glands and ending in sturdy knobs or levers easily worked with flabby fingers. In addition, there is an air valve. For my money it is essential that one be able to put a little pressure in his camera box. For deep dives in the Red Sea, Captain Cousteau used camera boxes which took on equalizing pressure from attached compressed air bottles as they descended. For deep work such an arrangement should be very good, but a valve to bleed off the pressure as the camera nears the surface again is also a vital necessity.

In any event, air pressure in the box is a good thing even in shallow dives. For our reef work we use from 8 to 10 pounds. This takes the strain off the box while it is submerged and also takes the strain off the

9. Fiberglass plastic case, with push-in flashlamp socket, built by Harry Pederson. The Fiberglass is easily worked into shape, has exceptional strength, does not corrode or conduct electricity.

10. Experimental strobe unit built by Dr. Harold Edgerton for underwater work. The diver wears an Aqualung. Photo courtesy Dr. Harold Edgerton.

diver. There is almost always a hair-sized leak somewhere in a camera box. When there is pressure in the case bubbles emerge from it in a tiny filmy stream. As long as these bubbles are coming out under pressure the photographer knows that his camera is dry, and he can spend his time worrying about other things. We often have our cameras on the bottom for 6 or 7 hours at a time, and after 6 years of undersea shooting we have yet to wet our first camera.

My latest box is made of a material that appears to have all the answers for undersea camera box construction—Fiberglass plastic. A very strong substance, it is unaffected by the action of sea water, is a nonconductor of electricity, and can be built into any desired shape by a tinkerer in a home workshop. It seems to have no weak points whatever and functions very successfully under water.

There is no provision in my box for changing either shutter speed or aperture. Since the Realist is synchronized to catch the peak of a wire-filled bulb at 1/25 to 1/50, and since the slower speed is almost out of the question undersea, we simply operate at the faster speed and let it go at that. Dr. Harold Edgerton is working on a strobe hookup for use on the Stereo Realist undersea, and when it is perfected, a box that allows for changing shutter speeds may be desirable. We found the lack of it no handicap in shooting wire-filled bulbs.

When it comes to a control for changing aperture, the same thing applies. The submarine photographer is always fighting for more light; consequently, unless he is using flash as basic illumination with no regard for daylight, he will almost invariably want to shoot with his lens wide open. The decision as to an aperture-changing mechanism will depend pretty largely upon the kind of stereos the photographer plans to make.

Focusing, of course, is essential. The focusing shaft ends in a plate with two pins. One pin fits in the center hole of the camera focusing knob, while the other slips into another small hole drilled near its outer edge. Such an arrangement assures that the focusing shaft will always engage the focusing knob at the same spot and makes it possible to use a scale on the outside of the box calibrated to underwater distances. It is neces-

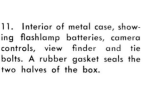
11. Interior of metal case, showing flashlamp batteries, camera controls, view finder and tie bolts. A rubber gasket seals the two halves of the box.

sary, of course, when setting up the scale, to take into account the greater refraction of sea water—roughly 30 per cent. In other words, when the actual distance to an object undersea is 6 feet, the Realist focusing knob should indicate 4 feet. It should be possible to work out a simple range finder to attach to the top of the camera box, but I have found that with a little practice it is quite simple to judge distances by eye. Of the many hundreds of stereos I have made undersea, a surprisingly small percentage have been out of focus. The great depth of field of Realist lenses doubtless had something to do with these results.

The flash setup is much simpler than one might imagine. Some people go to great lengths to keep flash from being shorted out by sea water. Some give it up as an impossible problem, since salt water carries current exceedingly well. However, the Woods Hole Oceanographic Institute has employed flashlamps in sockets open to sea water for many years when photographing sea bottom at great depths. Using their experience as a guide, we have found that only moderate precautions need be taken when using flash undersea.

The stereo box has room for 4 size D flash batteries. These are connected in series and are placed in the ungrounded side of the circuit. The socket is made especially for undersea work, and consists simply of a plastic base plate in which are three upright brass pins to hold the bulb base and make contact with the metal shell. The center contact is a sharp lead-coated brass stud. At the back of the base plate is the reflector holder. The reflector is brass, of course, heavily chromium-plated.

Screw-type sockets are of very little use undersea. Water softens the plastic coating on flash bulbs as well as the dope attaching them to their metal bases. This results in two unfortunate things: only the plastic coating turns when you try to screw the bulb into the socket; then, if greater pressure is applied, the glass comes loose from the metal bulb base and twists off the bulb wires—the sort of thing that makes an undersea photographer very unhappy.

The question of whether or not to use a tripod is one that always arises when one is setting up for undersea work. Personally, I'm all for it, especially for reef work in depths to 25 or 30 feet. The compact Stereo Realist box can be hand-held and the operator will come up with passable pictures. But at the slow shutter which must be employed, the most satisfactory stereos will be made from a tripod. I have tried both ways, and I find that my biggest pile of discarded stereo pairs results from hand-held shooting. We use heavy brass-bound wooden tripods with lead-weighted feet. When we set one up on the bottom it stays put—like a rock.

Final Underwater Tips

If you have never done any underwater work, here are a few tips that I will pass along for free.

Helmets have gone out of style now, and few photographers use them. They are cumbersome, offer limited vision, and the diver can't look at his feet without getting a face full of salt water. For short or deep dives the self-contained outfit is much better, or for long dives the air supply mask. Use hose that floats—you'll avoid having to unwind a hundred feet of it from assorted coral heads when you have been wandering about the bottom; besides, it will be up out of lens range. We use air-supply masks with an auxiliary hose running from the mask to an emergency air-supply tank. If the compressor stops, we have five leisurely minutes for getting up to the surface.

Two men on the bottom are of much more assistance to one another than one on the bottom and one in the boat trying to figure out what is happening to the man on the bottom. Rubber-soled sneakers make good

12. Fiberglass plastic box, side view, showing focusing lever and film-advance release lever on near side. Push-in flash socket, film-winding knob and carrying handle are on top; shutter cocking lever in front; shutter release on far side.

foot gear, and the sort of clothing that will keep you from being snagged on sharp coral is essential.

Don't believe one per cent of the stories about the dangerous denizens of the deeps. Most of them are straight poppycock. The dangers we have found are these: Stepping on or being thrown against sea urchin spines or stinging coral; getting out of air without figuring out what to do about it beforehand. (Air is one thing you have to have all the time—and if you run out down below, have a plan figured out for getting up to where it is in a hurry!) Octopi bother people in books only; barracudas have mean faces but appear to be only mildly curious about human beings; sharks are interested only in something that appears to be dead or *in extremis*. Try to be neither one of these things when you are shooting undersea pictures!

Have a good time. A reef in clear water is a world all its own, and it has more beauty than landlubbers dream exists anywhere on this planet. And if you want the thrill to last, box up your Realist and take it along down with you.

1. The fundamental principle of using stereo in business and industry is: when an object is *too big* to transport, *too small* to see comfortably with the naked eye, or *too intricate* to understand from an ordinary picture, then use stereo.

12. Stereo in Business, Science and Education

MARVIN L. RAND

Modern commercial usage of three-dimensional Stereo Realist slides literally started with the first roll of film taken with experimental models of the camera. The designer of the Realist actually used slides to "sell" himself and his hand-built model to the management of the ultimate manufacturer. When the camera was introduced to the photographic market, the pictures it took again sold the Realist to the American public. It is questionable whether any stereo camera has ever been sold without the prospect having first seen stereo slides in a viewer.

The success of this approach in marketing stereo equipment led sales-minded executives in other lines of business endeavor to add a third dimension to their own merchandising and promotional programs. In many cases, the first step was the purchase of a Stereo Realist camera by a business executive for his own personal use. Very quickly he would become enthusiastic over his own pictures (many times including shots relating to his business) and the inherent potential of three-dimensional slides as a visual sales aid. Shortly thereafter, his company's sales force would set forth equipped with complete sets of slides showing products, services, plant facilities, etc.

Three-dimensional slides have proved to be outstanding in sales and merchandising and have compiled a remarkable record in a wide variety of industrial and scientific applications, and as a visual training aid. The advantages of stereo photography in these fields are obvious. There is some application for stereo in virtually every field of professional endeavor.

Salesmen equipped with sets of slides showing their products, manufacturing facilities and/or services have many distinct advantages over salesmen using a portfolio of two-dimensional photographs or printed literature. It is difficult and often impossible for many salesmen on the road to transport their complete lines of merchandise to potential cus-

2. An outdoor substation of the Florida Light and Power Company. Such a stereo is valuable as a record for engineers, draftsmen and maintenance staff, saving time and money on field trips.

tomers. Realist pictures enable them to carry their lines in small sample kits weighing but 40 ounces. The product is photographed in favorable surroundings and in natural color and is illustrated life-size because of the magnification in the viewer lenses. When showing the slides to a prospect, the salesman has his undivided attention. While the customer is looking into the viewer, he can listen to a description of the product and its advantages to him. These same slides can be projected for sales meetings, or to a group of customers. Such advantages are of primary importance in present-day competitive selling.

One of the earliest and best examples of a three-dimensional sales program is that of the Hudson Pulp and Paper Corporation, which manufactures craft paper and various converted products such as grocery bags and gummed sealing tape. When the firm entered the field of Multi-Wall Shipping Sacks, it was faced with a market situation in which competition had already been well established for many years. Sales Manager S. W. Franklin made an analysis of the sales problems and determined that he needed a method of forcibly getting his story across to the trade in a manner that was unique but which would not detract from the basic sales story. The answer to this problem, which was proved conclusively by excellent results, was the use of a three-dimensional stereo presentation. From the beginning the Hudson sales force gave their enthusiastic support to the Stereo Realist slides, which made it easy for them to impress customers and prospects with the gigantic operation that stands behind the product of Hudson Multi-Wall Shipping Sacks. They were able to show with *realistic* depth, and in full color, segments of a million-acre, company-owned timber land, mammoth paper mill operations and the filled bulky Multi-Wall Sacks. The full color was particularly valuable in visualizing the powerful 4-color printing and design of the sacks.

The salesmen also discovered that with stereo presentations they were able to get their full sales story across in about 30 minutes. Previously, to cover this same amount of information required just about one hour. The salesmen thus got over the story of "buyer benefits" in much less time and were able to make a greater number of calls per day. Equally important, they were able to *prove* their ability to serve giant Multi-Wall industrial buyers by dramatically showing manufacturing facilities faster, easier and at a tremendous saving compared with transporting the buyers to the company's Florida mill location. They were also able to show that many nationally known manufacturers used Hudson sacks, and how they in turn had taken advantage of the firm's design and printing facilities to produce sales-building messages.

Stereo Program Costs

The cost of this particular sales program was surprisingly low. To equip one salesman with a complete presentation amounted to approximately $35.00. This included the cost of the Realist viewer, 35 slides,

3. Hazardous industrial operations can be studied safely in the office or classroom through the medium of stereo slides like this one. Stereo courtesy Realist, Inc.

4. Architects Welton Becket and Associates in Los Angeles use stereo pictures to record progress during construction, and unusual building techniques for future reference. Stereo by Douglas Simmonds.

and the convenient, small leatherette-covered case into which the entire presentation fits. One of the reasons it was possible to keep costs so low is that stereo photography is relatively simple with the Realist camera and all the photographs could be taken by the sales manager himself. Low-cost copies of the originals enabled them to equip each salesman with a set of slides, which were the basis for a unified sales program for the entire staff.

Coordinating the Sales Story

In making up the sets of slides, a number and a key sentence concerning the picture are printed for identification and continuity on the space provided on the face of the stereo slide. To provide each salesman with the essential and supplemental information upon which he could expand his sales story, a "leader's guide" was prepared and furnished with each kit. This is effective in insuring that all the necessary information is presented, and at the same time gives the salesman the opportunity to tell the sales story in his own words. Still another advantage is the ease with which additions or changes can be made by merely substituting or rearranging the order of the slide presentation. Salesmen obtain the greatest value from using this type of presentation when they are taught properly how to do so. In this case, the salesmen were instructed to insert their first slide in the viewer, give the few required instructions to the buyer on how to adjust the focus and interocular spacing, and

310

then hand the viewer to the buyer with the facing area in front. An opening key sentence by the salesman sets the scene for the slide which the buyer views for himself. When interest in that particular slide has waned, the buyer instinctively puts the viewer down and the salesman amplifies the point regarding the scene. Mr. Franklin is personally convinced that for the salesman to talk while the scene is being viewed would result in only partial attention and partial reception to the sales message. Mr. Franklin sums up his reaction to this type of stereo selling as follows: "Not only are our customers delighted with this type of presentation, but so are our salesmen. They look forward to the use of this sales tool with greater anticipation. It simply provides them with the ammunition for greater sales while enabling them to utilize their own personality, and their own choice of words."

Stereo Selling in Action

Another example of stereo photography as a selling tool is outlined by Ralph Fulbright, Vice-President in Charge of Sales of Timber Structures, Inc., of Portland, Oregon. Timber Structures is a leader in the comparatively new industry of laminating wood with waterproof glue to make timbers stronger for their size than a single piece of timber wood from virgin forests. When sales volume declined, Mr. Fulbright, who is convinced that good salesmen need good selling tools and "plenty of them," hit on the idea of using three-dimensional photographs. As an experiment he was granted an expenditure of $2,500 to set up a stereo sales program. Sales since the plan was put into effect have averaged at least 100 per cent over the average for the previous five years. In the first year of operation, sales reached 300 per cent above the previous year. The program proved so successful that over $12,000 was invested in Stereo Realist viewers and slides within the first four years.

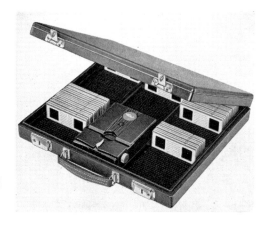

5. Handsome Stereo Realist cases are made in various sizes to hold small or large groups of slides, and the Realist viewer.

6. A stereo view of the completed building shows, in three dimensions, details that would be almost unnoticed in a flat picture. Building by Welton Becket and Associates, Los Angeles. Stereo by Douglas Simmonds.

Architectural concepts are always three-dimensional. No flat rendering, whether photograph or drawing, can give the complete feel of a structure as can the stereo photograph. When buildings are properly lighted and pictures well composed, the architect's stereo presentations are invaluable.

7. Even though architects' models are far smaller than the actual building, they cannot be carried around conveniently or mailed to prospective clients. Stereo slides can. Model by Welton Becket and Associates. Stereo by Douglas Simmonds.

Since the real building will be seen in daylight, it is always well to photograph architects' models outdoors, in sunlight, so that a single sharp strong shadow pattern is cast, and the natural lighting effect is maintained. A reflector or flashlamp will avoid inky black shadows and preserve detail.

313

8. Stereo recreates the mood and space of this lounge in Bullock's Pasadena department store, and shows the special circular treatment. Welton Becket and Associates design. Stereo by Douglas Simmonds.

Architects and builders who are still skeptical after sales talks about the advantages of glue-laminated wood timbers and trusses are entranced when they see three-dimensional pictures of new churches and other wood-laminated structures. In some cases, it was actually harder to persuade salesmen to use the new medium than it was to get customers to look at it. Mr. Fulbright tells the story of one regional sales executive who flatly refused to use stereo photography in sales and preferred give-away novelties as a selling aid. Mr. Fulbright accepted this as a personal challenge; with the sales executive he visited an architect's office where an order had not been placed for several months. In fact, salesmen could not get past the outer office. However, Mr Fulbright thrust the viewer into the architect's hands and said just one word: "Look." The result? The top man called in all of his department heads to take a look, too. The office became a regular account for Timber Structures for the first time and the regional sales executive now supplies all his salesmen with stereo kits.

Architects who specialize in schools, for instance, normally do not have time for lengthy sales talks, but Timber Structures salesmen often have audiences lasting hours while school specialists look at pictures of school projects through the 3-D viewer. Mr. Fulbright points out that to sell anything you have to keep the interest of the customer throughout the sales talk. The Realist viewer does just that. It literally walks them inside buildings constructed with laminated arches,

314

Viewers and slides are now in big demand by all salesmen, dealers and distributors in leading cities all over the United States. The stereo sales kits are versatile in that specific sets of slides of particular interest can be shown to specialized groups. Thus, if a firm is considering a new warehouse, slides of similar warehouse structures can be shown, or slides can be limited to airplane hangars, outdoor theaters, schools, or whatever structures are of interest to the client.

The Joy Manufacturing Company (Canada) Ltd. of Galt, Ontario, has developed a stereo sales program for its salesmen in much the same manner. This company manufactures and sells massive construction and industrial machinery. It is extremely important for the salesmen to show these machines in operation. President J. A. Drain purchased a Stereo Realist camera for himself, then added cameras for use in his business. His company has even been able to show their machinery operating underground in pictures made with the Realist flash attachment and single flashbulb. All of the branch offices in Canada are equipped with viewers, slide cases and up-to-date pictures of their equipment in actual operation. They also project their pictures at exhibitions and conventions in Canada. They have also made black-and-white negatives from the small stereo pictures and used enlargements of these pictures in their publication advertising. This alone has resulted in a considerable savings. Salesmen and executives of the company are furnished with cameras which they use to photograph new equipment and its application in underground operations. The cost of retaining a commercial photographer

9. Furniture buyers can see a complete season's line in one set of stereos, and place their orders directly from the slides, which show life-sized scale and proportions. Stereo by John Meredith.

10. Houses and other real estate can be presented in stereo with their best foot forward. A selection of structures and sites can be viewed by the client without driving around for hours. Stereo by John Meredith.

to make a trip of several hundred miles to a remote mine using the equipment would be almost prohibitive.

A firm in New England was one of the first to use stereo in selling real estate. The method employed was simple. Heads of the firm purchased Stereo Realist cameras and proceeded to take pictures of houses listed with them for sale. The pictures showed the houses as they really are and included exterior and interior shots, cellars, attics, heating systems, etc.

The use of three-dimensional color photography in merchandising real estate has many advantages both to the realtor and the prospect. Often prospective buyers make house hunting a sort of adventure which ends up in a hit-or-miss game involving many hours of strenuous work. The limitations in time and travel and the factor of fatigue are important. A method whereby prospective buyers can see and consider a great number of homes suitable in design, size, location and price range offers a tremendous advantage. Instead of driving around for hours to see a few houses, the buyer can sit comfortably, without distractions, and see many houses in a viewer. He can narrow his choice to one or two specific houses best suited to his needs and save days of personal inspection. Neither weather nor time make any difference. He can see houses at night, or appreciate a summer home viewed during February blizzards. The real estate firm can show individual properties to a greater number of potential buyers. Showing real estate in stereo eliminates the nuisance of having parties of sightseers tramping through a house occupied by

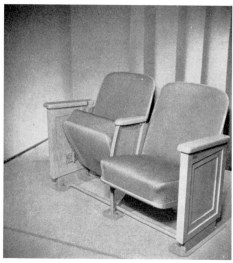

the seller. On-the-spot inspection of the property is then confined exclusively to sales and interested persons.

An increasing number of home owners are using the Realist camera to make insurance inventories of their homes. They photograph the entire contents of each room in the house, then place the slides in a safety deposit box. Insurance agents have hailed this idea because with a record of this type there is no question in case of fire, theft or other insured loss. Every article in the room is shown exactly as it looks. In the case of cabinets or other closed pieces of furniture, the owner can actually photograph the contents of drawers or shelves.

Does the addition of a third dimension to sales pay off? A large distributor of boats *knows* that it does. The firm is a warehouse distributor with 15 traveling salesmen serving five states. Early one spring, with little prior notice, a boat manufacturer displayed a sensational 20-foot family-type cruiser at a boat show. The distributor was asked to commit itself for a quota of 44 boats at $1,775 list price each, for delivery before Labor Day. No literature or bulletins covering the boat were to be available for some time, and since sample boats would not be available for several weeks, something drastic had to be done to get orders for the 44 boats from dealers. The firm took 20 Stereo Realist pictures each of four different shots of the boat at the show. (By shooting originals, it was not necessary to wait for duplicate slides to be made.) Within two weeks the salesmen and each branch manager and supervisor were supplied with a viewer, carrying case and set of slides. The only other sales tool was a rough draft of a bulletin listing some of the boat's features obtained verbally at the boat show. The whole program was explained to the sales force at a general sales meeting.

The entire quota of 44 boats was sold by stereo slides within 45 days—almost one boat per day—or $81,000 worth of boats at retail. And the factory catalogue sheet was not received until *after* all of the boats were sold. Needless to say, the stereo program was promptly expanded by this distributor to include the balance of his lines.

Furniture stores which generally cater to customers actually seeing and testing their merchandise have made excellent use of stereo photography by staging invitational 3-D projection shows. Even though the actual merchandise may be on hand at the store for customers to see, stereo slides have the advantage of showing how the furniture can be used in actual home settings. Decorators point out how decorating problems can be met through the use of color, fabrics, etc., or dramatically illustrate how a narrow room can be expanded by proper placement of furniture.

Even restaurants have been able to utilize stereo photography successfully. For example, at Keen's English Chop House in New York, patrons who want to see the specialties of the house before they order are offered a Realist viewer complete with color slides of the restaurant's famous meat dishes. The diner can then make his choice from the realistic

12. Hotels and restaurants use stereo slides to show arrangements of food and table decorations for people planning a large banquet, or just choosing dinner. Stereo at the Beverly Hills Hotel, Los Angeles, by R. B. Carter.

318

three-dimensional meals he sees. Patrons, of course, still get a two-dimensional printed menu to peruse in case they are interested in the less famous dishes—or in price!

Clothing salesmen have been particularly grateful for color stereo photography. For decades they struggled with the burden of mammoth sample cases which necessitated establishing headquarters in a hotel and then attracting store buyers to the hotel to view the merchandise. Even then the merchandise was not always shown to best advantage because it would be merely placed on tables or hung on hangers. With stereo sales kits, however, the same salesmen can go directly to the buyers' offices and present the line comfortably. Not only is the clothing shown in its true texture and color, but the slides have the added advantage of showing the merchandise as it actually looks on attractive models in ideal background conditions. This is particularly valuable for lingerie salesmen. Male buyers not only welcome the salesmen's visits, but look forward to seeing the slides!

Another use for stereo slides in the clothing industry, as well as in many, many others, is to show stores how to display merchandise on counters and in store windows to best advantage. Display houses make considerable use of stereo photography to show their actual displays and/or display know-how to prospects.

An accounting of just a few diversified commercial users of stereo pictures as selling aids illustrates more graphically than anything else just how stereo has swept the country as a vital sales tool.

319

14. While this one appliance might not be much trouble for a salesman to carry, a trunkful of them would be a burden. The stereo picture makes the most effective presentation. Stereo courtesy Sterno, Inc.

The Bastian-Blessing Mfg. Co. of Chicago manufactures soda fountain equipment. The firm photographs fountains after they are installed so that they can be presented in the most attractive surroundings to other customers. In three years the company photographed 80 different subjects, affording distributors an interesting and complete coverage. Advertising Manager Myron E. Steczynski says of stereo: "Many of our distributors join with us in proclaiming it the most successful sales aid that we have ever used."

Advertising Manager Fred G. Jones of the Creamery Package Mfg. Company of Chicago points out that in 1947 his firm "hopefully photographed several of its plants in three dimensions. Today, Creamery Package has more than 100 stereo viewers in use by 21 branches and at least eight export agents in foreign lands." Jones says stereo selling gives prospects a "highly realistic and dramatic look at our equipment in action—without going out of their own offices." He points out that "the novelty of three-dimensional color is an eye-opener and attention-getter for 'cold turkey' calls. The stereo slides pave the way for a signed order many times by clearing up questions in the prospect's mind as to appearance and design of machinery, and on installation details such as piping hookup or clearance." Jones calls his stereo slides an "office display room."

The Lambert Company of New Jersey, representing the Lambert Pharmacal Company and Pro-Phy-Lac-Tic Brush Company, uses stereo to illustrate its merchandising offers. Many of these merchandising offers are rather large in size and heavy in weight. Some showcases average

320

four feet in height, and obviously it would not be practical for salesmen to attempt to carry them. The stereo slide does all that work for the company.

There is actually no limit to the fields where stereo selling can be applied.

From the Centralab Division of Globe-Union, Inc., Milwaukee, comes another report of the success of stereo selling. The firm, which manufactures component parts for the electronic industry, found that it could not expect its salesmen to carry with them some of the finished products for which Centralab makes parts—such as huge television chassis. So the salesmen were equipped with stereo sales kits, which showed the complete line of products manufactured by the company. The sales manager calls stereo selling "the most successful visual sales aid we have ever had."

Florists have found that the use of stereo photography enables them to show prospective buyers floral arrangements for any occasion, with the resultant saving in time that would be normally spent touring the greenhouse.

Architects make excellent use of stereo photos as a permanent pictorial record and as a sales stimulant for prospects. To the eminent and critical Frank Lloyd Wright "the only photograph that can be made of architecture is three-dimensional." Quoted in a national photographic magazine,* he went on to explain: "In the kind of architecture that I represent, it's

*Photography, February, 1954

15. Outdoor storage of cotton bales in front of a Southern California cotton gin is effectively shown in this stereo by Willard D. Morgan.

that dimension—the depth—that gives it quality and effect. The ordinary camera eye can't penetrate, but can only give you the elevation. So I've never been much interested in photographs of my work until this three-dimension process came in. Now, I must say, you can get a photograph of a building that will really give you the experience of being in that building." The Museum of Modern Art in New York City had a special stereo exhibit of the Johnson Wax Company's Administration and Research Center, which was designed by Mr. Wright. A series of 38 Realist slides were mounted in individual Realist viewers to give thousands of weekly visitors a "realistic" tour of these buildings.

Bakers and other people in the food field take pictures of food items and show them to customers for special orders. Landscape gardeners use stereo slides of completed projects as realistic proof of the quality of their work.

Continued recitation of examples of the uses of stereo photography in sales would be endless—hotels . . . caterers . . . automotive manufacturers . . . foods . . . caskets . . . anything salable. Yes, even enterprising theatrical agents use stereo slides to secure bookings for their clients!

Scientific and Educational Applications

Stereo photography is exceptionally useful in the laboratories and engineering departments of American science and industry, and in the nation's classrooms. Whenever a visible record of tangible fact is desired,

16. A simple record shot of a small banquet room can be made with the Stereo Realist and flash attachment. Setup for a dinner party at the Beverly Hills Hotel. Stereo by R. B. Carter.

322

stereo photographs have proved superior to any other record. Because they duplicate the original object that was photographed, they are perfect as a reference.

One of the most exciting phases of stereo photography has been in the field of medicine. Major hospitals have established stereo slide libraries of surgical operations and pathological photographic conditions for doctors to use as reference and for students to study. Much in the same way, dentists have found stereo photographs to be highly satisfactory, particularly in the field of orthodontia and oral surgery.

The experience of a hospital on the campus of a large midwestern university is a specific example of the use of stereo slides in the medical field. In surgery, the hospital makes a complete collection of all of the various operative procedures as well as many record pictures. Thousands were taken in the first year of this program. The present use of the slides is primarily for reference in the medical library for resident physicians and interne aides. The slides are also frequently used for exhibits and meetings. They have made up sets of slides with recorded lectures for specific training which cannot otherwise be furnished. Nurses, medical students and internes rotate through surgical service a few at a time, and ordinarily it is difficult to give them complete instructions on such subjects as scrubbing, gowning, etc., for the operating room. Sets of stereo slides were made up to portray the correct procedure graphically, and the students learn the procedure from the pictures. The hospital has also made

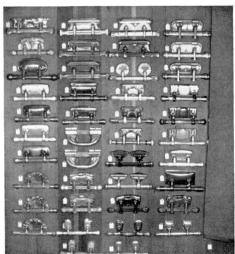

17. The stereo sample case is used even by distributors of casket hardware. This display panel would be too unwieldy to carry around. Stereo courtesy Hollywood Casket Company.

18. Ultra close-up stereo of normal eye is valuable, not only for detail, but for teaching the anatomy of the eye in depth. Stereo by Donald Tate.

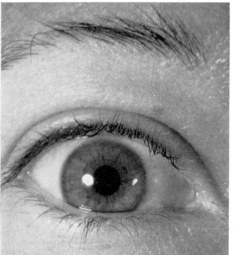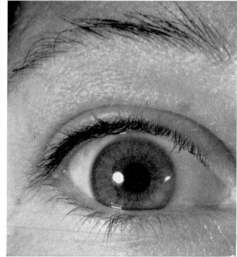

The use of the Stereo Realist in education often requires special techniques or accessories. An ultra close-up like that above must, of course, be taken with reduced interocular and the equipment and method may be adapted from information presented in Chapter 10: *Stereolusions*.

The equipment and methods used for the close-ups on these two pages can be used equally well for portraying small objects or mechanisms used in industry. The educational value of such slides in the training of workers in assembly or servicing of such devices is incalculable.

19. Ultra close-ups of small insects permit detailed study at the viewer's leisure, without danger of the subject's moving or being lost. Stereo by Donald Tate.

20. Another close-up insect stereo, made by the same technique as the two on previous pages. What would be a jumble of legs in a flat picture is structurally clear in stereo. Stereo by Donald Tate.

up sets of slides for patient instructions on such subjects as home treatment for arthritis, bandaging of knees and ankles for athletes, polio rehabilitation exercises, etc. Another interesting and effective subject is the blocking-in of anasthesia for both surgical and dental work where the angle of the injection needle is important; this shows up particularly well in stereo photography.

The medical artist has found stereo photography particularly valuable, especially where sketching over the surgeon's shoulder is futile. Now stereo pictures are taken at indicated steps in the operation, and the artist can work directly from them. Stereo pictures are also useful in anatomical dissections, both for training and records.

Enterprising dentists—in addition to using the Realist camera professionally to record unusual cases—have also found Realist slides an entertainment medium for patients waiting for consultation. Dr. Clifford L. Feiler of Lafayette, California, keeps a carrying case of travel slides and a viewer in the waiting room, and says, "They are wonderful to relieve tension in nervous patients as well as being great entertainment for those who must wait quite some time."

Optometrists and oculists have actually prescribed stereo to patients with weakened eye muscles. By placing a slide in a viewer, then moving the interocular adjustment or focusing knob, the muscles can be forced to move in a pattern which helps to correct certain deficiencies.

Veterans' Administration doctors make use of Realist slides on a mass audience basis in a teaching program for doctors and patients. Hundreds of stereo pictures were taken for the Physical Medicine and Rehabilitation Department showing the step-by-step treatment of various types of physically handicapped cases. The series covers the entire range of treatment, from the patient's interview with a psychologist through the physical treatment to his vocational training. The slides are projected to groups of doctors, and the treatment is explained in detail. Patients are also shown the slides to give them a very realistic idea of the nature of treatment and how they can help make it a success.

Service organizations, such as the Service Star Legion—a group of mothers who had sons or daughters in the service—have also collected great numbers of stereo slides which hospitalized veterans can view at their leisure. The slides are circulated the same as library books and help relieve the humdrum boredom of prolonged hospitalization by bringing the veterans a lifelike view of the world beyond the hospital.

Wedding Photography

The stereo slide box is rapidly replacing the family album of wedding photos, and professional wedding and portrait photographers are finding a great demand for stereo coverage of weddings. The fascination of wedding pictures in stereo is that the 3-D picture actually *recreates* an important event in the lives of two people; it does not just *record* it on a flat piece of paper as the ordinary photograph does.

Unless the stereo photographer has had much experience in the photography of weddings, he may run into a few pitfalls which will seriously hamper his work and reduce his effective coverage of the event. It is essential, always, to check with the church authorities in advance, so that the photographer will know exactly what he may and may not

21. Photography of weddings has long been a lucrative field for still photographers. Stereo slides add another dimension to the bride's recollection of a cherished event.

327

photograph, whether flash is permitted and various other local rules. Advance planning should also include a list of pictures to be taken—before the ceremony, during the actual event, and coverage afterward, either of the principals leaving or of the wedding dinner.

Those planning to enter this business without previous experience in professional photography should be cautioned that it *is* a business and must be run like one. Fees should be high enough to cover overhead, cost of getting business such as advertising, etc., materials, and a fair price for the photographer's labor.

Miscellaneous Applications

A typical engineering use of stereo photography is that of the Giddings and Lewis Machine Tool Company of Fond du Lac, Wisconsin. Engineers use stereo to make three-dimensional photo records of various constructions and operating devices used on the heavy machine tools which this company makes. The stereo slides are filed by subject matter and have been invaluable to the engineering department and others directly concerned with machine design and constructions. The chief engineer cites the use of the Stereo Realist camera for production records during the construction of 200-ton machines made for a large aircraft company. Several slides a week were taken during the development of the machine, and the engineers found they learned a great deal by referring to these pictures. The slides were particularly valuable as a record of conduit

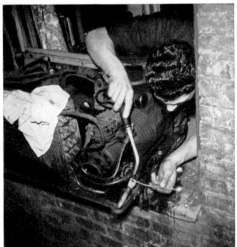

22. Servicing a window-type air conditioning unit; another example of the use of stereo both for record purposes and for the training of servicemen. Stereo by Dorothy S. Gelatt.

328

routing and hydraulic and lubrication lines which might not always be in the same position on each machine. The engineers found that changes could be made in the assembly after the slides were checked and drawings corrected accordingly. The company also makes stereo records of modifications and adaptions in design for specific applications. In many cases, the stereo slides actually augment blueprints, since they give a much clearer overall picture of the unit under construction. In the case of Giddings and Lewis, the engineers work on different problems almost every day, and it might be a year or more before a similar project is encountered. In these cases, a stereo slide is invaluable as a record of what has been done previously.

Stereo slides are also coming into their own in the service field. In the erection of a new machine or in the maintenance of that machine, service men in the field find stereo pictures to be real timesavers as a quick machine-part reference because the slides give a true picture of machine details.

The ease with which the stereo pictures are stored is also important to the engineers. The small space required to file the slides makes them easily accessible and handy to refer to.

The Physics Research Department of General Mills, Inc. has made extensive use of the Stereo Realist camera as a documenting instrument. Because this laboratory is primarily interested in food research, there are many instances where a three-dimensional photograph can save

329

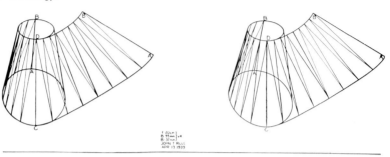

24. Development of frustum of cone. Stereos to explain difficult visual concepts can also be prepared by drawing, as in these stereo drawings by Prof. John T. Rule of Massachusetts Institute of Technology.

considerable description of material which is perishable and which can be examined and kept for only a few hours. The Realist is a "natural" for recording the color, texture and general shape of such perishable material as cake sections, breads, etc.

This research department has many other uses for the Realist. Photographer R. I. Derby applies photographic techniques to aid in the research problems throughout the laboratory, including high-speed cinematography and photomicrography. These often involve complex arrangements of equipment according to the specific problems at hand. A stereo record of the arrangement of the photographic apparatus (camera, lights and associated equipment) is a timesaver. With a few simple stereo shots, one can easily reassemble the same apparatus for a similar job without having to describe camera angles, type of lighting, light placement, etc. A planar shot of the same equipment is generally a jumble of confusion and does not show relative size or distance.

Among many other products, General Mills manufactures extremely complicated packaging machinery. Motion pictures are satisfactory for

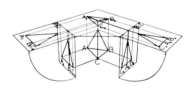

25. Projection of a pyramid on three planes and revolution of auxiliary planes to place all views on one sheet. A graphic demonstration of the basic principle of drafting, by Prof. John T. Rule.

26. Coloring a large museum display by reference to a Stereo Realist slide in hand viewer, bringing nature indoors and eliminating the fallibilities of memory.

making a photo record of the machinery for people who cannot examine the actual machine. Supplemented by stereo pictures, however, the story is really complete. Many of the stereo slides are used for instructions and sales as well as for record files. Research staff members often use the projected slides to illustrate scientific discussions. Mr. Derby has adapted the Realist and stereo techniques to stereo photomicrography. Using a specially designed stand and a standard modern wide-field stereo binocular microscope of low power (5X to 100X), he takes wide-field stereo photomicrographs in color. The results are such that when one views the final picture he sees almost exactly the quality visible in the stereo microscope. These slides are used for permanent records, for comparison,

27. The museum artist can color artificial flowers slowly and painstakingly, without danger of his model wilting, when the "model" is a stereo slide in color.

for the study of detail long after the original specimen has perished, and for teaching. For instance, slides are made of food contaminants microscopic in size, and the materials in these slides are identified by experts so that later others may learn to recognize and identify similar material.

Stereo photography has even found a role in art—from both an educational and practical application standpoint. Three-dimensional slides of architecture and sculptures are valuable to teachers in familiarizing students with various art forms. Projected stereo is excellent for group instruction, and slides of art objects give students a totally new and thrilling awareness of actual form and color.

The Milwaukee Public Museum, among others, has found stereo exceedingly practical in preparing museum displays. The artists and modelers for these institutions are noted for the authenticity of their displays. Their job has been made much easier with Realist slides taken of the original scene which they are assigned to duplicate. These slides are ideal as a reference in model work, and literally walk the museum craftsmen right into the specific spot on the globe they are to recreate.

Realist slides have even starred in criminal courts. The first known example took place September 27, 1950, in Chattanooga, Tennessee. The defendant was charged with murdering a man. Judges ordinarily are reluctant to permit a jury to be taken to the scene of the crime, so the public prosecutor obtained special permission to bring the scene to the

28. Mystery skeleton. The stereo camera preserves the exact position and place in which the bones were found for future study after the relics have been removed or disturbed. Stereo courtesy Realist, Inc.

jury by means of Realist slides and a stereo projector. The judge ruled favorably on the admission of such evidence. Several police departments now equip squad cars with Realist cameras so that three-dimensional pictures can be taken of automobile accidents and scenes of crimes.

State highway commissions, to cite another example, photograph proposed new highway routes in three dimensions to illustrate the extent of major cut-and-fill areas. Movie producers have files of "location" area slides to save countless hours and days searching for and checking possible outdoor sites where specific scenes can be photographed.

Applications of the Realist in science, industry and education are virtually unlimited. The list is endless—designers . . . production, mechanical and civil engineers . . . mathematicians . . . mineralogists . . . zoologists . . . biologists—all are successfully using Stereo Realist slides in order to advance American productivity and knowledge.

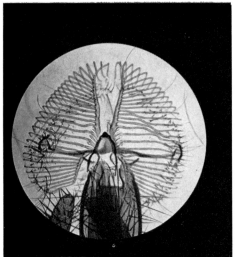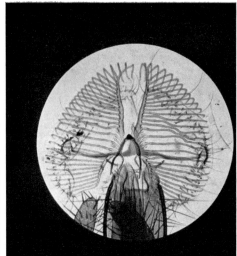

1. Proboscis of a house fly, magnified about 200x, photographed through monobjective binocular microscope adapted to stereo with Stereo Polarizer. From a color transparency by Henry M. Lester.

13. Stereos Through The Microscope

HENRY M. LESTER

OSCAR W. RICHARDS

Stereo photography through the microscope is an old and venerable art. It has been practiced for years, and many outstanding examples of the early work would be hard to match today. They were the result of the infinite patience and ingenuity of competent microscopists who were determined to share with others their disclosures of the appearance of things greatly magnified, and seen in true stereoscopic aspect. The methods used were as varied as they were complicated and difficult. The results, when excellent, were accomplished through many trials and many errors.

A comparatively simple method for efficient production of stereo photomicrographs in color and in black and white suggested itself recently through the availability of the Stereo Realist camera.

While skilled microscopists will be able to apply stereo photomicrography to the solution of current problems such as are encountered in industry, science, medicine, biology or botany, many an amateur photographer would like to know what would look pictorially interesting and aesthetically appealing through a stereoscopic microscope. In general, man-made things appear clumsy and crude even when only slightly magnified. The finest Swiss watch movement looks coarse when magnified only 10 or 15 times. A finely cut and polished diamond would never be bought if the prospective purchaser looked at it through a stereoscopic microscope magnifying it 20 or 25 times. On the other hand, the workmanship of nature is so superb down to its minutest details that its creations retain their unbelievable beauty high up on the scale of magnification. Some of these stereo photomicrographs are reproduced here, limitations of space making it impossible to show more of them.

For the benefit of readers interested in the aesthetics of things which would ordinarily pass unnoticed, here are a few suggestions for stereo photomicrography subjects:

A transistor . . . a thermistor . . . a worn phonograph needle or stylus . . . a small ball bearing . . . a piece from a broken record . . . chips of crazed or wrinkled paint surfaces . . . type face . . . copper engraving . . . fractured china . . . cracked or chipped enamel . . . a welded point . . . a soldered joint . . . sandpaper . . . emery cloth . . . ridges on bullets . . . firing pin marks on small shells . . . tool marks on wood or metal surfaces . . .

Seeds . . . sugar . . . salt . . . crystals of iodine, alum, hydroquinone or other substances . . . rye or corn bread . . . cake . . . cigarette tobacco or ash . . . silk or nylon stockings . . . human hair . . . moss . . . algae . . . pollen . . . insects . . . geological specimens . . . bits of soil . . . leaves . . . small flowers, such as forget-me-nots or baby breath . . . driftwood . . . paper surfaces . . . the skin of a peach or an orange . . . and hundreds more.

Types of Microscopes

There are two general types of microscopes which are suitable for making stereo photomicrographs with the Realist camera:

1. The Greenough stereo microscope, offering wide-field views at magnification not exceeding about 150X;
2. The conventional monobjective binocular microscope capable of yielding high magnification and great resolving power.

(Greenough, an American living in Paris towards the end of the nineteenth century, conceived the idea of combining two compound microscopes, one for each eye, modified to give an erect rather than an inverted image to obtain enlarged stereoscopic views of small objects. These

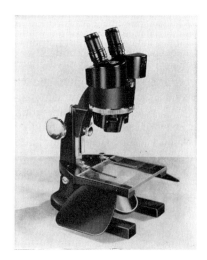

2. AO-Spencer binocular sterescopic microscope (Greenough type) with paired, wide-field inclined eyepieces, adjustable for varying interocular separation. Triple nosepiece accommodates 3 sets of paired objectives.

microscopes are often called "Greenough microscopes" or "stereoscopic microscopes." They are actually two microscopes combined into a unit on a single stand. Both are focused as one — two independent optical systems carefully matched to render true stereoscopic views.)

Each of the two basic types of microscopes, available in a great variety of models from a number of microscope makers, has its own sphere of applications more or less to the exclusion of the other. The Greenough-type instrument is specifically a stereoscopic viewing device, while the conventional binocular microscope is not, but it can easily be adapted to such application.

Photomicrography Without Focusing the Camera

When a microscope is focused upon a subject, the image-forming light rays emerging from the microscope ocular are made substantially parallel. If the camera lens, focused for infinity, is placed close to the microscope eyepiece, it will form from such rays an image in the camera film plane. Obtained under such conditions, the image will usually appear on film within a circular outline, and the diameter of the circle will be larger as the magnifying power of the microscope ocular increases.

Applying this simple principle to the Realist camera, both its lenses are set to infinity and this setting is secured with a bit of adhesive tape applied to the focusing knob. There is little to be gained from stopping

337

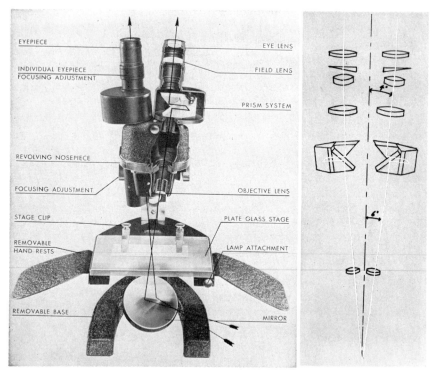

Labels on figure:

EYEPIECE
INDIVIDUAL EYEPIECE FOCUSING ADJUSTMENT
REVOLVING NOSEPIECE
FOCUSING ADJUSTMENT
STAGE CLIP
REMOVABLE HAND-RESTS
REMOVABLE BASE

EYE LENS
FIELD LENS
PRISM SYSTEM
OBJECTIVE LENS
PLATE GLASS STAGE
LAMP ATTACHMENT
MIRROR

4. The structure of the Greenough microscope; AO-Spencer microscope with straight (not in-clined) eyepieces, showing light path inverted by Porro prisms to make the subject appear erect.

5. Path of light through the binocular stereo microscope with objectives converging about 6°; after emergence from prism, the convergence is 4°. Auxiliary prisms over camera lenses make light beams parallel as required for Stereo Realist camera.

down the lens apertures more than one stop below the full aperture: no greater depth of field will be secured. The camera lens aperture should be left large enough so that it will not restrict the cone of light emerging from the microscope ocular, to avoid vignetting. Thus set, the camera is ready for stereo photomicrography with either type of microscope without further adjustments. It should be remembered that the interocular distance between the centers of its two lenses is 70mm (about 2¾ inches).

Adapting the Stereo Microscope

The two optical axes of the stereo microscope converge toward the specimen; this is obvious from a glance at the instrument itself. However, it is not so easy to see that some stereo microscopes have two angles of convergence, the light beams having been bent within the microscope body by prisms. In such microscopes, the eyepieces converge

338

more sharply than do the objectives, though the difference is quite small. When the two angles are the same — that is, when the eyepieces converge at the same angle as the objectives, the perspective is correct and normal. In some microscopes, however, the angles have been altered to produce an exaggerated effect of depth, quite useful in certain applications such as microsurgery. In general, the greater the angle of convergence, the greater the depth perception.

For photomicrography, the Realist camera must be placed in such a position that its back be at right angles to the light rays emerging from the two microscope eyepieces, or nearly so. To direct the two light rays from their diverging paths to parallel, ophthalmic prisms are used which have refracting powers appropriate to the actual angle of convergence. The refracting power of a prism is expressed in "prism diopters," the amount needed is easily found by dividing the tangent of the angle of convergence with the vertical by 0.01. The convergence angles (or angles of inclination) vary in different makes and models of stereo microscopes, as will be seen from the following listing of a few popular makes:

PRISMS REQUIRED FOR STEREO PHOTOMICROGRAPHY WITH
SOME POPULAR MICROSCOPES

Microscope	Angle of Inclination Approximate Degrees (*)		Prism Diopters
	Objectives	Eyepieces	
A. Biobjective binocular (Greenough):			
AO-Spencer	12	8	7.0
Bausch & Lomb	10	8	9.0
Leitz (straight eyepieces)	18	16	14.0
Leitz (inclined eyepieces)	—	°	°
Zeiss X	—	8	7.0
Zeiss XII	—	5	4.5
B. Monobjective binocular:			
Instruments with parallel (straight) eyepiece tubes do not require prisms			
AO-Spencer with convergent eyepieces	—	8	7.0

*Varying from 8.5° at 54mm interpupillary distance to 18° at 76mm. Prisms required would be that for camera interocular distance, e.g., for Stereo Realist of 70mm interocular use a 13.5 diopter prism.

A pair of prisms of the appropriate power must be placed between the camera lenses and the microscope eyepieces with their bases toward each other. To be effective, the prisms should be as close as possible to

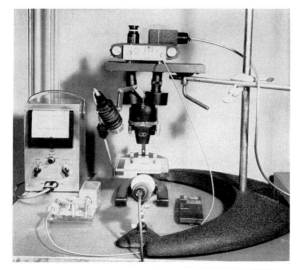

6. Laboratory stand, wide horseshoe base, and ¾″ diameter upright supporting Realist camera on U-shaped shelf (see Fig. 9). Probe of light meter and magnifier are shown on ground glass inserted in camera with back removed.

the camera lenses and to the exit pupils of the microscope. This is best accomplished when the prisms are secured to the camera lenses in simple slip-on mounts which are provided with reference marks on the outer edges of their rims for proper orientation and accurate alignment, easily done with a small straightedge (Fig. 8). When the camera is now centered over the properly focused microscope, a single exposure will produce simultaneously a photograph of the image emerging from each microscope eyepiece, the pair to be later viewed as a true stereoscopic rendering.

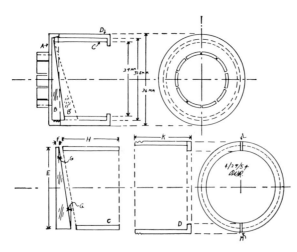

7. Slip-on prism mount to fit over lenses of Stereo Realist. A: slip-on collar; B B¹: prisms; C: spacer to hold prism in place; D: hood and light baffle; L and M: reference marks for alignment and orientation of prisms.

8. Stereo Realist camera provided with prisms in slip-on mounts, their reference marks lined up against a straightedge. Another set of prisms of 14 diopters is shown alongside for work with another microscope requiring greater prism power.

Some stand to support the camera in proper vertical and horizontal alignment with the microscope is desirable even though, with a little practice, it is possible to make the pictures with the camera hand-held. The stand can be either a laboratory stand (Fig. 6) which has a large horseshoe base with an 18-inch open work space and a ¾-inch diameter upright, or an adaptation of an enlarger baseboard with its substantial upright supporting a sliding arm to which the camera is secured in a true horizontal plane. A "U"-shaped, fork-like bracket (Fig. 9) is very effective as a camera support. The camera rests freely on it, with the lenses nesting snugly between the two tines of the fork; it can be easily lifted up for loading or unloading film and is just as easily returned to its proper position.

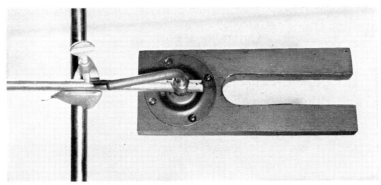

9. The "U"-shaped, fork-like shelf support for the Realist camera, the two lenses of which fit snugly between the tines of the "fork." This provides a practical way to support the camera above the microscope: it is readily removable and easily returned to its proper alignment for viewing or for photography.

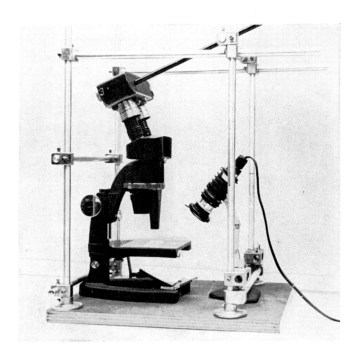

10. Microscope stand and camera support for stereo photomicrography, made up of lightweight rods and connectors of the Flexaframe Laboratory Stand System (Fisher Scientific Company). This arrangement is one of the great many possible for supporting the camera at any angle required by the microscope.

A suitable camera support, readily adaptable to the best position of the Realist, depending upon the microscope's 'working angle," can also be assembled from the lightweight rods, clamps and connectors of the Flexaframe Laboratory Stand System (Fisher Scientific Company), as shown in Figure 10.

Each microscope objective has a definite magnification and depth of field. In choosing the objective, it should be borne in mind that overall sharpness and good depth of field are important requirements of stereo photography. Best results are ordinarily secured with the lowest power which will give adequate rather than excessive magnification of detail. Stereo pictures will be more pleasing when the top of the specimen (point nearest the objective) is in good focus, rather than if the specimen goes out of focus toward the eye. A little loss of sharpness *away* from the observer is generally more tolerable than loss of sharpness *toward* the observer. However, the in-or-out-of-focus aspects of stereo photography must be permitted to remain as personal criteria of the photographer: what might be satisfactory to one person or one application may not be acceptable to another.

342

If the nature of the specimen is such that the top and bottom or right or left side are significant for identification or recognition, then the camera should be suitably oriented above the microscope or the subject arranged on the stage so that the top of the camera coincides with the top of the specimen. This is an important requirement for good stereo photomicrographs and should never be overlooked when the equipment is being readied for exposure.

When the camera lens is used as part of the optical system of the microscope, the magnification is reduced because a microscope normally produces a real image at a distance of about 10 inches above the eyepiece. If, then, the focal length of the camera lens is less than 10 inches, the magnification will be reduced in proportion; that is, if a camera lens of 5-inch focal length is used, the magnification will be only ½ that of the microscope alone. In the case of the Stereo Realist lenses, which have a focal length of 35mm, the magnification on the film is only ¼ that of the microscope alone. However, it must be remembered that the Stereo Realist pictures will be seen through the Stereo Realist viewer, which has a magnification of about 5½ times, so the original size of the microscope image is largely restored in the viewer.

Focusing the Stereo Microscope

The stereo microscope should be in proper adjustment before photographic work is started. A simple method of testing this is to focus the instrument upon a ruler or some other object having straight lines or

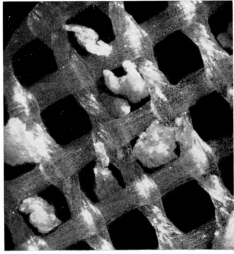

11. Flour on Bolting Silk 64XXX — magnified here about 25x. From a stereo transparency by Richard I. Derby.

12. Small pearl set in sterling, an ear ornament. From a stereo photomicrograph by Henry M. Lester.

12. Small pearl set in sterling, an ear ornament.
From a stereo photomicrograph by Henry M. Lester.

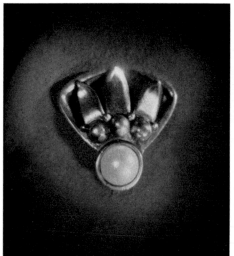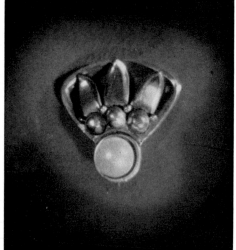

edges. When this is placed at the right outside edge of the field, it should be seen in the same position by each of the two eyes. Similarly, the top and bottom of the field should be tested for like position of the subject within the two fields. Though adjustment screws are provided, the alignment of the two objectives should be attempted only by those familiar with this procedure. It may be better to entrust this task to the maker of the microscope or to a competent repair man.

Securing critical focus with a stereo microscope is simple enough. However, when one of the two oculars has an adjustment for compensation of vision in one eye, focusing should be done with one eye first through the eyepiece which is not adjustable and then, *with the same eye*, through the adjustable eyepiece until the image matches the critical sharpness seen in the first eyepiece. If the observer uses eyeglasses for distance, he should also use them for focusing.

Since the interocular of the Realist camera is 2¾ inches (70mm), while the average interocular of the eyes is about 2½ inches (63mm), the microscope oculars must be moved farther apart for the camera than for visual observation. The rims of the prism mounts will assist in the proper spacing of the oculars, their inner diameter having been designed with this in mind. The prisms should be brought in contact with the edges of the two oculars and then raised a hair's breadth above them. The camera lenses should be left at their f/3.5 or f/4 apertures and focused to infinity.

344

It will be found convenient to use two Realist cameras for photomicrography. The cameras should be of the same model. One is loaded with film for photography, and the other is used for viewing or focusing. The camera used for focusing has its back removed and a piece of fine ground glass taped into the film channel. This "focusing camera" is handy for checking focus, measuring illumination, centering and composition of the image in the respective apertures of the camera. The ground-glass camera is removed after focusing, and the loaded one is substituted for the exposures. This arrangement saves a lot of time and wear and tear on the microscopist.

Lighting for the Stereo Photomicrograph

Depending on whether the subject is transparent or opaque, it will be lighted either from below the stage or from above. With transparent objects, lighted from below by means of the substage mirror, a large light source is necessary, since light must be provided for the specimen which is being viewed from two different angles. It may be necessary to place a piece of white paper or opal glass over the mirror to diffuse the light sufficiently, but some loss of light intensity must be expected.

Opaque specimens are lighted from above the stage, and in most cases the method of lighting will be much the same as that used for any small still-life object. Such light sources as the Spencer Universal Microscope lamp or similar small spotlights should be used, at a distance great

13. Fungi on wood, magnified about 12½x. From a stereo photomicrograph by Richard I. Derby.

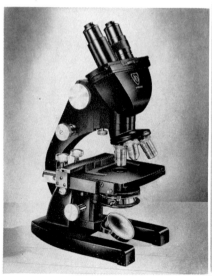

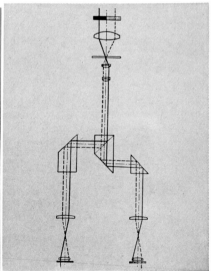

14. A monobjective binocular microscope (AO — Spencer) with inclined and divergent eyepieces. Note that left ocular tube is adjustable for observer's vision. The 3 objectives shown on nosepiece are used one at a time — hence, monobjective.

15. Light path through a monobjective binocular microscope as it is affected by the application of Schulman's Stereo Polarizer. The right half of the field covered by the objective is seen only through the right eyepiece; the left half, only through the left eyepiece.

enough to permit the beam spread of the light to cover the subject fully. In general, such subjects should be cross-lit by two of these lamps, one of them fairly high for general illumination, the other at a sharper angle for modeling. The two lights should both be aimed from a plane midway between the two objectives to avoid uneven illumination in the two stereo images. Except for this requirement, lighting from overhead for microscopic subjects differs very little from the approved method of lighting any type of picture for best modeling.

Adapting the Monobjective Binocular Microscope

The conventional microscope with a single objective and a binocular body is not a stereoscopic instrument, but it can be adapted to the needs of stereo observation and stereo photomicrography. The light gathered by the single objective is divided equally between the two eyepieces, transmitting through a system of prisms the identical view of the subject to each eye at one-half of its brightness. Ordinarily such an instrument gives no perception of depth; however, there are several ways of making this possible.

To secure a separate right-eye and left-eye view through a single objective, we want the light from the left-hand side of the objective to

346

reach only the left eyepiece and the light from the right-hand side of the objective to reach only the right eyepiece. This would give us a true stereoscopic view, even though only one objective is used.

This can be accomplished by various means which are extensively described in the literature of microscopy. For stereo photomicrography with the Realist camera, the most convenient method involves the use of a special "Stereo Polarizer" devised by Schulman (U.S. Patent No. 2,255,631) and supplied by the Bausch & Lomb Optical Company. This device consists of three Polaroid screens: the larger "polarizer" with a handle for the control of light reaching the single objective, and two smaller "analyzer caps," one for each of the two eyepieces. The polarizing screen in the polarizer is split through the center, one half polarizing in the direction of the handle, the other half at right angle to the first. The polarizer is placed below the diaphragm of the substage condenser with its handle pointing away from the observer. The analyzer caps are placed over the two eyepieces and oriented in such a manner that the right cap has its white line pointing away from the observer, while the white line of the left cap will point at right angles to the other. When two polarizing media are placed one over the other with their lines of polarization crossing each other at right angles, they will transmit no light; therefore, the right eyepiece will now extinguish the light transmitted by the left half of the objective and will transmit to the right eye only that which comes from the right half. Similarly, the left eyepiece cap will transmit to the left eye only the image which originates in the left half of the objective. Each eye then sees only the images

16. Stereo Polarizer devised by C. A. Schulman (U.S. Patent No. 2,255,631) for adaptation of monobjective binocular microscope to stereo observation and photomicrography. Available from Bausch & Lomb Optical Co.: polarizer with handle and two analyzer caps with orientation lines indicating direction of polarization.

17. Light path within the body of a monobjective binocular microscope (AO — Spencer): the beam of light emerging from the single objective (not shown) is divided by prisms into two equal beams delivering to the oculars two identical images of one-half the brightness.

18. Aphids, magnified here about 90 times. Stereo photomicrograph through a monobjective binocular microscope and Stereo Polarizer. Stereo by Oscar W. Richards.

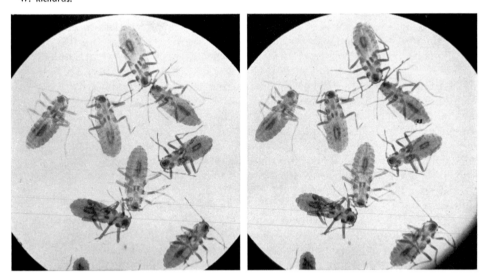

from their respective halves of the objective, and true stereoscopic vision is thus attained. The schematic diagram (Fig. 15) shows how this is accomplished.

The Realist camera can be conveniently used with this setup. The monobjective binocular microscope has the advantage of stereo rendering at higher magnifications than are available with the Greenough stereo microscope. The depth perception with this arrangement is quite remarkable even though specimens ordinarily prepared for observation under high magnification have little intrinsic depth — indeed, they are sliced very thin with a microtome.

When the ocular tubes of a monobjective binocular microscope are parallel, whether they be inclined or vertical, all that is necessary after focusing the microscope is to adjust the separation of the eyepieces to the interocular spacing of the camera. When the ocular tubes are of the diverging type, or when they do not remain parallel as the interocular distance is adjusted to 70mm, then it will be necessary to employ prisms in mounts of the same type as used with the Greenough microscope, but the prisms will have to be of a power appropriate to the angle of divergence of the particular microscope. Again, the power of the prism in prism diopters is obtained by dividing the tangent of the angle of convergence from the vertical by 0.01.

The camera may be supported or it may be hand-held; either method is accomplished in a manner similar to that suggested for use with the

348

Greenough stereoscopic microscope. When the ocular tubes are parallel and not inclined, the camera may be supported by the microscope.

Focusing the Monobjective Microscope

When the microscope is focused properly for the normal eye, it will usually be in focus on the film of a camera (which has *its* lens focused on infinity) when the camera lens is placed close to the microscope eyepiece. If the observer uses eyeglasses for distant viewing, he should wear them when focusing the microscope; otherwise a true infinity setting will not be obtained. Some observers do not get an infinity setting of a microscope even with glasses, due probably to their inability to relax the eye muscles completely. In this case, the eye can be forced to hold an infinity focus with the aid of a small telescope or field glass. The user first focuses the telescope on a distant object (several blocks away), then holds the telescope over the eyepiece of the microscope and focuses the microscope while looking through the telescope into the instrument.

Most modern binocular microscopes have an individual focusing adjustment on one eyepiece so that sharpness can be obtained in both when the observer's vision is not equal in both eyes. When the microscope is used with a camera, the two eyepieces should be adjusted alike, of course, and to do this the following procedure should be followed. First place one eye (aided by the telescope if necessary) over the non-

19. Polyplax spinulosa magnified as shown here about 200x through a monobjective binocular microscope and Stereo Polarizer. Stereo by Henry M. Lester.

349

adjustable eyepiece and focus the entire microscope in the normal manner. Then shift the same eye to the other eyepiece (the adjustable one), and without touching the focus of the microscope itself, proceed to adjust the eyepiece until the image is sharp also. Since the same eye is used over both eyepieces, the two will be alike in adjustment, and differences in vision between the two eyes will not affect the setting.

An additional suggestion for securing critical focus on film: the focus should be rechecked through each eyepiece with the same eye after the two oculars have been spread to the 70mm interocular setting, and if necessary a slight adjustment can be made before the camera is placed on the microscope for the exposure.

Lighting for the Monobjective Microscope

The best type of illumination for stereo photomicrography through the monobjective binocular microscope is the Köhler type; it is most likely to produce even distribution of light over the entire area of the specimen, which will insure equal amounts of light reaching both frames of the stereo photograph. Lack of space here makes it necessary to refer readers unfamiliar with this method of illumination to standard texts on photomicrography and the microscope.

The problem of evenness of lighting for the two views required for a good stereo is ordinarily not encountered in the monobjective binocular microscope. But if through accidental or inherent misalignment of the instrument the light appears to be unequally divided, there may be a

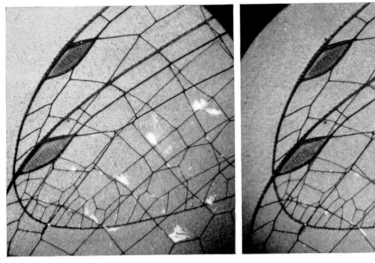

20. Dragon Fly Wings magnified here about 15x. Stereo photomicrograph through a stereo microscope. Stereo by Richard I. Derby.

350

21. Petunia Seeds and Needle Point magnified about 20x through a biobjective stereo microscope and 7 diopter prisms. Stereo by Henry M. Lester.

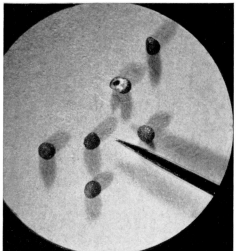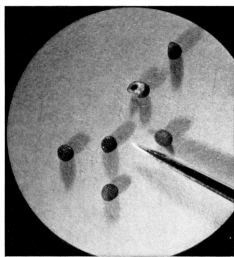

marked difference in the pair of views on film, which is far more sensitive to minute differences in brightness than the human eye. When such uneven brightness in the two fields becomes apparent, the alignment and proper centering of the stereo polarizer should be checked, and if that is found to be in order the instrument should be examined by its maker or a competent repairman.

The best way to insure equal and uniform illumination in both eyepieces is to check them individually with a sensitive light meter, such as is described here in the next section. If such an instrument is not available, one can look quickly with the same eye through both eyepieces. This may give a rough idea of the comparative brightness, but only very approximate results can be expected. The visual appraisal definitely cannot be recommended for the making of color stereo photomicrographs, where the slightest mismatch of light intensity will show up.

It should be further remembered that color photography requires proper color temperature of the light source. Correct rendering of the color of the subject and its background depends upon the color temperature of the light source. For instance, when Kodachrome Film, Type A, is used, the color temperature of the light source should be 3400°K at the film. A light source of 3200°K will impart a slight yellow cast over the entire field unless a suitable light balancing filter is employed in front of the light. (See PHOTO-LAB-INDEX, Section 16: Color Data, for guidance in the use of light, filters and color films.) If the light intensity is too great, neutral density filters should be employed

351

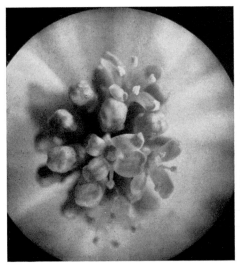 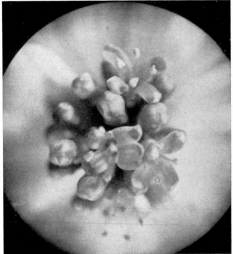

to reduce it. The use of rheostats or variable transformers is not suitable either for increasing or reducing the light intensity, since varying voltage will vary color temperature. A difference of 10 volts in a 115-volt line may produce a difference of as much as 100°K in color temperature, which will be discernible in a color picture.

For black-and-white photography, most 35mm photographic emulsions will be found suitable for stereo photomicrography, though the medium-speed panchromatic emulsions offer the best combination of contrast and fine grain which are so desirable for enlargements. Black-and-white negatives can be printed by contact in full lengths of film onto positive film, and then cut apart and mounted for viewing or for projection. These negatives can also be used to produce enlargements on paper, to be mounted on cardboards similar to those of the classical stereoscopic pictures of the earlier part of this century for viewing either through the parlor-type stereoscope or through the Stereo Viewer recently developed by Morgan & Lester, featured for the first time as an accessory to this volume. (See Chapter 14: *Stereo In Black and White.*) It should be noted that black-and-white prints on paper or on film, either contact prints or enlargements, can also be made from original color stereo photomicrographs. This service is available from certain custom photo-finishing organizations. Their names will be supplied on request by the publishers of this volume.

352

Stereo photomicrographs made with the Realist camera by methods outlined here are true stereos. As such they can be viewed or projected when mounted as any other stereos. Because these stereo pairs are made by the illumination of two light beams which are parallel, or nearly so, they can be mounted in the normal mounts. Only a few stereo photomicrographs may require mounting in medium or close-up masks, specifically those which were made through microscopes having hyperstereoscopic separation or through high-powered objectives of very short focal lengths.

Proper Exposure Is Important

Exposures for stereo photomicrography are rather critical; more so for color photography, but not unimportant in black-and-white work. The need for uniform brightness of both images is an indispensable condition. Visual evaluation is at its best not reliable. Conventional exposure meters are not sensitive enough for such critical work, but will be found useful in the absence of better means, and definitely superior to judgment rendered by the human eye. However, if a great deal of stereo photomicrography is done consistently, the observer gradually acquires the ability to estimate exposures with a fair degree of accuracy, just as one does in other applications of photography.

The usual trial and error methods, exposure tests and such can be applied, and when the light source employed is strong enough a fair

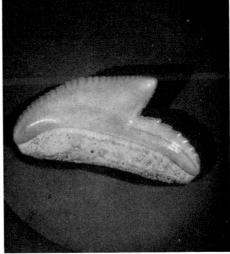

23. A Tiger Shark's Tooth magnified about 10x through a stereo microscope. Stereo by Henry M. Lester.

24. Probe of sensitive light meter displaying phototube through its "window." A d-c microammeter of 5 ranges. These are the two "business ends" of the light meter, the electronic circuit of which is shown in Fig. 26.

idea of the exposure can be obtained by holding an exposure meter, such as the General Electric, Hickok or other foot-candle measuring instrument, in such a manner that the entire light output emerging from one or the other eyepiece reaches the exposure meter cell. With the calculator of the meter set to the rated speed of the film employed, the exposure found opposite the f/2 aperture value will be quite close.

A Sensitive Light Meter

A satisfactory method for measurement of small amounts of light, capable of disclosing minute differences between the brightness of the two images and equally satisfactory for measurement of light in terms of correct exposure, is a light meter employed successfully during the past five years for all kinds and types of photography. The meter measures the brightness of the image as it appears in the film plane by means of a small probe which is applied to the ground glass. It has been found satisfactory and consistently dependable for photomicrography in color and in black and white, within the working range of the optical microscope. The light meter is an electronic instrument employing a circuit published by Radio Corporation of America for measurement of very small values of illumination (Fig. 26).

Capable of measuring illumination corresponding to the phototube current of only 10^{-10} amperes, this circuit, when operated with a vacuum phototube such as the Type 929, has a sensitivity of 45 microamperes per lumen. This type of tube, having a spectral sensitivity designated as S-4 (Fig. 25), has been found most suitable for the needs of stereo photomicrography in particular as well as photomicrography in general. The phototube, contained in a small metal housing, forms at the end of a shielded two-conductor microphone-type cable, a convenient probe with a window of about 0.75 square inch, effectively exposing the light-sensitive area of the phototube, which has an area of 0.6 square inch. Since the maximum circular area of an image projected upon the film seldom exceeds 0.7 square inch, the probe fully covers the image of one frame when centered upon the ground glass, without any exploratory movements.

The phototube current is measured by a sensitive multirange microammeter (1 to 1000 microamperes d-c, in 5 ranges) which, when suitably calibrated by a series of test exposures on a variety of subjects and magnifications, gives reliable indications for consistently correct exposures. Its linear characteristics make calculations simple. The instrument established the following fairly constant relationship between rated film speed, brightness of the image upon the ground glass and the correct exposure:

FOR KODACHROME, TYPE A FILM

10 microamperes	2½ seconds
100 "	¼ second
500 "	¹⁄₂₀ second

The circuit of this instrument is basically a d-c amplifier, which is stabilized by the incorporation of a balanced bridge circuit, with a resistor in one arm of the bridge corresponding to the phototube in the other arm. Since both arms of the bridge use identical tubes (within commercial limits), any drift due to change in temperature or voltage

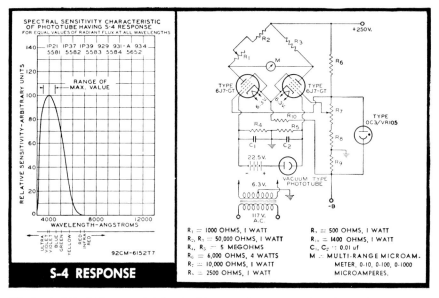

S-4 RESPONSE

25. Spectral Sensitivity curve S-4 for the RCA Type 929 vacuum phototube used in this work. By permission of RCA, copyright proprietor.

26. Circuit for measurement of very small values of illumination is used for the basis of sensitive light meter for stereo photomicrography. It is useful for balancing brightness of the two images and for determining correct exposure. By permission of RCA, copyright proprietor.

is nullified, since it occurs in the same direction in both arms of the bridge.

Some drift, of course, remains, and in any case there is considerable wandering of the zero point during warm-up. After about 15 minutes the instrument becomes reasonably stable, and only a slight adjustment of one of the two balance controls is needed to maintain the zero setting. Calibration stability is excellent; as long as the zero setting is properly adjusted, the instrument will consistently duplicate exposure readings. The slight inconvenience of the small residual zero drift is more than offset by the low cost of the instrument — less than $75, of which more than one-third is the cost of a good multirange microammeter. Upkeep is low, the instrument operating from the 115-volt a-c line with trifling current consumption, while phototube current is supplied by a 22½-volt hearing aid battery which usually lasts a year or more.

Identification of Stereo Photomicrographs

Whether the stereo photomicrographs are made on color film or on black-and-white emulsions, the importance of positively identifying the "right" and the "left" view of each pair cannot be overemphasized. Though the Realist camera has an identifying notch within the "right" film gate, which is automatically reproduced on the film, this mark may not be visible on photomicrographs, which may appear within a circular field, exactly duplicating the appearance of the field as it is seen through the microscope. Since the picture area may not extend to the edge of the full frame of the Realist camera, the notch will not be

356

visible. Any identification applied to all the "right" or to all the "left" images upon the entire length of the film before cutting, which will unmistakably mark at least one picture of each pair, will insure that the pictures will be correctly mounted for viewing or for projection so that the right eye will always see the picture as it was seen through the right ocular. The manner in which these pictures are identified is a matter of personal preference: a red or yellow crayon mark, a pin prick, a small punch notch—anything, as long as the pictures are identified. Unless the stereo pairs are correctly mounted so that the right eye will see the view which originated in the right eyepiece, the finished pictures may appear upon viewing or projection as pseudostereos, where cavities look like mounds and vice versa.

The perception of depth secured in stereo photomicrographs depends on the angles of inclination of the objectives and their inherent depth of field. It must be realized that the camera has no power of adjustment and accommodation, as the human eye has. Neither does the camera lens have the imagination which frequently enables us to visualize sharpness where it has all but gone. Thus the human eye will see a little more depth of field through the stereo microscope than the camera will reproduce on the photographic emulsion. Also, the eye will adjust itself as it wanders from the center to the edge of the field. But with the wide-field eyepieces, it may not be possible to get the entire field in sharp focus for the camera lens due to the curvature of field inherent in such oculars. However, these are problems common to all photo-

28. Dandelion Seed and Pappus shown magnified here about 11x. From a stereo photomicrograph by Richard I. Derby.

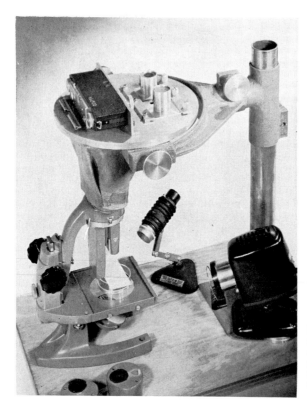

29. Interesting set-up for stereo photomicrography devised by Richard I. Derby of the Research Laboratories, General Mills, Inc. Minneapolis, Minnesota.

micrography, and the reader is referred for further guidance to standard texts dealing with these problems at length.

Other Ways

There are other ways to make stereo photomicrographs with the Realist camera. Richard I. Derby of the General Mills Research Laboratories, Minneapolis, Minnesota, has developed a method capable of producing excellent stereo photomicrographs at low magnification. A few of his stereos are reproduced here. Derby's approach requires a modification of the Realist camera to the extent that it is used without its lenses, diaphragms, shutters, or focusing mechanism. An ingenious stand provides a rigid support for the camera: a circular plate revolving in a horizontal plane supports the camera body, which has been provided with a dark slide. The opposite half of the revolving plate is provided with a ground glass screen in the focal plane of the camera and a pair of magnifiers for convenient focusing and composition. The circular plate is pivoted at its center on a lower plate which is stationary. The upper plate rotates to place either the camera or the viewing and focusing device over the microscope. The lower plate is connected to the microscope, a Greenough-type stereoscopic instrument, through a soft leather bellows which acts as a light shield. The microscope is ordinarily used without its eyepieces and ocular tubes. When higher magnifications are desired, the oculars can be used. Exposures are made by switching the light sources on and off with a timer. The complete setup as developed and used by Derby is shown in Figure 29. A sensitive electronic light meter plays an important part in Derby's work; his lighting and exposures are excellent and remarkably uniform.

Bibliography

Amateur Photomicrography with Simple Apparatus, Alan Jackson, Focal Press — Pitman, New York.

Exposure Control in Photomicrography, John A. Maurer; Journal, Biological Photographic Association; Vol. XII, June 1944, pp. 173-185.

Photography through the Microscope, Eastman Kodak Company, Rochester 4, N. Y.

Photo-Lab-Index, Henry M. Lester, Morgan & Lester, New York.

Photomicrography, R. M. Allen; D. Van Nostrand Co., Inc., New York.

Photomicrography, An Introduction to Photomicrography with the Microscope, Fourteenth Edition, 1944, Eastman Kodak Company, Rochester 4, N. Y.

Photomicrography in Theory and Practice, Chas. P. Shillaber, John Wiley & Sons, Inc., New York.

RCA Phototubes. Form PT-20R1, Radio Corporation of America, Harrison, New Jersey.

Stereo-Photography in Practice, E. F. Linssen, The Fountain Press, London.

Tridimensional Cytohistology, Oscar W. Richards; Journal, Biological Photographic Association; Vol. XIX, February 1951, pp: 7-15.

1. The old-fashioned paper stereo picture, used in the "parlor stereoscope." The image has been reduced in size for easy viewing, and card margins trimmed, but the antiquated "arched top" of the pictures is evident. In making paper copies of Stereo Realist pictures for these old viewers, no arch is necessary. Photo courtesy George Eastman House.

14. Stereo in Black & White

JOHN S. CARROLL

It is expected, of course, that the great majority of Stereo Realist pictures will be made in color, both for the ultimate in realism and the maximum convenience (since two manufacturers of color films provide mounting service at the time of processing).

However, there are some occasions when black-and-white stereo pictures may be either desirable or necessary. Some test and experimental work may be carried out economically on black-and-white film; in many cases, viewing the *negative* in the stereo viewer may provide all the information required. On other occasions, there may be reason to produce black-and-white stereos in quantity, either in standard Stereo Realist format or for the sake of using other types of viewing equipment which may be available. Finally, for special occasions, the Stereo Realist may be used as a fine miniature camera for single pictures by capping each lens alternately and using the double exposure release if necessary.

In general, it is necessary to remember that making black-and-white pictures with the Stereo Realist is a branch of miniature-camera photography, and all the meticulous care required to make a high-quality negative with any precision miniature camera will have to be exercised in black-and-white stereo work as well.

35mm Films Available

Any of the standard 35mm film cartridges for miniature camera use will fit the Stereo Realist. As in the case of color films, the 20-exposure cartridge will produce 15 stereo pairs, and the 36-exposure cartridge will produce 28 stereo-pair exposures.

All presently available 35mm films are panchromatic; that is, they are sensitive to light of all colors; darkroom work must be carried out in total darkness, and these films may be used with filters of nearly any color for correction of their spectral response or for special effects.

The available 35mm films fall into 3 classes:

1) Ultra-speed emulsions, for exposures under poor light conditions, when a picture must be achieved under any circumstances. Some graininess must be accepted as penalty for such speed. Films of this group include:

> Kodak Super-XX Panchromatic
> Ansco Ultra-Speed Panchromatic
> DuPont Superior-3 Panchromatic
> Gevapan 33
> Ilford HP-3

2) Medium-speed emulsions for all-around black-and-white photography. This group includes:

> Kodak Plus-X Panchromatic
> Ansco Supreme Panchromatic
> DuPont Superior-2 Panchromatic
> Gevapan 30
> Ilford FP-3

3) Slow, ultra-fine-grain emulsions for negatives which are to be enlarged to great size, and for copying. Such emulsions will seldom be required for stereo photography, but may be useful if the Stereo Realist is used for other purposes in an emergency. This group includes:

> Kodak Micro-File Panchromatic
> (high contrast for line work only)
> Gevapan 27 Microgran
> Ilford Pan F

Some special emulsions, such as infrared sensitive, are available from certain manufacturers, but their availability is generally limited, and it will be best to check with a local dealer if such film is required.

	A.S.A. Exposure Index		Weston Speed	
	Daylight	Tungsten	Daylight	Tungsten
Class 1 (Hi-speed films)	125	100	100	64
Class 2 (Medium-speed films)	64	50	50	32
Class 3 (Slow fine-grain)				
Ilford Pan F	16	10	12	8
Gevapan 27 Microgran	32	20	16	12
Kodak Micro-File	—	—	—	2.5*

*Taking reading from white card substituted for subject; use for line copying only.

While there will be some variation in speed between the several films of each group, the latitude of black-and-white films makes it possible to consider all films in groups 1 and 2 to be roughly equal to the average of the group in speed; the preceding table will provide a convenient starting point for exposure determination. If greater precision is required, refer to the PHOTO-LAB-INDEX for latest film speed ratings, or to the manufacturer's direction sheets.

Filters and Filter Factors

Since all 35mm films currently available are panchromatic, the results obtained, even without a filter, are usually excellent in tonality, closely approximating in tones of gray the aspect of the subject as seen by the eye. However, there are occasions when certain colors may be desirably rendered darker or lighter than they appear visually, and for this purpose filters are used. The rule for using filters is as follows:

1) A filter of the same color as the subject lightens the subject.
2) A filter of complementary color to the subject darkens it.

It is by the working of Rule 2 that a yellow filter, the complementary color to blue, is used to darken blue skies and make clouds more visible. Most black-and-white work with the stereo camera can be accomplished with, at most, 3 pairs of filters:

> Aero-2 or K-2 (medium yellow)
> X-1 (medium green)
> A (medium red)

The medium yellow filter is used for all general outdoor photography; it lightens grass and foliage slightly and darkens blue skies to a pleasing gray tone. The yellow filter should *not* be used when close-ups of people are being made outdoors, since it will render the skin tones and lips in too light a tone.

The medium green (X-1) filter is ued for interior work by incandescent light, particularly for portraiture where the normal tendency of panchromatic film is to render flesh tones quite light, lacking in modeling. Outdoors, the X-1 filter accomplishes much the same thing as the medium-yellow except for somewhat greater lightening of foliage; it is recommended where some darkening of the sky is desired and people appear in the scene. Here it will produce excellent modeling in the face and may be used in all such cases except for persons with deeply tanned skin, where it is better to omit the filter altogether.

The medium red (A) filter is strictly a special-effect filter. If exposure is carefully determined, it can produce white clouds on a nearly black sky. It will in general reproduce yellow, orange and red objects as white or nearly so, and blue or green objects as practically black. Such reproduction is highly unnatural, but may at times be desirable for dramatic emphasis or for certain scientific purposes.

363

All filters produce their characteristic effects by absorbing some of the light which would otherwise reach and affect the film. For this reason, additional exposure must always be given when a filter is used. The amount by which the exposure must be increased with a given filter and film is called the "filter factor," and complete tables of filter factors for most filters and films will be found in the PHOTO-LAB-INDEX, Section 9.

As a rough approximation only, the following table will provide usable factors for the three filters already mentioned with the principal types of film currently available.

	AERO 2 OR K-2		X-1		A	
	Day.	Tung.	Day.	Tung.	Day.	Tung.
Kodak Super-XX Kodak Plus-X	2	1.5	4	3	8	4
Ansco Supreme Ansco Ultra-Speed	2	1.5	4	3	8	5
DuPont Superior-3 DuPont Superior-2	2	1.3	4	3	5 3.2	2.5 2
Gevapan 27 Microgran	2	1.5	3	2	5	3
Gevapan 30	1.75	1.5	4	3	6	5.5
Gevapan 33	2	1.5	3	2	5	3

The filter factors given above are the amounts by which the basic exposure must be *multiplied* to secure the corrected exposure with the filter. The easiest way to use these factors, however, is to *divide* the film speed or Exposure Index by the filter factor and set the exposure meter calculator to the new speed resulting.

Thus, for example, if a film having a Daylight Exposure Index of 50 is used with a K-2 filter having a factor of 2, the meter calculator is set to the Exposure Index of 25, and no further calculation is required for use of this particular filter with this film — in daylight. Don't forget to reset the meter to the correct Exposure Index when the filter is removed, however!

Developing the Negatives

Black-and-white 35mm negatives made with the Stereo Realist camera may be developed by any *first-class* photofinishing house which offers a good fine-grain developing service for miniature-camera negatives. Ordinary drug store finishing will *not* do.

There is nothing difficult about developing these negatives at home, however, beyond the requirement for care and absolute cleanliness. The amateur who has already done any 35mm still photography will find nothing new in the handling of stereo pairs on 35mm film. Equipment already available in the amateur darkroom should prove adequate for this work.

As in the case of any miniature camera negative, fine-grain development is essential. One may use any of the standard developer formulas, such as Kodak D-76, D-23, D-25 or DK-20; Ansco 17 or DuPont 6-D, formulas for which will be found in the Photo-Lab-Index or in the manufacturer's literature. For those who prefer not to mix their own chemicals, Kodak Microdol or Ansco Finex-L are recommended for small negatives.

Good developing tanks are available at a wide variety of prices, and any one of these will be satisfactory; attempts at processing 35mm film by seesawing it in a tray will only result in disaster.

For those who have not done any amount of miniature film processing, methods for the handling of these small negatives will be found in the Leica Manual. If one is familiar with the development of larger negatives, there is little to learn except the mechanical handling of the smaller film and to become accustomed to the somewhat lower contrast required in small negatives. However, to avoid minor flaws which are painfully evident in these small negatives, the following technique is recommended and should be accurately followed:

After loading the film into the tank, fill the tank with plain water and agitate for about 1 minute. This will assure complete wetting of the film by the developer and will avoid small air bubbles, which may result in tiny undeveloped spots.

Then empty the water from the tank and immediately fill with developer. Agitate vigorously for the first minute, and then at 1-minute intervals for the remainder of the developing time. This is important for even, streak-free development. The developing time should be estimated accurately with the aid of a *good* thermometer and the manufacturer's instructions for the film and developer in question. If in any doubt as to development time, it is usually better to underdevelop miniature camera negatives slightly.

At the end of the development time, the developer should be poured off and the tank filled with a hardening stop bath, preferably a *freshly prepared* 3 per cent solution of Potassium Chrome Alum. Always use fresh hardener for each roll of film. Other more acid stop baths should be avoided; they may produce blisters in the soft film emulsion. Nonhardening stop baths or plain water rinses should likewise be avoided. In general, keep all solutions at a uniform temperature in the vicinity of 68° F where possible and avoid any plain water washes or rinses until the film has been thoroughly hardened.

Hardening takes about 5 minutes in 3 per cent Chrome Alum; this is followed by fixing in a hardening-fixing bath such as Kodak F-5 or the similar formulas of Ansco, DuPont, etc. While little additional hardening will take place in such a bath after a Chrome Alum treatment, these fixing baths have a longer life and are less likely to sludge than plain hypo baths.

After fixing is complete (about 10 minutes, or twice as long as the film takes to clear completely) the film should be washed in running water for about 30 minutes, or in 5 to 10 changes of still water for about 3 minutes each, with thorough agitation in each change. Water should be the same temperature as other solutions.

When washing is complete, the film may be *carefully* wiped with a soft, wet chamois or a viscose sponge and hung up to dry in a dust-free place. Some people prefer not to touch the emulsion of the film at all; in this case the film is given a final rinse in a wetting agent such as Kodak Photo-Flo and hung to dry without wiping.

When dry, the film should be rolled up at once and stored in one of the small containers sold for this purpose. The individual negatives may be identified and numbered along the edge before storing. Negatives should not be cut into individual images or into strips for filing; it is impossible to keep miniature films clean if this is done.

Instructions for identifying the right and left negatives of stereo pairs will be found in the chapter on slide mounting.

Direct Positive Films

Where only a single black-and-white transparency is needed from each subject, a black-and-white reversal film such as Kodak Direct Positive

2. A well-made copy negative from a Kodachrome original should make prints as good as original black and white shots, without appearing grainy, "duped" or copied. Stereo by James H. Calder.

Panchromatic Film may be used. This is a fast panchromatic film of low graininess which produces black-and-white *positive* transparencies directly on the film exposed in the camera.

The ASA Exposure Index of Kodak Direct Positive Panchromatic film is Daylight 64, Tungsten 50. The film is available only in 100-foot rolls and must be loaded into cartridges by the user. Filter factors for this film are the same as for Kodak Plus-X.

Kodak Direct Positive Panchromatic film may be processed by the user in the same type of equipment as is used for developing black-and-white negatives. However, the procedure is somewhat different, comprising 5 baths with rinses between each. Chemicals for preparing these 5 baths are sold in sets, called the Kodak Direct Positive Film Developing Outfits, containing a sufficient quantity of each bath to make one quart, which will process 5 rolls of 36-exposure film (28 stereo pairs). Complete instructions are furnished with the outfit.

Black-and-White Negatives from Color Transparencies

Black-and-white copy negatives may be made from color transparencies, including stereo pairs, either by contact printing or by enlargement. If the negatives are to be used for printing larger-size stereo pairs, they should be exposed and developed as pairs all the way through the process to insure identical gradation of left and right-eye images. If only a single negative is wanted from one of a stereo pair for black-and-white exhibition printing, this precaution is less necessary, though uniformity of treatment is still desirable.

Negatives of very high quality can be made from color transparencies by using a medium-speed panchromatic material for the copy negative. Exposure must be accurately determined; underexposure will cause loss of shadow detail, while excessive overexposure will cause blocking of the highlights and a "mousy" quality in the whites. Such films as Kodak Portrait Panchromatic Sheet film, Ansco Isopan Sheet film or DuPont X-F Pan Sheet film are suitable for this work. Optimum exposure will produce a negative looking very much like an original camera negative, except that there must not be any clear film even in the deepest shadow areas.

If negatives are being made by enlargement, the transparency should be placed in the negative carrier with its emulsion *up*—facing the lamp. This prevents the image from being transposed left-for-right in the final print. The sensitive film must be placed on the enlarger easel in complete darkness; any light leaks from the enlarger should be carefully covered to avoid degrading the quality of the negative with fog.

Because of the long density scale of a color transparency, the copy negative is developed for less than the normal time. As a starting point, development should be for about one-half the normal time, and exposure should be adjusted to secure a negative of average printing density. If the resulting negative is then too flat to produce an excellent print on No. 2 paper, development should be increased and exposure slightly reduced. One or two trials with a typical transparency will indicate the correct exposure and development for copy negatives from practically all normal transparencies.

One interesting possibility in making copy negatives from color transparencies is that of using filters while exposing the film to secure correction or contrast effects similar to those obtained when the same filter is used on the camera with black-and-white negative film. Thus if a darkened sky should appear desirable, an Aero-2 or K-2 filter may be used on the enlarger while making the enlarged negative. The proper filter factor (for tungsten light) should be used, of course. Likewise, flesh-tone modeling may be emphasized with the use of an X-2 filter on the enlarger, just as in black-and-white portraiture.

Printing the Black-and-White Negative

If only a few prints are required from black-and-white negatives, they can be made by any photofinisher. However, if the amateur already has the equipment for black-and-white printing and enlarging, there is little difference in technique when handling stereo pairs or duplicate negatives from color transparencies.

The following pages are simply an outline of the principal methods and materials for black-and-white contact printing and enlarging; more complete instructions for this work will be found in the LEICA MANUAL, GRAPHIC GRAFLEX PHOTOGRAPHY, PHOTO-LAB-INDEX, and BASIC PHOTO, Book 3: THE PRINT.

Contact Printing

Where small prints are satisfactory, or where the negative has been made by enlargement from an original color transparency, contact printing is the simplest means of preparing prints. Inexpensive printing boxes are available, or a printing frame may be used when only a few prints are made on occasion.

Some typical contact papers are Kodak Velox and Azo, DuPont Apex and Ansco Convira. These papers may be handled by means of a bright yellow light, making judgment of exposure and development easy. For the occasional user there is Kodak Velite paper, which is sufficiently insensitive to room illumination so that no darkroom is needed for its manipulation.

The negative is placed on the glass of the printer or frame, emulsion side up; then the paper is placed on the negative, emulsion side down—that is, the emulsion of the paper is in contact with that of the negative. This will insure correctly oriented prints. The printer back is closed and the exposure given; a few tests will indicate the correct exposure time for negatives of average density.

Contact papers are usually developed in a fairly strong developer such as Kodak D-72 or Kodak Dektol, diluted 1:1. Other similar developers are DuPont 53-D and Ansco 125. Developing time for contact papers is 45 seconds to 1 minute. It is best to develop for the full time without examining the print until it is just about finished; attempts at saving an overexposed print by cutting the development time usually result in greenish tones, streaky or mealy-looking prints. Forced development of an underexposed print is usually hopeless; development beyond the normal time adds little or no density, but usually causes fog or yellow stain.

After development, the action of the developer is stopped by immersing the print in a stop bath (a weak solution of acetic acid; see the PHOTO-LAB-INDEX or the manufacturer's instruction sheets) for about 30 seconds to one minute. It is then transferred to the fixing bath (Kodak F-5 or equivalent of other manufacturers). Here it should stay for about 15 minutes, since it is not possible to see the action of the fixing bath on papers.

At the end of fixation, the prints must be thoroughly washed for at least ½ to 1 hour in running water, or 6 to 12 changes of still water, with agitation. Drying may be done face down in blotter rolls; glossy papers may be ferrotyped if desired.

Enlarging

One advantage of enlarging over contact printing is the fact that it permits masking or cropping the negative and enlargement of only a desired area. If contact prints are made first, they may be studied and marked for cropping before enlargements are undertaken. However, as skill develops, one can learn to compose and crop the image in negative form directly on the enlarger easel.

If negatives have been made on 35mm film directly in the camera, any good miniature enlarger such as the Leitz Valoy or Focomat may be used; a wide variety of similar units is available. If larger negatives have been made by enlargement from color transparencies, then a bigger enlarger such as an Omega or the Kodak Precision may be used.

In any case, the enlarger to be used should first be tested to make sure that no light leakage from lamphouse vents or negative carrier causes stray light to reach the easel; otherwise a fogged and degraded image will result. The enlarger negative carrier, and pressure glasses if used, must be kept spotlessly clean, and if the enlarger is designed to take a larger negative than the one being printed, all area surrounding the negative in the carrier should be masked off to avoid stray light coming around the edges of the negative. Such stray light is often the cause of poor image contrast and dirty highlights in enlargements. Finally, a high-quality enlarger lens must be used if optimum print sharpness is to be maintained.

Maximum sharpness can only be obtained when the enlarger is critically focused and when the entire machine is free from vibration. Lenses of large aperture provide a higher brightness in the projected image and make focusing easier; after focusing, however, the lens should be stopped down to $f/11$ or $f/16$ so as to produce exposures of manageable length.

Enlarging papers come in several types: bromide, chlorobromide, and "fast" chloride papers, the latter being fast only in relation to the chloride papers used for contact printing. Actually the "fast" chloride papers are the slowest enlarging papers.

Bromide papers are the fastest of the three types and are used mainly for quantity printing and press work. They are seldom used by amateurs and are not usually available in the average supply store.

The popular enlarging papers today are all chlorobromides and fall into two subclasses. The faster types of chlorobromide, such as Velour Black, Kodabromide, Kodak Medalist and Ansco Brovira, produce neutral black tones when developed in the standard print developer (diluted 1:2) for about 45 seconds to 1½ minutes. The slower types, such as Ansco Cykora and Indiatone, DuPont Warmtone, Kodak Platino, Opal, Ektalure and Illustrators Special, produce tones from warm brown to black depending on exposure, developer dilution and development time. These papers have individual methods of handling which are explained at greater length in the instruction sheets to be found in the package.

Special papers include such emulsions as Varigam and High-Speed Varigam, which are enlarging papers whose contrast can be controlled by the use of filters over the enlarger lens. Varigam is particularly valuable to the amateur whose negatives vary considerably in contrast and who does not wish to keep a large stock of paper of different grades.

Enlargements are developed in exactly the same manner as contact prints except that they may not be handled under quite as bright a darkroom light as contact papers. A yellow-green safelight, such as the Wratten OA, is recommended for easiest judgment of print quality and contrast. After development, the prints are rinsed in an acid stop bath, fixed and washed in exactly the same manner as contact prints.

Transparencies

Positive transparencies may be made from black-and-white either by contact or enlargement. Contact-printed transparencies may be made in any standard contact printer, but the lamps should be replaced by much smaller ones, or several thicknesses of white translucent paper should be placed over the diffusing glass, since transparency films are much faster than contact printing papers, approaching bromide papers in speed. Contact prints on 35mm positive film may be made in the Leitz Eldia or Eldur printers, provided a mask is made for the exposure window to adapt it to the Stereo Realist format.

Safety Positive film for transparencies is available both in 35mm perforated and unperforated rolls, and in sheet-film form on the same thin (.005-inch) base as the roll film. It has about the same speed as a fast bromide paper, and may be used for making enlarged transparencies from negatives of normal contrast. A High Contrast Safety Positive film is also available for use with flat negatives or for line diagrams and drawings.

Positive film may be developed in any standard paper developer, diluted about 1:4, and exposures should be timed for complete development in not less than 2 minutes. Blacks should be nearly opaque when viewed by transmitted light; a very slight veil should appear over the highest light. Over or underexposed transparencies should be discarded; good quality cannot be attained by cutting development of an overexposed transparency short, or by trying to force the development of an underexposed one.

General Aspects of Printing Black-and-White Stereos

Before starting to print a set of black-and-white negatives made in the camera, it is important that the entire roll of negatives be identified in pairs, and that the left and right image of each pair be marked in some unmistakable manner along the perforated edge of the film. Most Realist cameras expose a small notch between two perforations of the right-hand picture, and this can be used for identification unless the exposure is very dark. As each print is exposed, and before development, it should be marked on the back with its number and the letter "L" or "R." Otherwise, if the final pictures are to be mounted as stereo pairs for viewing, identification of the correct pairs and positioning of the images will be a tedious trial-and-error process.

If the prints are being made only for display as single black-and-white pictures, they may be made any convenient size; good negatives, carefully developed, should make excellent prints up to 8x10 inches at least, and larger with care.

On the other hand, if the black-and-white images are being made for use in various types of stereo viewers, there are a few standard formats in general use, and the dimensions shown in the accompanying diagrams should be followed.

Most European viewers for larger stereo slides accommodate glass-plate transparencies of either 45x107mm or 6x13cm. (A few French cameras use glass plates 7x13cm, but these are rare.) For the smaller of the two sizes mentioned, the images should be made about 45mm square and mounted between glasses, with the image centers separated by 62mm. In U. S. measurements, this is equivalent to a pair of pictures 1¾ inches square, mounted between glasses 1¾x4¼ inches, with their centers separated 2½ inches.

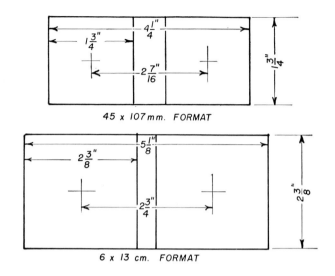

45 x 107mm. FORMAT

6 x 13 cm. FORMAT

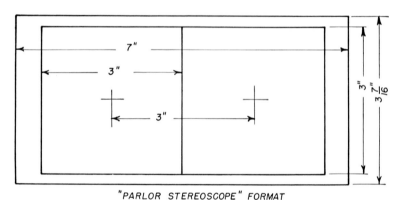

"PARLOR STEREOSCOPE" FORMAT

3. The three formats used in older stereo cameras. The upper two, 45 x 107mm and 6 x 13cm were usually used in the form of transparencies; the lower is the standard card-mounted paper print for "parlor stereoscopes." One odd size, sometimes found in Europe, was 7 x 13cm but it is very rare.

The larger size makes use of two pictures 6cm square (2⅜ inches) mounted between glasses 6x13cm (2⅜x5⅛ inches) with the centers of the images separated by 65mm (2⁹⁄₁₆ inches).

Practically all of the viewers for these two sizes of stereo images are designed for transparency viewing, and images for these viewers may be made on either film or glass plates (such as lantern-slide plates, provided they are obtainable in the proper size). If glass plates are used, it is particularly necessary to identify the negatives very carefully so that the right-eye image may be printed on the right edge of the plate and the left-eye image on the left — this is the reverse of the way they are arranged on the original negative roll. In addition, alignment of the images must be exact, or difficulty in fusion will be encountered when they are viewed. For this reason it is preferable to make these transparencies on film and mount them between glasses after development. In all cases, both images must have identical exposure and development for matched quality of left and right-eye images.

The majority of paper-printed stereo pairs will be made for viewing in the old-fashioned "parlor" or folding stereoscope, of which a great many are still in use in classrooms. For these, prints are made on glossy paper and mounted on cards. Most of the prints supplied for these sterescopes were made on die-cut paper having an arched outline, but this is un-necessary and looks antiquated. Prints should be approximately 3 inches square and mounted with their inner edges in contact on cards 3⁷⁄₁₆x7 inches.

Black-and-white stereo pairs for free viewing, or with the prism viewer supplied with this book, may be made of almost any convenient size. However, it has been found that the size and spacing of the illustrations in this volume is convenient for viewing, and it is recommended that prints for hand viewing be made in approximately this format.

If the prism viewer supplied with this book is used, the pictures are mounted in the same way as for a "parlor" stereoscope; that is, the right-eye image is placed on the right and the left-eye image on the left. A certain number of people can train themselves to view such images without any viewing apparatus at all, though this requires a good deal of practice, as described in Chapter 5.

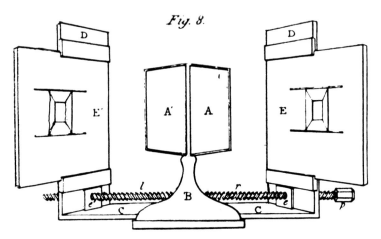

1. Wheatstone's original Stereoscope, as shown in his article in *Philosophical Transactions* of the Royal Society, 1838. (Plate X, page 372.)

15. Looking Back at Stereo

BEAUMONT NEWHALL

When Queen Victoria visited the 1851 World's Fair in the London Crystal Palace, she was so entranced by the stereoscopes on display in the French section that the exhibitors, Duboscq & Soleil, presented her with one. Her Majesty's interest precipitated popular enthusiasm for three-dimensional photography which, up to then, had been merely a scientific curiosity.

From that day until this, stereoscopic pictures have been the fascination of young and old. In the last century every well turned-out parlor had its basket of them, along with the skeleton viewer through which they appeared unbelievably real. Tourists bought slides wherever they went to add to their collections, and those who could not afford to travel found the stereoscope a splendid substitute. With the invention of dry plates and film towards the end of the century, stereo entered a second phase: amateurs, instead of buying ready-made slides, made their own. Today, with precision cameras, color films and self-illuminating viewers, three-dimensional photography is more popular than ever.

The stereoscope was invented in 1838 by Sir Charles Wheatstone, the famous English scientist. He first described it in an essay "On Some Remarkable, and Hitherto Unobserved, Phenomena of Binocular Vision," printed in the *Philosophical Transactions* of the Royal Society of London. Sir Charles maintained that we perceive depth because each eye sees different images, which are united by the mechanism of the brain. To prove this theory, he devised the instrument which he named the stereoscope "to indicate its property of representing solid figures." (Stereo = solid; scope = to see.) Wheatstone's was the first of a great variety of optical devices which enable us to reproduce the impression we get when we look at things with two eyes.

The illustration (Fig. 1), reproduced from Wheatstone's drawing, shows that the original stereoscope was a bulky device. It consisted of

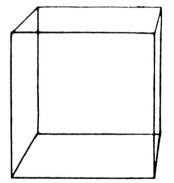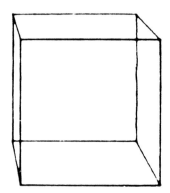

2a. One of Wheatstone's original Stereoscopic Drawings, from his article in *Philosophical Transactions* of the Royal Society.

a base, *C C*, with panels, *E E*[1], at each end of it. Mounted over the
center of the base are two mirrors, *A A*[1], set with their backs at 90° so
that each reflects one of the panels. On looking straight into the mirror,
therefore, the right eye will see panel E and the left eye panel *E*[1]. By
sliding the panels and adjusting their position from the mirror by the
screw *P*, pictures placed on them can be made to appear superimposed
when viewed in the mirrors.

On the panels of his stereoscope Wheatstone put pairs of geometrical
drawings (Fig. 2) of simple objects as seen from positions separated
by 2½ inches—the average distance between the eyes. Looking into the
mirrors he saw "instead of a representation on a plane surface . . . a
figure of three dimensions, the exact counterpart of the object from
which the drawings were made." He noticed that when he reversed the
pictures, so that the left-hand one was on the right, and vice versa,
space was reversed—that which was concave appeared convex, and
planes that normally receded seemed to project.

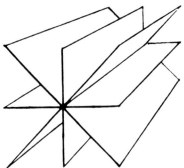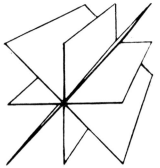

2b. Another of Wheatstone's original
Stereoscopic Drawings. Left and right drawings are transposed, resulting in a pseudoscopic image.

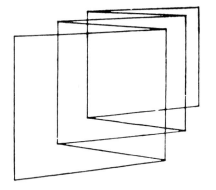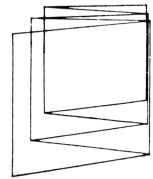

2c. A more complicated drawing from Wheatstone's paper. Considerable skill is required to make such drawings.

To test his theory further, Wheatstone made two identical cubes of wire. When these actual objects were put on the panels of the stereoscope so that each appeared the *same* to each eye, he saw no depth whatsoever, but merely a flat diagram!

"For the purpose of illustration," Wheatstone wrote about the drawings reproduced with the article, "I have employed only outline figures. . . . But if it be required to obtain the most faithful resemblances of real objects, shadowing and colouring may properly be employed to heighten the effects. Careful attention would enable an artist to draw and paint the two component pictures, so as to present to the mind of the observer, in the resultant perception, perfect identity with the object represented. Flowers, crystals, busts, vases, instruments of various kinds, &c., might thus be represented so as not to be distinguished by sight from the real objects themselves."

However, even the most skillful artist would shudder at such an assignment, for the difference between perspective drawings from points of

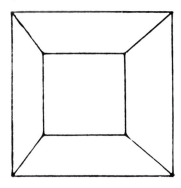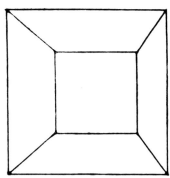

2d. A very simple drawing from Wheatstone's paper. This may eastily be copied and transposed for pseudoscopic effects.

3. Brewster's Stereoscope, invented in 1849. The slide is a glass positive of Niagara Falls. Collection of Mrs. Zelda Mackay, San Francisco. Photo by Ansel Adams.

sight separated by only 2½ inches is so minute as to be almost imperceptible. If stereoscopic pictures depended upon skill of hand, Wheatstone's invention would have remained a scientific curiosity.

But with timing so precise that it is difficult to dismiss it as coincidental, less than a year after Wheatstone announced the stereoscope a mechanical means of securing mathematically exact perspective pictures was made public. Photography made Wheatstone's prediction come true.

"It was at the beginning of 1839, about six months after the appearance of my memoir in the *Philosophical Transactions*, that the photographic art became known [Wheatstone wrote later]. Soon after, at my request, Mr. [Henry Fox] Talbot, the inventor, and Mr. [Henry] Collen (one of the first cultivators of the art) obligingly prepared for me stereoscopic

4. The Fairy Wedding Party. General Tom Thumb and wife, Commodore Nutt and Miss Minnie Warren. Negative by Mathew Brady. Eastman House, Rochester, N. Y.

Talbotypes of full-sized statues, buildings, and even portraits of living persons." Wheatstone sent these first stereoscopic photographs to the Royal Academy of Science in Brussels, where they were exhibited on October 9, 1841. "Messrs Collins [sic] and Wheatstone," we read in the *Bulletin* of the Academy, "have had the happy idea of taking at the same time two pictures of the same object, in positions suitable to be placed in the ingenious apparatus invented by the latter scientist to explain the effects of binocular vision. M. Quetelet [the secretary] saw two pictures of this kind produce, placed in the stereoscope, complete illusion. Thus it is possible, by two paper prints, to create portraits in relief of the most striking realism."

None of these first stereoscopic photographs appears to have survived, nor can any trace be found of the daguerreotypes which Wheatstone said had been made for him by Antoine Claudet and Hippolyte Louis Fizeau, two early experimenters.

Wheatstone's stereoscope was bulky. Because the paired pictures were viewed by their reflection in mirrors, they had to be reversed. The first improvement was made in 1849 by the Scottish scientist, Sir David Brewster. He not only did away with mirrors, but magnified the pictures with lenses. The Brewster stereoscope (Fig. 3) resembled somewhat a pair of opera glasses, and could be held in the hand. The twin pictures, mounted side by side, were put through a slot at the end of a tapering box which had a hinged lid on its top to admit light. The lenses, fitted in the other end of the box, were of a special kind. They were actually half-lenses. Brewster cut a lens of large diameter in half, so that he had

379

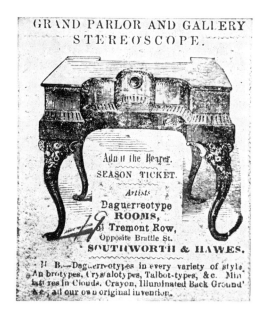

two semi-circular wedge-shaped pieces. These he ground to a circular shape, and placed them with the thick ends towards the *outside* in eyepieces. These half-lenses not only produced a magnified image, but they acted as prisms causing the line of vision to be toed out. He had a model made for him in Scotland by Andrew Ross. When he took it to London, in the hope of finding someone who would produce it commercially, he found no interest at all in the invention. But in Paris he had better luck. The optical firm of Jules Duboscq and Jean Baptiste François Soleil began at once to make both the instruments and daguerreotype slides to put in them.

These slides showed, Brewster said, "living individuals, statues, bouquets of flowers, and objects of natural history." A few such slides, bearing the monogram "D & S," have survived (Fig. 7): they may well be the very ones which so entranced Queen Victoria in 1851.

In that very year the daguerreotype process was challenged by the discovery of the collodion wet plate. This new technique had the advantage that quantities of paper slides could be produced which were cheaper and more convenient to look at than metal plates. But the daguerreotype lingered, particularly in America. In 1853 John F. Mascher of Philadelphia patented a case for stereo daguerreotypes which contained a built-in viewer: two lenses were mounted in a flap hinged to the inner side of the cover. Although these viewers were most inefficient, they must have been very popular to judge from the number now in existence. But the triumph of stereoscopic daguerreotyping was the work of Albert Sands Southworth and Josiah Johnson Hawes of Boston. They patented in 1854 a cabinet stereoscope of Wheatstone's pattern, specially designed to show daguerreotypes of the whole plate size (6½ x 8½ inches). Twelve pairs, mounted in metal frames, were contained in magazines at each end of a cabinet the size of a small piano; turning a crank brought a fresh pair into place. A V-shaped mirror of polished steel reflected the daguerreotype to the eyes of the viewer. The "Grand Parlor and Gallery Stereoscope" was a public attraction (Fig. 6). Season tickets were sold and Bostonians saw in three dimensions square-riggers at anchor, Niagara Falls in winter, portraits, and statues.

But already paper and glass stereo slides outnumbered the daguerreotypes by the thousand. Oliver Wendell Holmes, the famous writer, spoke for the first stereo fans when he wrote in the *Atlantic Monthly* for June, 1859:

> Oh, infinite volumes of poems that I treasure in this small library of glass and pasteboard! I creep over the vast features of Rameses, on the face of his rock-hewn Nubian temple; I scale the huge mountain-crystal that calls itself the Pyramid of Cheops. I pace the length of the three Titanic stones of the wall of Baalbec. . . . I look into the eyes of the caged tiger, and on the scaly train of the crocodile, stretched on the sands of the river that has mirrored a hundred dynasties. I stroll through Rhenish vineyards, I sit under Roman arches, I walk the

7. Stereoscopic Daguerreotype made by Duboscq and Soleil in Paris about 1850, showing scientific instruments made by them. Note Brewster stereoscope, lower right. George Eastman House, Rochester, N. Y.

8. A Holmes Stereoscope, made by Joseph Bates in Boston, about 1861. Viewing stereos with instruments like this was a popular home entertainment in the nineteenth century. The Holmes Stereoscope is still in use in many places. Photograph from the author's collection.

streets of once buried cities, I look into the chasms of Alpine glaciers, and on the rush of wasteful cataracts. I . . . leave my outward frame in the arm-chair at my table, while in spirit I am looking down upon Jerusalem from the Mount of Olives.

Holmes did more than collect and write about stereographs. He invented a simplified stereoscope which quickly became standard. He felt that the box-type viewer of Brewster's was needlessly bulky. With Yankee ingenuity he whittled out a skeleton model: hooded eyepiece, fitted with two prismatic half-lenses, slotted support for the cards, and a brad awl as a handle to support the whole. He turned his design over to Joseph L. Bates of Boston, who manufactured a slight modification as the "Holmes Stereoscope." Cheap, convenient and efficient, this instrument (Fig. 8) made "stereoscope" a household word.

From 1860 to 1880 there was hardly a photographer who did not make stereo negatives. No special camera was needed; the common view box of the 5x8-inch size could be fitted with twin lenses and an accordion-like partition to divide the bellows in two. The collodion process, then standard, was miserably insensitive, and exposures were usually so long that action photographs could not be taken. But the short focal length lenses of the stereoscopic camera had the great advantage that they could be made of larger relative diameter to admit more light; and furthermore the images they formed of moving objects traveled at a given exposure a relatively short distance across the plate. It was just possible to take with them instantaneous photographs. In these first "snapshots" of 1859 we can see Broadway choked with traffic and pedestrians (Fig. 9), yachts under sail, and even the intrepid Blondin balancing on his tightrope above Niagara Falls.

11. Civil War bulletin board and crowds.
Eastman Historical Photographic Collection.

12. Building the Central Pacific Railroad,
Dixie Cut, Gold Run Station, Placer County,
California. Photographed by Alfred A. Hart.
Collection of G. L. Howe, M. D., Rochester,
N. Y.

Stereographic cameramen documented the Civil War (Fig. 11). They went west with the railroads (Fig. 12). They were present when the golden spike was driven to join the the rails of the first transcontinental railroad. They accompanied explorers, and sent back to the east exact records of the far west. They lugged their equipment up mountains and across deserts (Fig. 10). Stereographs provide a rich, detailed and remarkably lifelike record of the world and its activities.

When printing presses finally caught up with photography in the 1890's and it became possible to reproduce photographs along with type, the demand for ready-made stereo slides dropped. There had been an overproduction of stock subjects. Writing of the state of photography in 1888 (the year the Kodak camera was introduced) John Werge, an Englishman, said that the year was "chiefly remarkable for the attempted revival of the stereoscope. As to its immense popularity thirty to thirty-five years ago, that was due to its novelty . . . but it soon ceased to be popular when the views became stale, and people grew tired of looking at them; to keep up their interest they had to be continually buying fresh ones. . . . When hosts saw that their guests were bored with sights so often seen, they put them out of sight altogether."

But a new era was already commencing with the invention of the dry plate and roll film. Now anyone could make his own photographs. Excellent cameras, specially designed for taking stereoscopic photographs, were soon offered in great variety. They ranged from inexpensive fixed-focus models for the casual snapshooter to precision instruments for the

13. Stereo cameraman, about 1860. Collection of G. L. Howe, M.D., Rochester, N. Y.

14. The Jules Richard Verascope, with magazine holding 12 glass plates, changed by pulling out drawer and pushing it back in. Drawer shown extended.

advanced amateur. The French took the lead in designing cameras that looked like opera glasses and were held like them at eye level. "Jumelles," they called them, using the very word for binoculars. Glass replaced paper for slides, and the box form of viewer with corrected lenses made the Holmes stereoscope obsolete.

Stereo-jumelles were made in two standard sizes, to take plates 60x30 mm (2⅜x5⅛ inches) and 45x107 mm (1¾x4¼ inches). The cameras were all metal, with beautifully made magazines to hold a dozen plates which were changed simply by pulling out a sliding box and pushing it back into place.

The smaller size was championed by Jules Richard, who called his inexpensive camera, first marketed in 1896, the "Verascope." (Fig. 14.) He claimed that the small negatives could give results equal to the larger

15. The Richard Taxiphote, a magazine viewer for stereo transparencies. Fifty slides were placed in each box, and changed by pressing a lever.

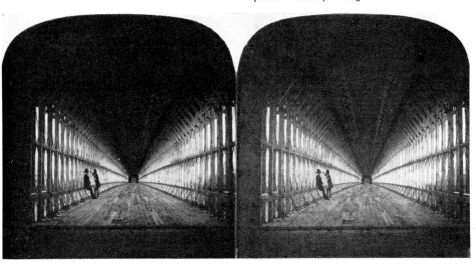

17. Another view of the pedestrian deck and carriageway of the Niagara Falls Suspension Bridge showing gatehouse and entrance. George Eastman House.

18. The Stereo Graflex, 1904. Using 5 x 7-inch plates, this camera made two 3½ x 5-inch negatives. The image on the ground glass was seen in relief through viewing prisms in the hood. George Eastman House.

sizes, and proudly announced that 30x40-inch enlargements from single Verascope negatives could be seen in his Paris shop.

Glass positives from the negatives were preferred for viewing, and the long forgotten Brewster stereoscope was revived. In 1900 Richard brought out an ingenious magazine viewer, the "Taxiphote." (Fig. 15.) Unmounted glass positives were held in slotted boxes of fifty each. The boxes were inserted in a cabinet viewer, and merely by pressing a lever the slides were brought into viewing position one after the other. When the last slide was brought into place a bell rang, indicating that a fresh box of views should be put in the machine. A numbered knob on the side of the cabinet made it possible to select any desired view and, on some models, supplementary lenses could be raised in front of the normal eyepieces to give a magnified view of any slide. Still another lever brought a prism opposite one eyepiece through which the title, written across the slide in the blank space between the two pictures, could be read. The simplicity of Richard's stereo system made stereoscopic photography the delight of thousands of French amateurs during the first two decades of the century.

In America, the leading manufacturers introduced adaptations of their cameras for stereoscopic work. Folmer & Schwing announced in 1898 that their Graphic cameras, for plates 5x7 and 6½x8½ inches, could be had on special order with a wide lens board to accommodate twin lenses. And a stereo model of the Graflex camera, in the 5x7-inch size, was put on the market in 1904. (Fig. 18.) This popular reflex camera had the advantage over the ordinary hand camera that a full-size image on a ground

388

19. The Stereo Kodak Model 1, a folding, roll-film stereo camera. George Eastman House.

glass screen could be seen right up to the moment of exposure. The Stereo Graflex went a step further. The picture could be previewed *stereoscopically*, in depth. The 1907 catalogue stated: "The hood at the top is practically a stereoscope, as it contains a pair of stereo prisms. These prisms are arranged to give a stereoscopic effect, when focusing, as the operator sees but one image on the ground glass screen—right side up— not inverted. The object is viewed just as one would see the finished stereogram through a stereoscope."

The Eastman Kodak Company began in 1901 to manufacture stereo cameras for roll film. The No. 2 Stereo Kodak, which took 6 pairs of pictures 4½x3½ inches, was a box type; it was replaced by the more convenient No. 2 Brownie Folding Stereo camera in 1905.

One of the Graphic cameras—the box-type Triple Lens Stereo Graphic Telescopic of 1900—was fitted with three lenses of exactly the same focal length. The function of the extra lens was to form an image on a ground glass, placed vertically at the back of the camera and hooded; thus the operator could see a single image of what he was photographing. This

20. The Stereo Brownie, another roll film stereo camera. George Eastman House.

389

21. Climbing the lower glacier of Grindelwald, Switzerland. Women went in for mountain climbing even then, though the costume must have been a hindrance! George Eastman House.

22. Another mountain climbing shot, apparently taken considerably later. Snow and sky rendition would seem to indicate the use of orthochromatic plates and a yellow filter. George Eastman House.

principle was later used by Franke & Heidecke in their Heidoscope camera of 1924. The ground glass, however, was at the top of the camera, and the image was thrown upon it by a mirror placed at an angle of 45°. Glass plates were used in the Heidoscope, which was furnished in the two standard Continental sizes—45x107mm and 60x130mm. The same principle was employed in the Rolleidoscope (1927), which owed its name to the fact that standard roll film was used in it.

In the meantime Jules Richard advertised in 1920 the prophetic Homeos camera. This was the first stereo camera to use 35mm film. Twenty-six pairs of 1x¾-inch negatives could be taken with it on one meter of standard cinema film, specially spooled for daylight loading. Film positives made from these negatives by contact printing could be viewed in a special stereoscope. The little camera—predecessor of countless "miniatures" of today—did not seem to appeal to photographers. The attitude of most of them to this new development was summed up as late as 1936 by J. Moir Dalzell in his fine book: "As for 'still' stereography on cine-film—well, let us smile indulgently."

Today, thanks to the perfection of 35mm color films and precision cameras, stereography has become more popular than ever, and the indulgence of the experts has given way to the astonishment of thousands who have never before experienced the thrill of taking and viewing color photographs in three dimensions.

Among the pioneers in this new development is the David White Company of Milwaukee (presently known as Realist, Inc.), which ever since

391

24. Stereo photographers ranged far and wide —to foreign lands for this shot of the tomb of the Caliphs, Cairo, Egypt. George Eastman House.

25. But homely scenes, like this farmyard activity, were equally popular with stereo viewers of Grandpa's time. George Eastman House.

26. Wherever there were pictures to be made the stereo photographer went, often risking life and equipment, like this photographer at the rapids of St. Anthony. George Eastman House.

it was founded in 1890 has been manufacturing surveying and drawing instruments. In 1942, with no previous experience in the manufacture of photographic equipment, the company decided to explore the possibilities of bringing out a complete stereo system: camera, viewer and mounting service. When the first market survey was made, an official of the company has stated, "the reaction from photographic dealers was even less than lukewarm." However, the reaction from potential users was encouraging enough to warrant the development of the program, and the first Stereo Realist camera was introduced to the market in May, 1947.

The camera incorporates three novel features. First, the lenses are stationary and the film plane moves for focusing, thus assuring lens alignment. Second, the range finder and view finder eyepieces are located at the bottom of the camera so that it can be held steadily against the forehead. Third, the viewing lens is set directly between the taking lenses to eliminate parallax.

The slide viewer, fitted with achromatic lenses, contains built-in illumination, powered either by a dry cell or by a transformer. As color film is almost invariably used to make the transparencies, uniformity of illumination is thus assured.

The third link in the system is a slide mounting service, which relieves the owner of the burden of preparing his photographs for viewing. At first, arrangements were made with the Eastman Kodak Company for

393

forwarding customers' Kodachrome films after processing to Realist, Inc., for mounting. In 1952 the Eastman Kodak Company undertook to introduce a special packaging of Kodachrome film in lengths sufficient for 20 pairs of Realist stereo pictures; the price includes processing and mounting.

These innovations have brought about a renaissance of three-dimensional photography, and countless people are daily discovering a new joy through stereography.

BIBLIOGRAPHY

Brewster, Sir David. *The Stereoscope, its History, Theory, Construction, and Application to the Fine and Useful Arts and Education.* London, 1856.

Dalzell, J. Moir. *Practical Stereoscope Photography.* London, 1936.

Drouin, F. *The Stereoscope and Stereoscopic Photography.* London, 1897.

Holmes, Oliver Wendell. "The Stereoscope and the Stereograph," *Atlantic Monthly,* III (1859), 738-48.

――― "Sun Painting and Sun Sculpture," *Ibid.,* VIII (1861), 13-29.

――― "History of the 'American Stereoscope,'" *Philadelphia Photographer,* VI (1869), 1-3.

Judge, Arthur W. *Stereoscopic Photography: its Application to Science, Industry and Education.* 2d Ed. London, 1935.

Taft, Robert. *Photography and the American Scene.* New York, 1938. (Chapter X: "The Stereoscope.")

Wheatstone, Sir Charles. "Contributions to the Physiology of Vision. Part the First: On Some Remarkable, and Hitherto Unobserved, Phenomena of Binocular Vision," *Philosophical Transactions of the Royal Society,* 1838, Part I, pp. 371-94. (Reprinted in *The Scientific Papers of Sir Charles Wheatstone,* London, 1879, pp. 225-259.)

Index